THE LIBRARY OF
PHILOSOPHY AND THEOLOGY

NEW ESSAYS IN
PHILOSOPHICAL THEOLOGY

NEW ESSAYS
IN PHILOSOPHICAL
THEOLOGY

edited by

ANTONY FLEW
*Professor of Philosophy
in the University College
of North Staffordshire*

ALASDAIR MACINTYRE
*Lecturer in the Faculty of Theology
in the University of Manchester*

SCM PRESS LTD
56 BLOOMSBURY STREET
LONDON

First published 1955
Reprinted December 1958

Made and printed in Great Britain by
William Clowes and Sons, Limited, London and Beccles

GENERAL INTRODUCTION

ONLY a short generation ago it was still customary for theological thinking to be carried out within the framework of avowedly philosophical concepts, and philosophical theology was a fairly well-defined *genre* within the whole field of theology. The great work of nineteenth-century theology was carried out for the most part by scholars who had undergone intensive training in the idealist movement in philosophy. It is no derogation of the achievement of that time to say that this simple conjunction of two disciplines is no longer possible today. Many things have contributed so to change the picture of the work which theologians and philosophers have to do that it seems to be not so much a modified picture as an entirely new one. The strong blasts of positive and empirical dogmatic theology blowing down from Switzerland upon Europe and America, the immense changes which have overtaken philosophy, especially in Britain, so that the very ways of thinking seem to have altered, and the changes which have taken place in the world in which we all live—have all contributed to bring about this revolution. We live in a post-liberal, post-idealist, atomic age in theology. Philosophy and theology alike are being compelled to face their traditional problems in such a radical way that the question even arises: are our traditional problems the real ones?

In this situation it seems possible, however risky, to attempt a new facing of the problems of living in the mid-century world, not in the strength of isolated disciplines, but in a meeting of those disciplines on the common ground offered by our life in this world. The present Library of Philosophy and Theology, therefore, desires to offer a meeting-place for the thought of contemporary theologians and philosophers, Continental and Anglo-Saxon, yet without partisan or *a priori* assumptions about the way in which such a meeting may best be used.

Among the early volumes in the Library will come a study of existentialist theology as revealed in the work of Rudolf Bultmann; a collection of papers in philosophical theology as seen from the standpoint of the philosophers of logical analysis; an unfinished, posthumous work on ethics by Dietrich Bonhoeffer; and a volume of essays on philosophical, literary and theological themes by Rudolf Bultmann.

No doctrinaire scheme underlies this first choice of titles, or the editorial plans. If the matter may be summed up provocatively and negatively, the editorial assumption of the series is that neither the idealist nor the linguistic philosophy, neither the liberal nor the neo-Calvinist nor the neo-Thomist theology, is able by itself to speak properly to the needs of our time, or to the demands which we are aware of as flowing out of our historical situation from the Renaissance onwards. We may hope that the volumes to be produced in this series, whether coming from the philosophical or the theological camp, will in fact not speak of or to any mere 'camp'. They will have as their concern the possibilities offered to the world through the tradition both of philosophical thinking and of Christian history.

R. Gregor Smith

CONTENTS

Contents

PREFACE

THIS is a collection of twenty-two papers by sixteen different philosophers working in the British Commonwealth. The first thing which all the contributors have in common is a familiarity with and a great indebtedness to the recent revolution in philosophy. They are therefore certain to be labelled 'Logical Positivists' by most laymen, including many professional theologians; and even by most philosophers outside the English-speaking countries. This label is entirely inappropriate: if it is to be taken, as it is and should be, to imply a toeing of the party line of the now defunct Vienna Circle; a position brilliantly epitomized by the Ayer of *Language, Truth and Logic* (First Edition, 1936: Gollancz, London). This is not the place to describe or discuss the revolution in philosophy or to estimate the part played in it by the Vienna Circle.[1] It should be sufficient here simply to repudiate the popular misconception that 'all the philosophers are Logical Positivists nowadays': and to ask that this volume be judged on its arguments, and not be forced into some preconceived matrix of misunderstanding. The second thing which the contributors share is a concern with theological questions, and a conviction that these call for serious and particular treatment. (Whereas the Logical Positivists used to reject all theology holus-bolus as so much meaningless metaphysics.) But this common conviction and concern is not accompanied by a community of religious belief. One Editor is a Christian and one is not: while the contributors and contributions are likewise divided just about equally.[2]

[1] Anyone interested might refer to: *The Revolution in Philosophy* (Macmillan, 1955), essays on the history of recent developments edited by D. F. Pears; and *Logic and Language* (Blackwell, Oxford: First Series, 1951, and Second Series 1953), and *Essays in Conceptual Analysis* (Macmillan, 1956), anthologies of recent philosophical articles edited by Antony Flew.

[2] It will perhaps be of interest to some to mention that though we made our selection with no thought of denomination in mind it has turned out that the majority of our Christian contributors are within the Anglican communion. To our great regret the one Roman Catholic whom we approached felt unable to co-operate.

Our title perhaps calls for some explanation. The word 'new' is put in: not because the papers included are here published for the first time—for the majority have already appeared before somewhere; but because it is only in the last few years that attempts have been made to apply these latest philosophical techniques and insights to theological issues, while this is probably the first time that a whole book has been devoted to this enormous job. We should like to have used the expression 'Philosophy of Religion' for its analogy with 'Philosophy of History', 'Philosophy of Science', and so on: since the questions discussed here are philosophical and bear the same sort of relation to religious thought and practice as the questions of the philosophy of history and of science bear to the thought and practice of working scientists and historians; the relation, that is, of arising out of or being posed by these empirical disciplines, while being themselves philosophical and not factual questions (see Chapter III). But this expression has become, and seems likely for some time to remain, associated with Idealist attempts to present philosophical prolegomena to theistic theology. So we have adapted as an alternative the expression 'Philosophical Theology'; which has a welcome analogy to 'Philosophical Ethics' and 'Philosophical Aesthetics', occasionally used to cover the parallel philosophical inquiries which arise out of moral and critical thought and practice. We realize that many will be startled to find the word 'theology' so used that: the expression 'theistic theologian' is not tautological; and the expression 'atheist theologian' is not self-contradictory. But unless this unusual usage of ours is adopted we have to accept the paradox that those who reach opposite conclusions about certain questions must be regarded as having thereby shown themselves to have been engaged in different disciplines: the paradox that whereas St. Thomas's presentation of the *quinque viae* is a piece of (Natural or Philosophical) Theology, Hume's *Dialogues concerning Natural Religion* must belong to some other and nameless discipline.

A very little needs to be said about our principles of

selection. We have tried to include papers covering as many as possible of the most important problems. We have not included John Wisdom's 'Gods', the paper from which much of the present discussion arose, because it has already been twice reprinted and we preferred to make room for less well-known papers.[3] We have included contributions to the 'Theology and Falsification' controversy by Flew, Hare and Mitchell and pieces on 'Death' by MacKinnon and Flew: in spite of the fact that all these are much shorter and slighter than the rest of the contents; and because they are often referred to, though they originally appeared in a journal now unfortunately defunct and consequently unobtainable.

Those of the essays which have been previously published appeared originally in the following journals:

(i) 'Can Religion be Discussed?', *Australasian Journal of Philosophy*, 1942.
(ii) 'The Existence of God', *Church Quarterly Review*, 1955.
(iii) 'Can God's Existence be Disproved?', A-D, *Mind*, 1948 and 1949.
(iv) 'A Religious Way of Knowing', *Mind*, 1952.
(v) 'Theology and Falsification' (i), A-D, *University*, 1950–1.
(vi) 'Theology and Falsification' (ii), *Socratic Digest*, V.
(vii) 'Religion as the Inexpressible', *Philosophy and Phenomenological Research*, 1954 (under another title and in a version directed to a different public).
(viii) 'Divine Omnipotence and Human Freedom', *Hibbert Journal*, 1955 (in a much abbreviated version).
(ix) 'Creation', *Church Quarterly Review*, 1955.
(x) 'The Perfect Good', *Australasian Journal of Philosophy*, 1955.
(xi) 'Demythologising and the Problem of Validity', *Theology*, 1955 (in a much abbreviated version).
(xii) 'Miracles', *Hibbert Journal*, 1952.
(xiii) 'Death', A-B, *University*, 1951–2.

We want to thank all our contributors, and all the editors

[3] *P.A.S.*, 1944–5, reprinted in *Logic and Language* (First Series) and *Philosophy and Pychoanalysis* by John Wisdom (Blackwell, Oxford, 1953).

of the journals mentioned, in which the items previously published originally appeared, for their permission to print, or reprint, the papers included in this volume. A particularly warm word of thanks is due: both to Ian Crombie, who consented to the reprinting of his essay on 'Theology and Falsification' although it is shortly to reappear in another volume; and to the officers of the Oxford University Socratic Club, which has been so largely responsible for encouraging the sort of thinking represented in this book, to which drafts of many of the chapters in it were first read, and which generously waived its claims to publish 'Divine Omnipotence and Human Freedom' and 'Tertullian's Paradox' for the first time in its occasional journal *The Socratic*.

ANTONY FLEW
ALASDAIR MACINTYRE

June, 1955.

I

CAN RELIGION BE DISCUSSED?[1]

A. N. PRIOR

My characters are Barthian Protestant, Modernist Protestant, Catholic, Logician and Psychoanalyst. The footnotes are by myself. Modernist Protestant is not much more than a foil or butt for the rest. Barthian Protestant may be an unfamiliar figure to philosophical readers; for whose benefit it may be explained that Karl Barth is a Swiss theologian with a considerable following in Europe, most notably in the German Confessional Church, which, under the leadership of Martin Niemöller, offered persistent resistance to Nazi interference in ecclesiastical affairs. The play begins.

BARTHIAN PROTESTANT. I ought to explain that I was in two minds about coming here at all. You see, I'm doubtful of the value of religious discussions between Christians and non-Christians; for there is no point of contact for argument between them. The truth of Christianity cannot be proved; faith is a gift of God; so what can I say that would be of any interest here?[2]

CATHOLIC. My own creed is commonly charged by Protestants with inhumanity; but it is hardly as inhuman as the Protestantism I have just heard. You appear, Barthian, to divide mankind into two rigid groups between which no intercourse is possible. On the one hand are believers, and on the other unbelievers, and never the twain shall meet. It is a

---

1 [This dialogue was written over a decade ago, and no character in it represents the present opinions of the author. Even the writer of the footnotes slips at times.—A.N.P. (1955).]

2 When invited to be a Gifford Lecturer, Barth at first declined, on the ground that he was an avowed opponent of all natural theology.

sort of spiritual racialism. We Catholics, however, affirm at least the *initial* spiritual equality of all men. Belief is a possibility that is open to everyone, and reasons for believing can be set out objectively for all to see.

PSYCHOANALYST. Before you two go any further with this little private discussion about whether Logician and I are human beings or not, might I chip in with a question to Barthian? I am wondering just why he did decide to come after all.

BARTHIAN PROTESTANT. I am glad you asked me that, as it will give me an opportunity also of answering Catholic's charge of inhumanity. What I was leading up to was a confession that I have come here with the deliberate intention of breaking the rules and, instead of arguing against unbelief, preaching to you—confessing my faith before you, in the hope that it may awaken an answering faith in yourselves. For I do believe there is one point of contact between us; though it is not one which enables us to discuss whether Christianity is true or false; and it is not a point that lies within ourselves. The point of contact that does bind us all together is the fact that we are all sinners for whom Christ died, wholly dependent on God's grace. And it is not for *me* to say that the grace of faith has been denied to anyone here; still less is it for me to claim that the grace of faith has been put into my own possession for ever, so that I no longer need God's help to go on believing. On the contrary, I know that I do go on needing it always, and continue always to be nothing in myself but a sinner and unbeliever. I hold also that the help I need may come through you—that it may be given to you not only to believe, but to confess your faith (perhaps without realizing that that is what you are doing) and so help me. I have come not only to convert but, knowing that I need conversion again and again, to be converted. In that perhaps I hold to our 'spiritual equality' even more firmly than Catholic does.

LOGICIAN. Perhaps—but you haven't come to be converted to a different point of view—which is the only sort of conversion that I can understand. Never mind that, though. You apologized at the outset for breaking some 'rule' or other. I wasn't aware that any rules had been made in connection with this gathering, but I imagine you have in mind those Laws of Thought or Laws of Reasoning of which I am popularly supposed to be the guardian. I can give you my professional assurance that these Laws don't in the least forbid you to 'confess your faith', as you put it. In fact, that is what I would particularly like you to do. I've never been much worried about the difficulty of 'proving' the truth of Christianity; and I would agree that most of our basic convictions have to be taken on trust. The real intellectual difficulty for the believer or would-be believer is not the problem of proof but the problem of meaning. The characteristic propositions of religion seem to me to be meaningless. So if you three Christians can tell me exactly what it is that you believe—and I presume that that is what you mean by 'confessing your faith'—I'd be more than grateful.

MODERNIST PROTESTANT. Yes, and when we've told you, you'll analyse and analyse and then tell us there's nothing left. You logicians forget that life is larger than logic. Religion is a deep experience, a matter of profound feeling, something that the rapture of poetry can catch, but that eludes *your* methods; and life is like that too, and love, and lots of things.

CATHOLIC. Yes, life is like that, and love, and lots of things. 'Lots of things' are impressive and moving and mysterious, but that hardly makes them proper objects of religious adoration. When a man worships, he should know what he is doing —it is too solemn and responsible an act for him to perform without applying any criterion of worthiness and unworthiness, truth and falsehood. For that reason Logician's request seems to me a fair one. We must be able to state with some precision the difference between God and all other beings— to explain, in other words, exactly what we mean, and still more exactly what we do not mean, when we confess 'I believe in God'—or we may find ourselves worshipping merely one object among the many which make up the universe, instead of him who made all. The charge of idolatry is often flung at us Catholics, but we certainly guard against that sin more carefully than the Protestant who has just

3

spoken. What the medieval schoolmen said—and I have yet to learn that their work in this field has been improved upon —was that the Being of God is necessary, while that of all other beings is contingent. All the objects we commonly encounter can be imagined not to exist—they exist, so to speak, by chance—but for God there is no such possibility of non-existence. He occupies the field of Being securely; his dislodgment from it is unthinkable; indeed, the supposition of his dislodgment is nonsense—it cannot even be talked about; we are not really speaking of God when we say such things. God *is* his own Being.[3] Similarly, all other beings are *what* they are 'by chance'; at least their 'properties' are contingent; one could imagine them being otherwise; all other good things, for example, even some supremely vast and good being whose vastness and goodness tempt us to worship him, are good 'by chance'; they might have been otherwise. But God couldn't have been other than good, and there is no chance of his losing his goodness; the supposition of his losing it is nonsense, because God *is* his own goodness, and all goodness. All our goodness flows from his and is dependent on it; while his is perfect and underived and sure, because it is himself.

LOGICIAN. Excuse me—in that sentence of yours, 'God is his own goodness', which you insist is no poetic fancy but strictly logical discourse, what part of speech, what kind of noun, is the word 'God'?

CATHOLIC. Proper or common, I suppose—a bit of both— does it matter?

LOGICIAN. No, *that* doesn't matter. The alternatives I had in mind were proper or common on the one hand, and *abstract* on the other. On the face of it, as you say, 'God' looks like a proper or common noun. Qualities are predicated of him— 'God is good'; and in the sentence we are considering, you speak of 'his own goodness'. But then you say that God *is*

---

[3] This proposition is not only in Anselm but in Aquinas, who holds that God's existence, though necessary, is not self-evident to man. I have not equated Catholic's position with the acceptance of the ontological argument; though I think Kant has shown that he *ought* to accept the ontological argument— that the cosmological depends on it.

this 'goodness'; that is, he is not a thing or person at all, but an abstraction.

CATHOLIC. I see you have the modern nominalistic prejudice against abstractions.

LOGICIAN. Oh no—on the contrary, I have often wished that this word 'abstraction' were changed for some other, first because it tends to give rise to the prejudice you mention —the prejudice that good objects are real while 'goodness' is somehow just imaginary. If God is an 'abstraction', he is none the less real for that—I mean, *that* doesn't make sentences about him meaningless. There are many different ways in which we can convey the same information, all of them making sense, and I have no prejudices against any of them. We may say the same thing with abstract nouns or common ones, and either way does equally well. We may, for instance, say 'The people were very happy' or 'The people's happiness was great'. The second sentence isn't 'meaningless' because its subject is an abstraction; on the contrary, it means exactly the same as the first. I do insist, however, that the second sentence doesn't *add* anything to the first. We are not first given information about the happy people and then new information about their happiness— the sentence about their happiness is just another way of telling us about the people, and the sentence about the people is just another way of telling us about their happiness. We can talk sense either way, but we *must* decide which way we will talk. We cannot have it both ways, and use a word as an abstract noun and a common noun at once,[4] as you try to do in your sentence 'God is his own goodness'—that's just bad grammar, a combining of words which fails to make them *mean*—like 'Cat no six'. You have indeed established a complete difference between God and all other beings, so that there is no danger of any idolatrous confusion; or rather, you have

[4] This insistence that abstract and common nouns must be subjects of different sentences is only a modern variant of Kant's insistence that it takes *two* propositions, or at least a complex proposition and not a simple one, to express necessity ('If . . ., then . . .' propositions expressing 'logical' necessity are translations from one way of describing a situation into another).

2   5

established a complete difference between 'God' and all the other words we use for naming things; but the difference is that this word, as you use it, does not and cannot name anything whatever—you refuse to put it through the proper motions of 'naming'.[5]

BARTHIAN PROTESTANT. It would seem, Logician, that your 'professional assurance' that the Laws of Thought would allow us to confess our faith, was a little premature.

PSYCHOANALYST. I was thinking something of that sort myself. Logician hasn't proved such a liberal fellow as his first promises led us to expect. I agree with him that the supreme intellectual problem for the believer is to show that his propositions have any meaning; but he shouldn't forget that the unbeliever has his problems too; and the chief of these is to explain just how it is that intelligent and civilized men ever come to believe, or imagine they are believing, these apparently meaningless things. Perhaps nothing makes an unbelieving view of the universe more difficult than this simple fact that men do believe—which believing, as Logician has made clear, is a most prodigious performance. And belief on a social and historical scale is if anything more prodigious still. The kind of clear and sharp and anti-idolatrous belief that we have been considering is hardly to be found outside ancient and modern Israel and the Christian Church (with Mohammedanism as a sort of sideshow); and this 'people of God', going back to the dawn of time and forward —who knows how far?—is a Body which sticks in the gullet of world history as Catholic's nonsense sticks in Logician's gullet now.[6] Leaving the historical problem aside for the

5 Logician's whole argument applies to Hegel's pantheistic 'concrete universal' as well as to Catholic's theistic one. Hegel is not concerned to establish an absolute difference between 'God' and all other names, but he eliminates this difference not by using 'God' sensibly but by using all names non-sensically, i.e. as Catholic uses 'God'. 'Pantheism' lays itself open either to this objection or (if it rejects the Hegelian 'logic') to that of Catholic— that it worships, in 'the Universe', an object we have no right or reason to worship.

6 Freud's *Moses and Monotheism* is, as far as I know, the only anti-religious work which treats the uniqueness of the Hebrew-Christian tradition as a serious problem for unbelief to solve and does not evade it with chatter about all religions being the same, or evolving along a single line.

moment, I would say in reference to Catholic's propositions about God that in fact they are not meaningless at all, but refer to a very real being or beings. God does exist, if you like to put it that way, but he is not what he purports to be. When men talk about 'God', they are really talking about such beings as their parents, the primeval father of the race, or Moses, the father of the Jewish Church-nation; and when they speak of their 'sin' or murderous hostility to God, it is their hostility to these persons that they are describing.[7] This, however, they do not know, and do not want to know, and in various ways they keep the knowledge from reaching their consciousness. Not the least ingenious of these tricks of their inner 'censor' is that of defining 'God' in ways which on inspection prove to be meaningless. Thus if we ask, 'Is "God" a name for your father?', the answer is, 'Oh no—to worship one's father is idolatry, which we have surely repudiated as plainly as it is possible to do'. 'Then who is he?' 'He is his own goodness'—this senselessness forms an opaque wall which bars the way to further inquiry and keeps the secret buried.

BARTHIAN PROTESTANT. I'm rather glad to hear all this, because it confirms a suspicion I have long had, though I have never followed it up. I have always felt that it must be possible to give an adequate explanation of religious faith on the hypothesis that it is an illusion[8]; and now you have shown me in a broad way how it might be done. It is also possible, however, to explain the fact of faith, and the corresponding sociological fact of Israel and the Church, on the assumption that it is *not* an illusion—that God is real, and faith is his gift, and 'sacred history' the story of his strategy. Without being familiar with the non-Christian explanation in detail, I have held that it is probably just as good as the other—that there is nothing to choose between the two, and

---

[7] 'Rabbi' Duncan, a nineteenth-century Scottish Calvinist who has been compared with Barth, said that sin 'designs deicide' and seeks 'to slay Being at its root'. A better description of parricide could hardly be found.

[8] Barth has always been interested in Feuerbach from this point of view, though he seems relatively unfamiliar with Freud. His theology might have started, like Marx's, from some 'Theses on Feuerbach'.

one just jumps the way one has to. Faith is not the product of superior intellectual discernment; it is not a thing on which we are in *any* way entitled to compliment ourselves; it is an inward miracle of God's mercy, and that is all we can say about it.

LOGICIAN. I can understand this idea of taking 'leaps of faith' when confronted with two standpoints between which there seems to be nothing to choose. I don't object to it at all—we are always doing it, and there is nothing in such 'leaps of faith' that contravenes the 'Laws of Thought'— unless one is half-hearted about it, and pretends to be able to 'prove' what cannot be proved (then, of course, I claim the right to criticize the 'proof'). The validity of inductive inference, on which Psychoanalyst's 'explanation' of religion ultimately depends, can only be affirmed as a leap in the dark.[9] That's what I meant by the liberty I allowed you at the beginning. But I'm afraid we are *not* in this case confronted with two hypotheses between which 'there is nothing to choose'. There is everything to choose between *these* two hypotheses; for one of them makes sense and the other doesn't —the believing hypothesis is meaningless, and so isn't a hypothesis at all. The chances are not fifty-fifty but a hundred to nothing against belief. The 'choice' which you imagine you have is illusory—unbelief is inevitable. Unless you have evolved a form of faith which isn't open to the objections which I have raised against that of Catholic—a form of faith, that is, which can be expressed in good grammar.

BARTHIAN PROTESTANT. No, I can't oblige you there. In fact, my main difference from Catholic is that I have never pretended to be able to do so. I do not begin, as he does, with doctrines which look rational but prove not to be so, but present you with the 'nonsense' right from the jump. If asked to define God—or in the language of Psychoanalyst,

---

9 H. Reichenbach, in *Experience and Prediction*, formulated a 'wager' argument for induction which bears an astonishing resemblance to Pascal's 'wager' argument for religion.

which I prefer, to say who he is[10]—I would say that God is he whom we encounter in Jesus Christ, as he is brought before us in the Bible and in the preaching of the Church. And when that definition, or personal identification, begins to be elaborated, we are immediately landed in the realm of paradoxes and contradictions. 'Jesus Christ'—we can only say what that name means by talking about the trinity and the incarnation, paradoxes both. The Bible—how can we explain its proper authority except by saying that it is both the Word of God and the words of men, divinely infallible and humanly fallible at once?[11] The Church's preaching or confession of its faith—this faith also is a paradox; it is we men who believe and confess our faith; and yet it is not us at all, but God speaking for us and in us. And this last paradox explains how my withers are unwrung by all the senselessness which Logician may be able to demonstrate in my language. *Of course* we can only talk nonsense when we try to talk about God—our language is the language of sinful men, and is utterly unfitted for such use. *Of course* the laws of thought, and the laws of grammar, forbid us to confess our faith—we try to speak of God, and it is impossible even to begin. But God, with whom all things are possible, comes to our rescue, and takes up our words and our thoughts and *makes* them carry his meaning and his message to men.[12] So my

10 In a work of early Scottish Protestantism, with which Barth has strong affinities, occurs this sentence: 'The poets say, Oedipus knew that he had a father, but knew not that Laius was his father; so the heathen know that there is a god, but know not the true God.' It is from this point of view that Mohammedanism is a 'sideshow'; for while it may be a purer form of abstract 'monotheism' than Judaism or Christianity, it is not so definite and unambiguous (and so 'monotheistic') in its identification of God's person by his concrete presence and action in history.

11 I can find no better way of expressing Barth's curiously ambiguous relation to 'Fundamentalism'.

12 This is not a wild guess at what Barth might reply to a criticism such as Logician's. The idea that nonsense may be given sense by an act of sheer omnipotence is repeated again and again in his *Prolegomena to Church Dogmatics*. On this miracle, for him, the very possibility of a science of theology depends. And on this miracle *alone*. Barth refuses explicitly and absolutely to try and justify his 'nonsense' by criticizing or qualifying or revising the laws of thought (like Hegel; and Modernist; and perhaps even Kant, to whom Barth is obviously close). Nor, however, does he consider it any part of his business to affirm or accept their validity. The Miracle is his one standing-ground.

9

confession of faith can only take the form, 'Lord, I believe; help Thou mine unbelief.' *Of course* unbelief is inevitable, to me as well as to Logician; and yet—God's grace is irresistible.

PSYCHOANALYST. That's true in a way too. Only I'd put it differently—it's the religious illusion that's irresistible, and cannot be removed either by demonstrating the absurdity of the objects of belief or by describing psychologically how belief works. This discussion will not 'cure' Barthian; all we can do by it is prove him wrong. *This*, indeed, we can do, and have done. I think, Logician, it's time we were going home.

LOGICIAN. I am reminded, Psychoanalyst, of the beginning of this conversation, when Barthian and Catholic were debating whether you and I were human beings or not. We now appear to be doing the same with them, and asking, are they sane human beings like ourselves, or are they mad? And like Catholic in his argument with Barthian, I feel like bringing a charge of 'inhumanity' against you—of failing to respect the humanity of others. You hold that our opponents are mad, and that it's useless to argue with them; while I assume that discussion with them is possible, at least until the contrary is completely proven.

PSYCHOANALYST. And like Barthian, I would plead that I am not as inhuman as you paint me. I *haven't* said that our opponents are mad; at least they're not any madder than you or I. These 'irresistible' illusions are things we all suffer from; sometimes they're large and sometimes they're trivial. One can hardly use so alarming a word as 'madness' to describe a phenomenon so universal. And what is more important, the 'irresistibility' or incurability of these illusions is only relative —they cannot be cured by the methods we are employing just now, and maybe not by you or me at all. Barthian and Catholic are not mad—yet. But a time may come—though on the other hand, of course, such a time may never come; we cannot foresee these things—when circumstances will push them into an emotional crisis in which they *will* go mad unless they do something about it, and then in the painful process of their own analysis they will see for themselves the roots of their urge to believe. Only in this way are genuine atheists made. Atheists by pure persuasion are usually, perhaps always, afflicted with a guilty conscience; the urge to believe is still in them, and they either try to quench it by becoming violent or unfair in their attacks on religion, or try to satisfy it by inventing milk-and-water religions like that of Modernist here, using religious language to describe anything they find impressive or moving or mysterious. Barthian and Catholic may be mad, if you choose to use the word that way; but there are many worse forms of insanity, even among atheists. German Catholicism and Confessional Protestantism are infinitely saner than the racial mysticism they oppose— that's as true on my theory as it is on their own.[13] They can take this, if they please, as a compliment to their creed from an outsider, or even a 'confession of faith' by one who does not realize what he is confessing—or they may take it as a new argument for unbelief, since it shows that unbelievers as well as believers can take due account of the German Church struggle and of the relative justification of the Church's position in it.

BARTHIAN PROTESTANT. Lord, I believe; help Thou mine unbelief!

Canterbury University College
Christchurch

NEW ZEALAND

13 Barth's most frequently reiterated argument against Modernism is that it is the beginning of a road which leads in the end to the wrong side of the German Church conflict. This is, of course, merely a particular and very topical application of Catholic's general objection that Modernism cannot guard against the worship of unworthy objects.

II

METAPHYSICS, LOGIC AND THEOLOGY [1]

J. J. C. SMART

BLACK. I teach philosophy in a theological College. I have read and admired many of the writings of Wittgenstein and Ryle and other people of that sort. They seem to be right in suggesting that philosophy is concerned with concepts, not with things, that philosophy is an investigation of the logic of our language, the classification of concepts into various categories. Philosophy, it seems, is not the discovery of profound truths about the universe, unattainable by the methods of the special sciences. It is the logical investigation of the concepts of common sense, of science, of history, of ethics, of law, and (might I add) of religion and theology. All this, no doubt, is very interesting, and very valuable in academic circles, but what worries me is whether it is the sort of thing we ought to teach here. In the old days some of us thought that philosophy could prove the existence of God, and so on, but I agree with you that all such hopes were delusory and based on mistaken logic. No doubt philosophy, in its modern form, is a wonderful wit sharpener, and is good for teaching people to think clearly, and to prevent them from falling into certain confusions. But is it specially valuable for *us*?

WHITE. I think I can see what is worrying you. Of course, there is one short answer that could be given to your question.

[1] In writing this paper I am much indebted to discussions with members of the Society of the Sacred Mission, St. Michael's House, Crafers, South Australia, and especially to Father Marcus Stephens, S.S.M., who will recognize many of his own remarks in those of 'Black'.

Some philosophers would say that philosophy is of the greatest importance for prospective theologians simply because a logical analysis of theological concepts would show theology to be a mass of confusion, a system of statements which either are obviously false or else are nonsensical. So on their view the study of philosophy would be of importance because it would lead you to change your way of life and to close down your institution. (Needless to say I do not number myself among these philosophers.) Other philosophers of the modern type take a more moderate line. They hold that philosophy is theologically neutral, just as it is scientifically and ethically neutral. According to them the analysis and clarification of the concepts of religion and theology can be as legitimate a sphere of philosophical activity as is the analysis and clarification of the concepts of science and ethics. This, I think, is the view that you yourself are inclined to take. And, clearly, on this view it is difficult to see how philosophy is *specially* relevant to your students. We do not expect all scientists to be trained in the philosophy of science or all historians to have studied the philosophy of history. Why, then, should we expect that ordinands should be versed in the logic of theological discourse?

BLACK. Yes, why should they? After all, it is only a proportion of our people who are academically minded. They have a lot of work to do here. It would no doubt be a good intellectual exercise for them if they learned some philosophy, something of the logic of our language, but I cannot see that this is specially important for us. On the old view that philosophy is a sort of super-science, that it consists of a body of factual propositions of a rather profound sort, it would have seemed that not to teach philosophy to our men is to send them out without a most important body of information about the universe. But if philosophy is only the investigation of the logic of language, then it is possibly an entertaining and even useful subject of study, but not something that everybody ought to do here. We want our people to know what is right and what is wrong, but is it necessary for them to engage in philosophical investigations, such as the

13

investigation of whether goodness can be reduced to non-ethical properties?

WHITE. When people began saying that philosophy is logical grammar, that it is the investigation of concepts or the distinguishing of categories (in Ryle's sense) and things of that sort, what they said was valuable and illuminating. For one thing, it helped to get rid of the old idea that philosophy is a sort of super-science,[2] that it examines the truth of certain propositions that the special sciences have to treat as assumptions. For that matter, it also neatly expresses disagreement with certain other hoary stories, for example that philosophy is the study of the mind (though the rise of psychology as an experimental science also helped to put that one out of court) or that it is the study of a separate world of Platonic essences. You can see why philosophers should now want to say that philosophy is logic.

BLACK. Wait a minute. By 'logic' you don't mean, A, E, I and O, do you?[3]

WHITE. No. I am using 'logic' in a very wide sense. Any conceptual investigation, such as the discovery of what Ryle calls 'category distinctions', is what I am here calling logic. I don't mean 'A, E, I and O', and nor do I mean modern symbolic logic either. I mean the logic of *all* words, including such ones as 'cause', 'know', 'good', 'happy', and 'God'. 'A, E, I and O' only investigates rather easy words like 'all' and 'some' and 'none'.

BLACK. Yes. I see. But I thought I'd better raise the point. For 'A, E, I and O' is what 'logic' tends to mean for us here.

WHITE. Well, then, you see how attractive is the statement that philosophy is logic. And yet it is seriously misleading. It does not do justice to the way in which philosophical problems in fact arise and to the motives that impel people to study philosophy. (Not only to begin to study philosophy but to go on studying it). In order to make my point clear I

---

[2] See the article on 'Philosophy' in *Encyclopedia Britannica* (13), Vol. XXI, p. 41, part of which is quoted by W. H. Watson in *On Understanding Physics*, pp. 7–8. Watson's comments are very much to the point.

[3] [The traditional formal logic with its examination of the four figures of the syllogism.—Eds.]

propose to make a distinction between *metaphysical* questions and *logical* questions. Remember that I am still using 'logic' in the wide sense that we agreed on a few moments ago. Examples of metaphysical questions are: 'How do mind and matter interact?' 'Is the will free?' 'What would it be like if time went backwards?' 'Do we see things as they really are or do we only see appearances?' As an example of a logical question we can take the one you mentioned: 'Is goodness reducible to a set of non-ethical properties?' Other examples of logical questions are: 'Is looking related to seeing as running is to winning? (Is "see" an "achievement" word?)'[4] 'Is the concept of legal responsibility a defeasible[5] concept?' 'Can the analytic-synthetic distinction be usefully applied to the propositions of theoretical science?'[6] Notice that the logical questions, if you understand the terminology of them, are fairly clear, but the metaphysical questions put us in a bit of a whirl. Notice also that the metaphysical questions have at any rate the appearance of being about the world, whereas the logical questions are overtly conceptual. I shall make it the definition of a metaphysical question that (1) it has at any rate the appearance of being factual, (2) it is in some way puzzling—we don't quite know how to get clear about the question, how even to set about answering it. The logical questions, on the other hand, do not have any appearance of being about the world, and they do not give us the dizzy feeling the metaphysical ones do: there are techniques for answering them, and though we may not in fact be able to answer them we know roughly what sort of answer would be required.

BLACK. Do you mean to say, then, that the metaphysical questions are one thing, the logical questions quite another?

WHITE. No. For it is my opinion that if we engage in certain conceptual investigations, that is, if we try to answer some of the logical questions, we can eventually (if we are clever enough) dissolve away a metaphysical question so that

4 Cf. Ryle, *Concept of Mind*, pp. 149–53 and 222–3.
5 In Hart's sense. See H. L. A. Hart, 'The Ascription of Responsibility and Rights', *Logic and Language* (*First Series*), edited by A. G. N. Flew.
6 Cf. my article on 'Hertz', *Australasian Journal of Philosophy*, 1951.

either no question remains at all or else what remains is a straight question of one of the special sciences, or of history, or perhaps of practical ethics or of revealed theology. This straight question may or may not be easy to answer but it will have replaced the metaphysical one. So you see, when we ask the metaphysical question the conceptual investigations are of interest to us because we hope that they will enable us to see the metaphysical question in a new light, perhaps to transform it utterly, or even to make it vanish.

BLACK. How could a question vanish?

WHITE. Well, the old example of the dog that runs round the cow will do. Suppose the dog runs round and round in a complete circle with the cow in the middle. The cow, however, is pivoting round so that she is always facing the dog. Does the dog run round the cow or not? A very naïve person might consider that this was a question of fact. He might even think that it was worth-while to make delicate measurements of the angular velocity of the dog. Psychologists often seem to me to be like this. They have a simple faith that experiments will always help them when in fact their puzzles are often due to conceptual muddles. Now, of course, we can see that there is no straight answer to the question of the dog and the cow. We see that the question vanishes: we no longer want to answer it. In a sense the dog runs round the cow, for he runs in a complete circle with the cow in the middle. But in a sense the dog does not run round the cow. For he never gets behind her.

BLACK. Yes, naïve people might argue both sides of the dog and cow case as though they were rival factual hypotheses. But is the dog and cow question a metaphysical one? I don't feel like saying that it is, and yet it satisfies your two criteria. For to naïve people it appears to be a factual question, and it is also the sort of question that makes them dizzy: none of the usual techniques such as measurement or observation or deduction seem to help them to answer it.

WHITE. Perhaps I should add a third criterion for calling a question 'metaphysical'. For normally we feel inclined to

16

call a question 'metaphysical' only if it is ideologically significant, that is, if we feel that it *matters* what the answer is. The questions about mind and body, free-will, time and the reality of matter have connections (or seem to have connections) with the general question of the destiny of the human soul. It is partly because the dog and cow question is *not* ideologically significant that I chose it for an example of how a question can vanish. We are much more likely to see what is happening if we take a case where our emotions are not involved. Another reason for choosing that example is, of course, the obviousness of what has gone wrong when people treat it as a factual question.

BLACK. Do you mean to say that no metaphysical questions are factual?

WHITE. Not exactly. It may well be that when the metaphysical question is clarified it will be replaced by one from one of the special sciences or humanities. In this case it may well be factual. To take a simple example, suppose people are puzzled about the localization of mental functions, and are wondering whether something mental can really be located in something material, a lump of grey matter. The clear question that replaces this one is something like this; given a certain mental function, are there bits of the brain that can be chopped out so that this mental function disappears while the other mental functions are unaffected? Only experiment can answer this question for us. Where the philosopher's job ends the neurophysiologist's begins.

BLACK. In this case, then, the metaphysical question is replaced by one of neurophysiology. One might say that the original question was metaphysical-cum-neurophysiological. Are there any questions that are metaphysical-cum-theological?

WHITE. Now you are getting down to brass tacks. Your point, I take it, is that it is only if some metaphysical questions turn out to be also theological that there is any point in the study of metaphysics here?

BLACK. Yes. And of logic in your sense of the word too. For our interest in logic would be that it is the tool for transforming the metaphysical-cum-theological questions (if there are any).

WHITE. Here is an example of a metaphysical question that is also a theological one. 'Why should there be anything at all?' This seems to me to be a question I very much want to ask. And yet it is certainly a metaphysical question. It puts my head in a whirl. I don't feel at all clear about just what sort of question it is, what are the ways to set about answering it. It is not like a question in mathematics or science or history. In mathematics or science or history the question is easy to understand. What is difficult is discovering the answer. But in the case of 'Why should anything exist at all?' I feel that the question itself is most unclear. And yet I do want to go on asking it.

BLACK. Has your question got anything to do with the cosmological argument for the existence of God?

WHITE. Something to do with it. As an argument the cosmological argument cannot pass muster at all. Nevertheless it does appeal to something deep-seated in our natures. It takes its stand on the fact that the existence of you or me or this table is not logically necessary. Logic tells us that this 'fact' is not really a fact at all, but is a truism like the 'fact' that a circle is not a square. The cosmological argument tries to base the existence of you or me or this table on the existence of a logically necessary being, and hence commits a rank absurdity, for the notion of a logically necessary being is a self-contradictory one. So the only rational thing to say if someone asks, 'Why does this table exist?' is to say some such thing as that a certain carpenter made it. But now let us ask my question, 'Why should anything exist at all?' This is not like asking why some specific thing such as this table exists, and it cannot have the same sort of answer. Logic seems to tell me that the only answer which is not absurd is 'Why shouldn't it?' Nevertheless, though I know how any answer on the lines of the cosmological argument can be pulled to pieces, I feel I still want to go on asking the question.

BLACK. Your question 'Why should anything exist at all?'

is certainly, according to your criteria, a metaphysical question. But in what way is it also a theological question?

WHITE. It seems to me to be a theological question for the following reason. There are many philosophers—perhaps they are the majority of philosophers—who see no problem here. They would say quite cheerfully that the only retort that could be given to the question is the one I mentioned: 'Why shouldn't it?' Now if another philosopher took such a line I should not be inclined to accuse him of lack of intelligence. Normally when another philosopher cannot see the point of a philosophical puzzle one is inclined to accuse him of lack of intelligence and acumen. But not in this case. What I should be inclined to accuse such a philosopher of would not be lack of intelligence but a certain superficiality, a lack of seriousness, a lack of reverence for reality. That is why I want to say that the question 'Why should anything exist at all?' is not only a metaphysical question but is also a theological one. It is no doubt a muddled question, and logical analysis might make it disappear, or perhaps transform it into another question. What I want you to notice, however, is that it does not present itself to us as a conceptual question: our motives for trying to answer it are not those of logical tidiness.

BLACK. You have given an example of a metaphysical question that you are also inclined to call a theological question. It is not, however, a very typical theological question. What about the question at issue between Arius and Athanasius? Is this metaphysical?

WHITE. Certainly. It satisfies my criteria for 'metaphysics'. The doctrine of the trinity is certainly lacking in conceptual clarity. And yet Christians still affirm that it is a doctrine which is basically true.

BLACK. Apart from its conceptual character, what sort of question is it? Is it scientific, is it historical, or what is it?

WHITE. In order to find out what sort of question it is you must see what sort of considerations would settle it. How was this question settled? Something like this: Arius regarded

Christ as created by God. But if Christ was created by God then he is only a very big thing, divine but not himself God, worthy perhaps of our profoundest admiration but not of worship. Now if we accept the premiss that Christ *is* a worthy object of worship *and* the premiss that no created being, however big, is a worthy object of worship, then we must deny that Christ is a created being.

BLACK. And we get the first premiss, that Christ is a worthy object of worship, from our reading of the Gospels. It is a value judgment that those of us who are convinced by the Gospels feel we just have to make. What about the premiss that no created being, however big, is a worthy object of worship? Isn't that a value judgment too?

WHITE. Yes, in the sense that if someone who appeared to understand the issues involved did say that a created being could be a proper object of worship, we should not criticize him on the score of lack of intelligence but on the score of the lack of some sort of insight.

BLACK. We might say that it all depends on experience. By this, of course, I don't mean the usual 'argument from religious experience'. By 'experience' I don't mean 'special experiences'.

WHITE. The doctrine of the trinity is far too big a question, of course, for us to do justice to now. But by asking this question, 'How do we think the controversy between Arius and Athanasius should be settled?' we provide ourselves with a tool for deciding what sort of question it is that lurks behind the metaphysics, the logical unclarity. Athanasius expressed himself in the terminology of Greek philosophy, but however he expressed it, he was trying to do justice to the question of what is a proper object of worship, and to the fact that, on our reading of the Gospels, we are constrained to acknowledge that Christ is a proper object of worship.

BLACK. No one would deny that the doctrine of the trinity is metaphysical in your sense: there appear to be contradictions however we formulate it. But in principle, I hope, these contradictions could be resolved and a clear doctrine propounded which would do justice to all our theological insights. But are theological questions all metaphysical, all tinged with conceptual confusion?

WHITE. Not at all. The question of the virgin birth is a theological question in that it is the sort of question discussed by theologians. But it is not in the least metaphysical. It can be quite clearly stated, the whole thing is perfectly conceivable, and our belief in its truth is based on personal testimony. Of course, many people do not believe in the virgin birth, but I think no one would say that it wasn't the sort of thing that can be *imagined* or *described* with clarity. In fact it is a straight historical question.

BLACK. If any historical question is straight. Clearly someone with materialist presuppositions will assess the historical evidence differently from someone who believes in the divinity of Christ. If you believe in the divinity of Christ there is, of course, no strong compulsion to believe that Christ was born in the normal way. After all, Christ is unique, and our usual rules about what normally happens can't be expected to apply. If you are not inclined to believe in the general Christian doctrine you will on the other hand take a very different view of the very same historical evidence. After all, the historical evidence is only a lot of marks on paper—e.g. the Codex Sinaiticus. If you find the Christian story hard to swallow you can always fall back on the known fact of the credulity and mendacity of mankind to explain it away. So our reading of history depends on our presuppositions.[7] Even in settling a question of theological history, faith is involved. Where we do differ here from the Roman Catholics is that while we recognize the impotence of historical data apart from faith, we do stress that faith must not run on ahead of the historical data. Thus in the doctrine of the Immaculate Conception the Roman Church shows very plausibly how fitting and appropriate the Immaculate Conception is, in a sense how it conforms to reason. But because we have no warrant for it in Scripture we do not

[7] F. H. Bradley's 'Presuppositions of Critical History', published in his *Collected Essays*, Vol. I, is of great interest in this connection.

make it an article of faith. That it appears fitting and appropriate is not, by itself, enough for us.

WHITE. You said, '*if* any historical question is straight'. Surely some historical questions *are* straight. Whether you were a Christian or an atheist you wouldn't expect that to matter in deciding whether, say, Napoleon lost the battle of Waterloo.

BLACK. True enough. There has been much dispute about the historical truth of the story of the resurrection, but no serious historian, to my knowledge, has questioned the truth of the crucifixion. After all, crucifixions are not contrary to our common experience. We could produce one for you now (though it would be hard on the victim). But we couldn't in the same sort of way produce a resurrection for you now.

WHITE. Anyway, we are losing the thread of our argument. Whether an historical question like that of the virgin birth or the resurrection is a 'straight' historical question or not, it is an historical question without any tinge of metaphysics. Occurrences like the virgin birth and the resurrection are quite clearly *conceivable*, even by those who regard them as *unbelievable*. It is not like the doctrine of the trinity, which contains elements of conceptual difficulty. Some people might say that there was no clear doctrine at all, nothing which was clearly enough stated to be either believable or unbelievable. In this case there is much work for the theological logician to do!

BLACK. So here logic is the handmaid of theology! And putting it more generally: logic is the handmaid of metaphysics. The questions we puzzle over may resolve themselves into conceptual questions, or perhaps leave a non-metaphysical residue (say of science, history or revealed theology), but, you say, they do not present themselves to us *as* conceptual questions.

WHITE. Yes, that is the point. People begin to study philosophy because they ask questions that are *not* overtly conceptual. They ask questions like 'Have we free-will?' not questions like 'Can goodness be reduced to non-ethical properties?' Even though their questions turn out to be

22

conceptual in nature, or at any rate to be very largely conceptual in nature, that is not how they present themselves to us in the first place. And that is why the layman is liable to be slightly misled when philosophers tell him that philosophy is logic, the sorting out of categories, that sort of thing. Admittedly professional philosophy tends to become more and more overtly conceptual—more logical and less metaphysical. This is for two reasons. In the first place conceptual investigations help to clarify metaphysical disputes. Now there is no way of telling beforehand just what logical distinctions are going to clarify a given metaphysical question. Hence it is good policy to engage in overtly conceptual investigations over as wide a field as possible even though at the time some of them may not appear to have any obvious metaphysical relevance. In the second place philosophers tend to get an intellectual and aesthetic delight in the study of the logical structure of language, and so tend to study philosophy, in its logical guise, even though they do not feel the impact of metaphysical problems. Some philosophers study philosophy mainly from the metaphysical motive; some philosophers study it mainly from the logical motive. But most philosophers have mixed motives. There are some questions which they feel metaphysically, that do not present themselves in overtly conceptual form, and there are other questions which are quite clearly questions of logical grammar. For example, I am interested in the following metaphysical puzzle: 'Why is the universe markedly asymmetrical in the time dimension in a way in which it is not markedly asymmetrical in space dimensions?'[8] (What worries me is that I can't make up my mind whether or not the asymmetry in question is just a 'brute fact' that must be accepted.) But I am also interested in, say, the resolution of the 'heterological' paradox, which does not appear to be a metaphysical question at all.[9] It is overtly conceptual.

BLACK. So you think that we should teach logic here

[8] See 'The Temporal Asymmetry of the World', *Analysis*, Vol. 14 (1954), pp. 79–83.

[9] See, G. Ryle, 'Heterologicality' in *Analysis*, Vol. 11, (1951), pp. 61–9.

because some of the theological questions we ask are meta-physical in nature, and we can clarify them only by learning to understand the logical issues involved?

WHITE. Yes. For you the interest of logic is its application to the clarification of metaphysical questions. Logic is the servant of metaphysics. Of course, the reverse thing happens sometimes. Sometimes we can treat metaphysics as the servant of logic. For example, when Parmenides deduced that there could be only one thing in the world, and that this thing could have no specific qualities, we can turn his argument round. We can say: 'The conclusion is obviously false. There is more than one thing. So what has gone wrong with the argument?' We can treat Parmenides' argument as a *reductio-ad-absurdum* proof of the necessity for distinguishing different senses of 'is', namely that of existence ('God is'), that of identity ('God is the ruler of the universe'), and that of predication ('God is good'). Every metaphysical argument for an absurd conclusion can be turned round in this way into a *reductio-ad-absurdum* argument for a conceptual truth.

BLACK. When you say that metaphysics in these cases can be turned into *reductio-ad-absurdum* proofs of conceptual truths I suspect that you are not using 'metaphysics' in the same way as you were before. For you were using 'meta-physical' as an adjective to the noun 'question', whereas we don't talk about Parmenides' question but about his argument and conclusion.

WHITE. Yes, you are right there. In talking about Parmenides I was using 'metaphysics' in the sense of 'deduc-tive metaphysics'. And since I don't believe that there can be any such thing as a deductive science of metaphysics this application of the word 'metaphysics' is pejorative in a way in which my previous application of the word was anything but pejorative. Admittedly the latter use of the word implied 'confused', but confusion is not always something to be ashamed of: sometimes it is to our credit that we wade into deep waters. I only wanted to mention the old deductive metaphysics in order to show you that even this can be turned inside out and made into something philosophically valuable.

BLACK. Let me see if I have got your point right. You hold that the study of philosophy—that is, of logic, in your sense of the word 'logic'—is of first-rate importance to us because many of our theological questions are metaphysical, in your sense of the word 'metaphysical'. That is, they are somehow confused, and we must transform them by seeing them in the light of logical knowledge before we can get anywhere with them.

WHITE. Yes. Scientists, historians and critics sometimes find themselves entangled in metaphysical questions born of conceptual muddles. But in theology you very frequently, not just sometimes, find that your questions are philosophical in nature. Hence you need to study philosophy. I shall use one final example to make my point clear. Do you not agree that the question of how you can reconcile the existence of evil in the world with that of an omnipotent and benevolent God is a question with which you ought to be concerned?

BLACK. Yes, of course it is.

WHITE. Well, Professor J. L. Mackie of Otago recently discussed this problem in a paper he read in August at a philosophical conference in Melbourne.[10] Let me try to recollect the outline of his argument. He distinguished different orders of evil. First of all there are the first-order evils: pains, discomforts, distress of every kind. Still, he said, the theist might argue that there were second-order goods which it would be logically impossible for us to have if you didn't have the first-order evils. These second-order goods are virtues like sympathy, kindness and helpfulness. Clearly these cannot (*logically* cannot) exist without first-order evils. (Though one might wonder whether it is necessary for there to be *as much* of the first-order evil as there appears to be. However, we'll waive this point now.) Now the goodness of these second-order goods might outweigh the badness of the

10 This paper is to be published in *Mind*. There is a similar line of argument in Professor Flew's paper on 'Divine Omnipotence and Human Freedom', in this volume (Ch. VIII).

first-order evils. But Mackie then went on to ask: how would you explain the existence of second-order evils? Not only do we find in the world sympathy, kindness and helpfulness but we also find selfishness, unkindness and cruelty.

BLACK. Couldn't you say that forgiveness is a third-order good? You couldn't have forgiveness without second-order evils.

WHITE. That's a suggestion that Mackie didn't specifically consider. But his reply would be that you couldn't then explain unforgiveness. This would be a third-order evil.

BLACK. If you could only be forgiving, never unforgiving, there wouldn't be free-will.

WHITE. This is the suggestion that Mackie goes on to consider. He says that you can explain the second-order evils (as I said, he didn't consider the possibility of forgiveness as a third-order good) by reference to free-will. We might hold that free-will is of such transcendent value that God buys it at the price of second-order evils. But then the question arises: is it logically necessary for there to be free-will that there should be second-order evils? Could God not make people so that they always freely chose the right?

BLACK Surely there is a contradiction here. If God made people so that they always chose right then they couldn't choose freely.

WHITE. This is the point up to which I was trying to lead. You say that it is a contradiction to say that man could be made so that they always freely chose the right. Mackie thinks that there is no contradiction here and I for one cannot see that he is wrong. The more one examines the question of freedom the more it comes to seem that free-will is not necessarily incompatible with determinism.[11] However, you can see that this question: 'Is there a contradiction in saying that God could have made us so that we always freely chose right?' is in my sense a *logical* question. And you also see how we were brought up against it in discussing the theological problem of evil. And I think that this sort of thing will happen

[11] Flew argues for this point briefly in Ch. VIII, 'Divine Omnipotence and Human Freedom'.

in nearly every theological problem you discuss. You will be brought up sooner or later against some question of logic : some question of the sort that earlier on you felt inclined to say could not be of much importance for your students.

University of Adelaide
    AUSTRALIA

III

THE EXISTENCE OF GOD[1]

J. J. C. SMART

This lecture is not to discuss whether God exists. It is to discuss reasons which philosophers have given for saying that God exists. That is, to discuss certain arguments.

First of all it may be as well to say what we may hope to get out of this. Of course, if we found that any of the traditional arguments for the existence of God were sound, we should get out of our one hour this Sunday afternoon something of inestimable value, such as one never got out of any hour's work in our lives before. For we should have got out of one hour's work the answer to that question about which, above all, we want to know the answer. (This is assuming for the moment that the question 'Does God exist?' is a proper question. The fact that a question is all right as far as the rules of ordinary grammar are concerned does not ensure that it has a sense. For example, 'Does virtue run faster than length?' is certainly all right as far as ordinary grammar is concerned, but it is obviously not a meaningful question. Again, 'How fast does time flow?' is all right as far as ordinary grammar is concerned, but it has no clear meaning. Now some philosophers would ask whether the question 'Does God exist?' is a proper question. The greatest danger to theism at the present moment does not come from people who deny the validity of the arguments for the existence of God, for many Christian theologians do not believe that the existence of God can be proved, and certainly nowhere in the Old or New Testaments do we find any evidence of people's religion having a metaphysical basis. The main

[1] A public lecture given at the University of Adelaide in 1951.

danger to theism today comes from people who want to say that 'God exists' and 'God does not exist' are equally absurd. The concept of God, they would say, is a nonsensical one. Now I myself shall later give grounds for thinking that the question 'Does God exist?' is not, in the full sense, a proper question, but I shall also give grounds for believing that to admit this is not necessarily to endanger theology.)

However, let us assume for the moment that the question 'Does God exist?' is a proper question. We now ask: Can a study of the traditional proofs of the existence of God enable us to give an affirmative answer to this question? I contend that it can not. I shall point out what seem to me to be fallacies in the main traditional arguments for the existence of God. Does proving that the arguments are invalid prove that God does not exist? Not at all. For to say that an argument is invalid is by no means the same thing as to say that its conclusion is false. Still, if we do find that the arguments we consider are all fallacious, what do we *gain* out of our investigation? Well, one thing we gain is a juster (if more austere) view of what philosophical argument can do for us. But, more important, we get a deeper insight into the logical nature of certain concepts, in particular, of course, the concepts of deity and existence. Furthermore we shall get some hints as to whether philosophy can be of any service to theologians, and if it can be of service, some hints as to how it can be of service. I think that it can be, but I must warn you that many, indeed perhaps the majority, of philosophers today would not entirely agree with me here (see Ch. II above).

One very noteworthy feature which must strike anyone who first looks at the usual arguments for the existence of God is the extreme brevity of these arguments. They range from a few lines to a few pages. St. Thomas Aquinas presents five arguments in three pages! Would it not be rather extraordinary if such a great conclusion should be got so easily? Before going on to discuss any of the traditional arguments in detail I want to give general grounds for suspecting anyone who claims to settle a controversial question by means of a short snappy argument.

My reason for doubting whether a short snappy argument can ever settle any controversial question is as follows: *any argument can be reversed*. Let me explain this. A question of elementary logic is involved. Let us consider an argument from two premisses, *p*, *q*, to a conclusion *r*:

$$p$$
$$q$$
$$\overline{}$$
$$r$$

If the argument is valid, that is, if *r* really does follow from *p* and *q*, the argument will lead to agreement about *r* provided that there already is agreement about *p* and *q*. For example, if we have the premisses

p All A, B and C grade cricketers are entitled to a free pass to the Adelaide Oval for Test matches, Sheffield Shield matches, etc. (quite uncontroversial, it can be got from the rules of the South Australian Cricket Association).

q John Wilkin is an A, B or C grade cricketer. (Quite uncontroversial, everyone knows it.)

we may conclude

r John Wilkin is entitled to a free pass to the Adelaide Oval for Test matches, Sheffield Shield matches, etc.

But we now consider this argument[2]:

p Nothing can come into existence except through the activity of some previously existing thing or being.

q The world had a beginning in time.

therefore

r The world came into existence through the activity of some previously existing thing or being.

If this argument is valid (as it certainly is) then it is equally the case that

(not-*r*) The world did not come into existence through the activity of some previously existing thing or being

implies that either

---

[2] I owe this illustration, and the whole application to the idea of 'reversing the argument', to Prof. D. A. T. Gasking of Melbourne.

(not-*p*) Something *can* come into existence otherwise than through the activity of a previously existing thing or being

or

(not-*q*) The world had no beginning in time.

That is, if $\dfrac{\substack{p \\ q}}{r}$ is valid $\dfrac{\substack{\text{not-}r \\ q}}{\text{not-}p}$ and $\dfrac{\substack{\text{not-}r \\ p}}{\text{not-}q}$ must be equally valid.

Now it is possible that a person might think that we have *fewer* reasons for believing *r* than we have for believing (not-*p*) or (not-*q*). In which case the argument $\dfrac{\substack{p \\ q}}{r}$ though perfectly valid will not convince him. For he will be inclined to argue in the opposite direction, that is, from the falsity of *r* to the falsity of either *p* or *q*.

This last example is perhaps itself a—not very good— argument for the existence of God, but I have given it purely as an example to show *one* of the things to look out for when criticizing more serious arguments. The other thing to look out for, of course, is whether the argument is *valid*. It is my belief that in the case of any metaphysical argument it will be found that if the premisses are uncontroversial the argument is unfortunately not valid, and that if the argument is valid the premisses will unfortunately be just as doubtful as the conclusion they are meant to support.

With these warnings in mind let us proceed to the discussion of the three most famous arguments for the existence of God. These are:

(1) The Ontological Argument.
(2) The Cosmological Argument.
(3) The Teleological Argument.

The first argument—the ontological argument—really has no premisses at all. It tries to show that there would be a contradiction in denying that God exists. It was first formulated by St. Anselm and was later used by Descartes. It is not a convincing argument to modern ears, and St. Thomas Aquinas gave essentially the right reasons for rejecting it. However, it is important to discuss it, as an understanding of what is wrong with it is necessary for evaluating the second argument, that is, the cosmological argument. This argument does have a premiss, but not at all a controversial one. It is that something exists. We should all, I think, agree to that. The teleological argument is less austere in manner than the other two, It tries to argue to the existence of God not purely *a priori* and not from the mere fact of *something* existing, but from the actual features we observe in nature, namely those which seem to be evidence of design or purpose.

We shall discuss these three arguments in order. I do not say that they are the only arguments which have been propounded for the existence of God, but they are, I think, the most important ones. For example, of St. Thomas Aquinas' celebrated 'Five Ways' the first three are variants of the cosmological argument, and the fifth is a form of the teleological argument.

The Ontological Argument. This as I remarked, contains no factual premiss. It is a *reductio-ad-absurdum* of the supposition that God does not exist. Now *reductio-ad-absurdum* proofs are to be suspected whenever there is doubt as to whether the statement to be proved is *significant*. For example, it is quite easy, as anyone who is familiar with the so-called Logical Paradoxes will know, to produce a not *obviously* nonsensical statement, such that both it *and* its denial imply a contradiction. So unless we are sure of the significance of a statement we cannot regard a *reductio-ad-absurdum* of its contradictory as proving its truth. This point of view is well known to those versed in the philosophy of mathematics; there is a well-known school of mathematicians, led by Brouwer, who refuse to employ *reductio-ad-absurdum* proofs. However, I shall not press this criticism of the ontological argument, for this criticism is somewhat abstruse (though it has been foreshadowed by Catholic philosophers, who object to the

*also
Leibniz* —

ontological argument by saying that it does not first show
that the concept of an infinitely perfect being is a *possible*
one). We are at present assuming that 'Does God exist?' is
a proper question, and if it is a proper question there is no
objection so far to answering it by means of a *reductio-ad-
absurdum* proof. We shall content ourselves with the more
usual criticisms of the ontological argument.

The ontological argument was made famous by Descartes.
It is to be found at the beginning of his Fifth Meditation. As
I remarked earlier it was originally put forward by Anselm,
though I am sorry to say that to read Descartes you would
never suspect that fact! Descartes points out that in mathematics we can deduce various things purely *a priori*, 'as for
example', he says, 'when I imagine a triangle, although
there is not and perhaps never was in any place . . . one such
figure, it remains true nevertheless that this figure possesses a
certain determinate nature, form, or essence, which is . . . not
framed by me, nor in any degree dependent on my thought;
as appears from the circumstance, that diverse properties of
the triangle may be demonstrated, for example that its three
angles are equal to two right, that its greatest side is sub-
tended by its greatest angle, and the like'. Descartes now
goes on to suggest that just as having the sum of its angles
equal to two right angles is involved in the idea of a triangle,
so *existence* is involved in the very idea of an infinitely perfect
being, and that it would therefore be as much of a contradiction to assert that an infinitely perfect being does not
exist as it is to assert that the three angles of a triangle do not
add up to two right angles or that two of its sides are not
together greater than the third side. We may then, says
Descartes, assert that an infinitely perfect being *necessarily*
exists, just as we may say that two sides of a triangle are
together *necessarily* greater than the third side.

This argument is highly fallacious. To say that a so-and-so
exists is not in the least like saying that a so-and-so has such-
and-such a property. It is not to amplify a concept but to say
that a concept applies to something, and whether or not a
concept applies to something can not be seen from an

33

examination of the concept itself. Existence is not a property. 'Growling' is a property of tigers, and to say that 'tame tigers growl' is to say something about tame tigers, but to say 'tame tigers exist' is not to say something about tame tigers but to say that there are tame tigers. Prof. G. E. Moore once brought out the difference between existence and a property such as that of being tame, or being a tiger, or being a growler, by reminding us that though the sentence 'some tame tigers do not *growl*' makes perfect sense, the sentence 'some tame tigers do not *exist*' has no clear meaning. The fundamental mistake in the ontological argument, then, is that it treats 'exists' in 'an infinitely perfect being exists' as if it ascribed a property existence to an infinitely perfect being, just as 'is loving' in 'an infinitely perfect being is loving' ascribes a property, or as 'growl' in 'tame tigers growl' ascribes a property : the verb 'to exist' in 'an infinitely perfect being exists' does not ascribe a property to something already conceived of as existing but says that the concept of an infinitely perfect being applies to something. The verb 'to exist' here takes us right out of the purely conceptual world. This being so, there can never be any *logical contradiction* in denying that God exists. It is worth mentioning that we are less likely to make the sort of mistake that the ontological argument makes if we use the expression 'there is a so-and-so' instead of the more misleading form of words 'a so-and-so exists'.

Russell's Theory of Descriptions

I should like to mention another interesting, though less crucial, objection to Descartes' argument. He talks as though you can deduce further properties of, say, a triangle, by considering its definition. It is worth pointing out that from the definition of a triangle as a figure bounded by three straight lines you can only deduce trivialities, such as that it is bounded by more than one straight line, for example. It is not at all a contradiction to say that the two sides of a triangle are together less than the third side, or that its angles do not add up to two right angles. To get a contradiction you have to bring in the specific axioms of Euclidean geometry. (Remember school geometry. how you used to prove that the angles of a triangle add up to two right angles. Through the vertex *C* of the triangle *ABC* you drew a line parallel to *BA*, and so you assumed the axiom of parallels for a start. <u>Definitions, by themselves, are not deductively potent</u>. Descartes, though a very great mathematician himself, was profoundly mistaken as to the nature of mathematics. However, we can interpret him as saying that from the definition of a triangle, *together with the axioms of Euclidean geometry*, you can deduce various things, such as that the angles of a triangle add up to two right angles. But this just shows how <u>pure mathematics is a sort of game with symbols</u>; <u>you start with a set of axioms, and operate on them in accordance with certain rules of inference</u>. All the mathematician requires is that the axiom set should be *consistent*. Whether or not it has application to reality lies outside pure mathematics. Geometry is no fit model for a proof of real existence.

We now turn to the *Cosmological Argument*. This argument does at least seem more promising than the ontological argument. It does start with a factual premiss, namely that something exists. The premiss that something exists is indeed a very abstract one, but nevertheless it *is* factual, it does give us a foothold in the real world of things, it does go beyond the consideration of mere concepts. The argument has been put forward in various forms, but for present purposes it may be put as follows:

Everything in the world around us is *contingent*. That is, with regard to any particular thing, it is quite conceivable that it might not have existed. For example, if you were asked why you existed, you could say that it was because of your parents, and if asked why they existed you could go still further back, but however far you go back you have not, so it is argued, made the fact of your existence really intelligible. For however far back you go in such a series you only get back to something which itself might not have existed. For a really satisfying explanation of why anything contingent (such as you or me or this table) exists you must eventually begin with something which is not itself contingent, that is, with something of which we cannot say that it might not have existed, that is we must begin with a necessary being. So the first part of the argument boils down to this. *If anything exists an absolutely necessary being must exist. Something exists. Therefore an absolutely necessary being must exist.*

The second part of the argument is to prove that a necessarily existing being must be an infinitely perfect being, that is, God. Kant[3] contended that this second stage of the argument is just the ontological argument over again, and of course if this were so the cosmological argument would plainly be a fraud; it begins happily enough with an existential premiss ('something exists') but this would only be a cover for the subsequent employment of the ontological argument. This criticism of Kant's has been generally accepted but I think that certain Thomist philosophers have been right in attributing to Kant's own criticism a mistake in elementary logic. Let us look at Kant's criticism. Kant says, correctly enough, that the conclusion of the second stage of the cosmological argument is 'All necessarily existing beings are infinitely perfect beings'. This, he says, implies that 'Some infinitely perfect beings are necessarily existing beings'. Since, however, there could be only one infinitely perfect, unlimited, being, we may replace the proposition 'Some infinitely perfect beings are necessarily existing beings' by the proposition 'All infinitely perfect beings are necessarily existing beings'. (To make this last point clearer let me take an analogous example. If it is true that some men who are Prime Minister of Australia are Liberals and if it is also true that there is only one Prime Minister of Australia, then we can equally well say that all men who are Prime Minister of Australia are Liberals. For 'some' means 'at least one', and if there is only one Prime Minister, then 'at least one' is equivalent to 'one', which in this case is 'all'.) So the conclusion of the second stage of the cosmological argument is that 'all infinitely perfect beings are necessarily existing beings'. This, however, is the principle of the ontological argument, which we have already criticized,

[3] *Critique of Pure Reason*, A 603.

and which, for that matter, proponents of the cosmological argument like Thomas Aquinas themselves reject.

Kant has, however, made a very simple mistake. He has forgotten that the existence of a necessary being has already been proved (or thought to have been proved) in the first part of the argument. He changes 'All necessary beings are infinitely perfect beings' round to 'Some infinitely perfect beings are necessary beings'. If this change round is to be valid the existence of a necessary being is already presupposed. Kant has been misled by an ambiguity in 'all'. 'All X's are Y's' may take it for granted that there are some X's or it may not. For example if I say, 'All the people in this room are interested in Philosophy', it is already agreed that there are some people in this room. So we can infer that 'Some of the people interested in Philosophy are people in this room'. So 'All the people in this room are interested in Philosophy' says more than 'If anyone were in this room he would be interested in Philosophy', for this would be true even if there were in fact no people in this room. (As I wrote this lecture I was quite sure that *if* anyone came he would be interested in Philosophy, and I could have been quite sure of this even if I had doubted whether anyone would come.) Now sometimes 'All X's are Y's' does mean only 'If anything is an X it is a Y'. Take the sentence 'All trespassers will be prosecuted'. This does not imply that some prosecuted people will be trespassers, for it does not imply that there are or will be any trespassers. Indeed the object of putting it on a notice is to make it more likely that there won't be any trespassers. All that 'All trespassers will be prosecuted' says is, 'If anyone is a trespasser then he will be prosecuted'. So Kant's criticism won't do. He has taken himself and other people in by using 'all' sometimes in the one way and sometimes in the other.

While agreeing thus far with Thomist critics of Kant[4] I still want to assert that the cosmological argument is

---

[4] See, for example, Fr. T. A. Johnston, *Australasian Journal of Philosophy*, Vol. XXI, pp. 14–15, or D. J. B. Hawkins, *Essentials of Theism*, pp. 67–70, and the review of Fr. Hawkins' book by A. Donagan, *Australasian Journal of Philosophy*, Vol. XXVIII, especially p. 129.

radically unsound. The trouble comes much earlier than where Kant locates it. The trouble comes in the *first* stage of the argument. For the first stage of the argument purports to argue to the existence of a necessary being. And by 'a necessary being' the cosmological argument means 'a *logically* necessary being', i.e. 'a being whose non-existence is inconceivable in the sort of way that a triangle's having four sides is inconceivable'. The trouble is, however, that the concept of a logically necessary being is a self-contradictory concept, like the concept of a round square. For in the first place 'necessary' is a predicate of *propositions*, not of things. That is, we can contrast *necessary* propositions such as '3+2=5', 'a thing cannot be red and green all over', 'either it is raining or it is not raining', with *contingent* propositions, such as 'Mr. Menzies is Prime Minister of Australia', 'the earth is slightly flattened at the poles', and 'sugar is soluble in water'. The propositions in the first class are guaranteed solely by the rules for the use of the symbols they contain. In the case of the propositions of the second class a genuine possibility of agreeing or not agreeing with reality is left open; whether they are true or false depends not on the conventions of our language but on reality. (Compare the contrast between 'the equator is 90 degrees from the pole', which tells us nothing about geography but only about our map-making conventions, and 'Adelaide is 55 degrees from the pole', which does tell us a geographical fact.) So no informative proposition can be logically necessary. Now since 'necessary' is a word which applies primarily to propositions, we shall have to interpret 'God is a necessary being' as 'The proposition "God exists" is logically necessary.' But this *is* the principle of the ontological argument, and there is no way of getting round it this time in the way that we got out of Kant's criticism. No existential proposition can be logically necessary, for we saw that the truth of a logically necessary proposition depends only on our symbolism, or to put the same thing in another way, on the relationship of concepts. We saw, however, in discussing the ontological argument, that an existential proposition does not say that one concept is involved in another, but that a concept applies to something. An existential proposition must be very different from any logically necessary one, such as a mathematical one, for example, for the conventions of our symbolism clearly leave it open for us either to affirm or deny an existential proposition; it is not our symbolism but reality which decides whether or not we must affirm it or deny it.

The demand that the existence of God should be *logically* necessary is thus a self-contradictory one. When we see this and go back to look at the first stage of the cosmological argument it no longer seems compelling, indeed it now seems to contain an absurdity. If we cast our minds back, we recall that the argument was as follows: that if we explain why something exists and is what it is, we must explain it by reference to something else, and we must explain that thing's being what it is by reference to yet another thing, and so on, back and back. It is then suggested that unless we can go back to a logically necessary first cause we shall remain intellectually unsatisfied. We should otherwise only get back to something which might have been otherwise, and with reference to which the same questions can again be asked. This is the argument, but we now see that in asking for a logically necessary first cause we are doing something worse than asking for the moon. It is only *physically* impossible for us to get the moon; if I were a few million times bigger I could reach out for it and give it to you. That is, I know what it would be *like* to give you the moon, though I cannot *in fact* do it. A logically necessary first cause, however, is not impossible in the way that giving you the moon is impossible; no, it is *logically* impossible. 'Logically necessary being' is a self-contradictory expression like 'round square'. It is not any good saying that we would only be intellectually satisfied with a logically necessary cause, that nothing else would do. We can easily have an absurd wish. We should all like to be able to eat our cake and have it, but that does not alter the fact that our wish is an absurd and self-contradictory one. We reject the cosmological argument, then, because it rests on a thorough absurdity.

Having reached this conclusion I should like to make one or two remarks about the necessity of God. First of all, I think that it is undeniable that if worship is to be what religion takes it to be, then God must be a necessary being in some sense or other of 'necessary'. He must not be just one of the things in the world, however big. To concede that he was just one of the things in the world, even a big one, would reduce religion to something near idolatry. All I wish to point out is that God can not be a *logically* necessary being, for the very supposition that he is is self-contradictory. (Hence, of course, to say that God is not logically necessary is not to place any limitations on him. It is not a limitation on your walking ability that you cannot go out of the room and not go out. To say that someone cannot do something self-contradictory is not to say that he is in any way impotent, it is to say that the sentence 'he did such and such and did not do it' is not a possible description of anything.) Theological necessity cannot be logical necessity. In the second place, I think I can see roughly what sort of necessity theological necessity might be. Let me give an analogy from physics. It is not a *logical* necessity that the velocity of light in a vacuum should be constant. It would, however, upset physical theory considerably if we denied it. Similarly it is not a logical necessity that God exists. But it would clearly upset the structure of our religious attitudes in the most violent way if we denied it or even entertained the possibility of its falsehood. So if we say that it is a *physical* necessity that the velocity of light *in vacuo* should be constant—(deny it and prevailing physical theory would have to be scrapped or at any rate drastically modified)—similarly we can say that it is a *religious* necessity that God exists. That is, we believe in the necessity of God's existence because we are Christians; we are not Christians because we believe in the necessity of God's existence. There are no short cuts to God. I draw your attention to the language of religion itself, where we talk of *conversion*, not of *proof*. In my opinion religion can stand on its own feet, but to found it on a metaphysical argument *a priori* is to found it on absurdity born of ignorance of the

40

logic of our language. I am reminded of what was said about the Boyle lectures in the eighteenth century: that no one doubted that God existed until the Boyle lecturers started to prove it.

Perhaps now is the time to say why I suggested at the beginning of the lecture that 'Does God exist?' is not a proper question. Once again I make use of an analogy from science. 'Do electrons exist?' (asked just like that) is not a proper question. In order to acquire the concept of an electron we must find out about experiments with cathode-ray tubes, the Wilson cloud chamber, about spectra and so on. We then find the concept of the electron a useful one, one which plays a part in a mass of physical theory. When we reach this stage the question 'Do electrons exist?' no longer arises. Before we reached this stage the question 'Do electrons exist?' had no clear meaning. Similarly, I suggest, the question 'Does God exist?' has no clear meaning for the unconverted. But for the converted the question no longer arises. The word 'God' gets its meaning from the part it plays in religious speech and literature, and in religious speech and literature the question of existence does not arise. A theological professor at Glasgow once said to me: 'Religion is "O God, if you exist, save my soul if it exists!"' This of course was a joke. It clearly is just *not* what religion is. So within religion the question 'Does God exist?' does not arise, any more than the question 'Do electrons exist?' arises within physics. Outside religion the question 'Does God exist?' has as little meaning as the question 'Do electrons exist?' as asked by the scientifically ignorant. Thus I suggest that it is possible to hold that the question 'Does God exist?' is not a proper question without necessarily also holding that religion and theology are nonsensical.

The cosmological argument, we saw, failed because it made use of the absurd conception of a *logically* necessary being. We now pass to the third argument which I propose to consider. This is the *Teleological Argument*. It is also called 'the Argument from Design'. It would be better called the argument *to* design, as Kemp Smith does call it, for clearly that the universe has been designed by a great architect is to assume a great part of the conclusion to be proved. Or we could call it 'the argument from apparent design'. The argument is very fully discussed in Hume's *Dialogues concerning Natural Religion*, to which I should like to draw your attention. In these dialogues the argument is presented as follows: 'Look round the world: Contemplate the whole and every part of it: You will find it to be nothing but one great machine, subdivided into an infinite number of lesser machines. . . . The curious adapting of means to ends, throughout all nature, resembles exactly, though it much exceeds, the productions of human contrivance. . . . Since therefore the effects resemble each other, we are led to infer, by all the rules of analogy, that the causes also resemble; and that the Author of nature is somewhat similar to the mind of man; though possessed of much larger faculties, proportioned to the grandeur of the work which he has executed.'

This argument may at once be criticized in two ways: (1) We may question whether the analogy between the universe and artificial things like houses, ships, furniture, and machines (which admittedly are designed) is very close. Now in any ordinary sense of language, it is true to say that plants and animals have *not* been designed. If we press the analogy of the universe to a plant, instead of to a machine, we get to a very different conclusion. And why should the one analogy be regarded as any better or worse than the other? (2) Even if the analogy were close, it would only go to suggest that the universe was designed by a *very great* (not infinite) architect, and note, an *architect*, not a *creator*. For if we take the analogy seriously we must notice that we do not create the materials from which we make houses, machines and so on, but only *arrange* the materials.

This, in bare outline, is the general objection to the argument from design, and will apply to any form of it. In the form in which the argument was put forward by such theologians as Paley, the argument is, of course, still more open to objection. For Paley laid special stress on such things as the eye of an animal, which he thought must have been contrived by a wise Creator for the special benefit of the animal. It seemed to him inconceivable how otherwise such a complex organ, so well suited to the needs of the animal, should have arisen. Or listen to Henry More: 'For why have we three joints in our legs and arms, as also in our fingers, but that it was much better than having two or four? And why are our fore-teeth sharp like chisels to cut, but our inward teeth broad to grind, [instead of] the fore-teeth broad and the other sharp? But we might have made a hard shift to have lived through in that worser condition. Again, why are the teeth so luckily placed, or rather, why are there not teeth in other bones as well as in the jaw-bones? for they might have been as capable as these. But the reason is, nothing is done foolishly or in vain; that is, there is a divine Providence that orders all things.' This type of argument has lost its persuasiveness, for the theory of Evolution explains why our teeth are so luckily placed in our jaw-bones, why we have the most convenient number of joints in our fingers, and so on. Species which did not possess advantageous features would not survive in competition with those which did.

The sort of argument Paley and Henry More used is thus quite unconvincing. Let us return to the broader conception, that of the universe as a whole, which seems to show the mark of a benevolent and intelligent Designer. Bacon expressed this belief forcibly: 'I had rather beleave all the Fables in the Legend and the Talmud and the Alcoran than that this Universal Frame is without a Minde.' So, in some moods, does the universe strike us. But sometimes, when we are in other moods, we see it very differently. To quote Hume's dialogues again: 'Look around this Universe. What an immense profusion of beings, animated and organized, sensible and active! You admire this prodigious variety and fecundity. But inspect a little more narrowly these living existences, the only beings worth regarding. How hostile and destructive to each other! How insufficient all of them for their own happiness! ... the whole presents nothing but the idea of a blind Nature, impregnated by a great vivifying principle, and pouring forth from her lap, without discernment or parental care, her maimed and abortive children!' There is indeed a great deal of suffering, some part of which is no doubt attributable to the moral choices of men, and to save us from which would conflict with what many people would regard as the greater good of moral freedom, but there is still an immense residue of apparently needless suffering, that is, needless in the sense that it could be prevented by an omnipotent being. The difficulty is that of reconciling the presence of evil and suffering with the assertion that God is both omnipotent and benevolent. If we *already* believe in an omnipotent and benevolent God, then some attempt may be made to solve the problem of evil by arguing that the values in the world form a sort of organic unity, and that making any *part* of the world better would perhaps nevertheless reduce the value of the whole. Paradoxical though this thesis may appear at first sight, it is perhaps not theoretically absurd. If, however, evil presents a *difficulty* to the believing mind, it presents an *insuperable* difficulty to one who wishes to argue rationally from the world as we find it to the existence of an omnipotent and benevolent God. As Hume puts it: 'Is the world considered in general, and as it appears to us in this life, different from what a man ... would *beforehand* expect from a very powerful, wise and benevolent Deity? It must be a strange prejudice to assert the contrary. And from thence I conclude, that, however consistent the world may be, allowing certain suppositions and conjectures, with the idea of such a Deity, it can never afford us an inference concerning his existence.'

The teleological argument is thus extremely shaky, and in any case, even if it were sound, it would only go to prove the existence of a very great architect, not of an omnipotent and benevolent Creator.

Nevertheless, the argument has a fascination for us that reason can not easily dispel. Hume, in his twelfth dialogue, and after pulling the argument from design to pieces in the previous eleven dialogues, nevertheless speaks as follows:

44

'A purpose, an intention, a design strikes everywhere the most careless, the most stupid thinker; and no man can be so hardened in absurd systems as at all times to reject it . . . all the sciences almost lead us insensibly to acknowledge a first Author.' Similarly Kant, before going on to exhibit the fallaciousness of the argument, nevertheless says of it: 'This proof always deserves to be mentioned with respect. It is the oldest, the clearest and the most accordant with the common reason of mankind. It enlivens the study of nature, just as it itself derives its existence and gains ever new vigour from that source. It suggests ends and purposes, where our observation would not have detected them by itself, and extends our knowledge of nature by means of the guiding-concept of a special unity, the principle of which is outside nature. This knowledge . . . so strengthens the belief in a supreme Author of nature that the belief acquires the force of an irresistible conviction.' It is somewhat of a paradox that an invalid argument should command so much respect even from those who have demonstrated its invalidity. The solution of the paradox is perhaps somewhat as follows[5]: The argument from design is no good as an argument. But in those who have the seeds of a genuinely religious attitude already within them the facts to which the argument from design draws attention, facts showing the grandeur and majesty of the universe, facts that are evident to anyone who looks upwards on a starry night, and which are enormously multiplied for us by the advance of theoretical science, these facts have a powerful effect. But they only have this effect on the already religious mind, on the mind which has the capability of feeling the religious type of awe. That is, the argument from design is in reality no argument, or if it is regarded as an argument it is feeble, but it is a potent instrument in heightening religious emotions.

Something similar might even be said of the cosmological argument. As an argument it cannot pass muster at all; indeed it is completely absurd, as employing the notion of a

5 See also N. Kemp Smith's Henrietta Hertz Lecture, 'Is Divine Existence Credible?', *Proceedings of the British Academy*, 1931.

logically necessary being. Nevertheless it does appeal to something deep seated in our natures. It takes its stand on the fact that the existence of you or me or this table is not logically necessary. Logic tells us that this fact is not a fact at all, but is a truism, like the 'fact' that a circle is not a square. Again, the cosmological argument tries to base the existence of you or me or this table on the existence of a logically necessary being, and hence commits a rank absurdity, the notion of a logically necessary being being self-contradictory. So the only rational thing to say if someone asks 'Why does this table exist?' is some such thing as that such and such a carpenter made it. We can go back and back in such a series, but we must not entertain the absurd idea of getting back to something logically necessary. However, now let us ask, 'Why should anything exist at all?' Logic seems to tell us that the only answer which is not absurd is to say, 'Why shouldn't it?' Nevertheless, though I know how any answer on the lines of the cosmological argument can be pulled to pieces by a correct logic, I still feel I want to go on asking the question. Indeed, though logic has taught me to look at such a question with the gravest suspicion, my mind often seems to reel under the immense significance it seems to have for me. That anything should exist at all does seem to me a matter for the deepest awe. But whether other people feel this sort of awe, and whether they or I ought to is another question. I think we ought to. If so, the question arises: If 'Why should anything exist at all?' cannot be interpreted after the manner of the cosmological argument, that is, as an absurd request for the nonsensical postulation of a logically necessary being, what sort of question is it? What sort of question is this question 'Why should anything exist at all?' All I can say is, that I do not yet know.

University of Adelaide
AUSTRALIA

IV

CAN GOD'S EXISTENCE BE DISPROVED?

A

J. N. FINDLAY

The course of philosophical development has been full of attempted proofs of the existence of God. Some of these have sought a basis in the bare necessities of thought, while others have tried to found themselves on the facts of experience. And, of these latter, some have founded themselves on *very general facts*, as that something exists, or that something is in motion, while others have tried to build on *highly special facts*, as that living beings are put together in a purposive manner, or that human beings are subject to certain improbable urges and passions, such as the zeal for righteousness, the love for useless truths and unprofitable beauties, as well as the many specifically religious needs and feelings. The general philosophical verdict is that none of these 'proofs' is truly compelling. The proofs based on the necessities of thought are universally regarded as fallacious: it is not thought possible to build bridges between mere abstractions and concrete existence. The proofs based on the general facts of existence and motion are only felt to be valid by a minority of thinkers, who seem quite powerless to communicate this sense of validity to others. And while most thinkers would accord weight to arguments resting on the special facts we have mentioned, they wouldn't think such arguments successful in ruling out a vast range of counter-possibilities. Religious people have, in fact, come to acquiesce in the total absence of any cogent proofs of the Being they believe in: they even

47

find it positively satisfying that something so far surpassing clear conception should also surpass the possibility of demonstration. And non-religious people willingly mitigate their rejection with a tinge of agnosticism: they don't so much deny the existence of a God, as the existence of good reasons for believing in him. We shall, however, maintain in this essay that there isn't room, in the case we are examining, for all these attitudes of tentative surmise and doubt. For we shall try to show that the Divine Existence can only be conceived, in a religiously satisfactory manner, if we also conceive it as something inescapable and necessary, whether for thought or reality. From which it follows that our modern denial of necessity or rational evidence for such an existence amounts to a demonstration that there cannot be a God.

Before we develop this argument, we must, however, give greater precision to our use of the term 'God'. For it is possible to say that there are nearly as many 'Gods' as there are speakers and worshippers, and while existence may be confidently asserted or denied of *some* of them, we should feel more hesitant in the case of others. It is one thing, plainly, to pronounce on God's existence, if he be taken to be some ancient, shapeless stone, or if we identify him with the bearded Father of the Sistine ceiling, and quite another matter, if we make of him an 'all-pervasive, immaterial intelligence', or characterize him in some yet more negative and analogical manner. We shall, however, choose an indirect approach, and pin God down for our purposes as the 'adequate object of religious attitudes'. Plainly we find it possible to gather together, under the blanket term 'religious', a large range of cases of possible action, linked together by so many overlapping[1] affinities that we are ready to treat them as the varying 'expressions' of a single 'attitude' or 'policy'. And plainly we find it possible to indicate the character of that attitude by a number of descriptive phrases which, though they may err individually by savouring too strongly of particular cases, nevertheless permit us, in their

[1] This word is added to avoid the suggestion that there must be *one* pervasive affinity linking together all the actions commonly called 'religious'.

48

totality, to draw a rough boundary round the attitude in question. Thus we might say, for instance, that a religious attitude was one in which we tended to abase ourselves before some object, to defer to it wholly, to devote ourselves to it with unquestioning enthusiasm, to bend the knee before it, whether literally or metaphorically. These phrases, and a large number of similar ones, would make perfectly plain the sort of attitude we were speaking of, and would suffice to mark it off from cognate attitudes which are much less unconditional and extreme in their tone. And clearly similar phrases would suffice to fix the boundaries of religious *feeling*. We might describe religious frames of mind as ones in which we felt ready to abase ourselves before some object, to bend the knee before it, and so forth. Here, as elsewhere, we find ourselves indicating the *felt* character of our attitudes, by treating their inward character as, in some sense, a concentrated and condensed substitute for appropriate lines of action, a way of speaking that accords curiously with the functional significance of the inward.[2] But not only do we incorporate, in the meanings of our various names for attitudes, a reference to this readiness for appropriate lines of action: we also incorporate in these meanings a reference to *the sorts of things or situations to which these attitudes are the normal or appropriate responses*. For, as a matter of fact, our attitudes are not indifferently evoked in *any* setting: there is a range of situations in which they normally and most readily occur. And though they may at times arise in circumstances which are not in this range, they are also readily dissipated by the consciousness that such circumstances *are* unsuitable or unusual. Thus fear is an attitude very readily evoked in situations with a character of menace or potential injury, and it is also an attitude very readily allayed by the clear perception that a given situation isn't really dangerous. And anger, likewise, is an attitude provoked very readily by perverse resistance and obstructive difficulty in some object, and is also very readily dissipated, even in animals, by the

---

2 Whatever the philosophical 'ground' for it may be, this plainly is the way in which we *do* describe the 'inner quality' of our felt attitudes.

consciousness that a given object is innocent of offence. All attitudes, we may say, *presume* characters in their objects, and are, in consequence, strengthened by the discovery that their objects *have* these characters, as they are weakened by the discovery that they really haven't got them. And not only do we find this out empirically: we also incorporate it in the *meanings* of our names for attitudes. Thus attitudes are said to be 'normal', 'fully justified' and so forth, if we find them altered in a certain manner (called 'appropriate') by our knowledge of the actual state of things, whereas we speak of them as 'queer' or 'senseless' or 'neurotic', if they aren't at all modified by this knowledge of reality. We call it abnormal, from this point of view, to feel a deep-seated fear of mice, to rage maniacally at strangers, to greet disasters with a hebephrenic giggle, whereas we think it altogether normal to deplore deep losses deeply, or to fear grave dangers gravely. And so an implicit reference to some standard object—which makes an attitude either normal or abnormal —is part of what we ordinarily mean by all our names for attitudes, and can be rendered explicit by a simple study of usage. We can consider the circumstances in which ordinary speakers would call an attitude 'appropriate' or 'justified'. And all that philosophy achieves in this regard is merely to push further, and develop into more considered and consistent forms, the implications of such ordinary ways of speaking. It can inquire whether an attitude would still seem justified, and its object appropriate, after we had reflected long and carefully on a certain matter, and looked at it from every wonted and unwonted angle. And such consideration may lead philosophers to a different and more reasoned notion of the appropriate objects of a given attitude, than could be garnered from our unreflective ways of speaking. And these developments of ordinary usage will only seem unfeasible to victims of that strange modern confusion which thinks of attitudes exclusively as hidden processes 'in our bosoms', with nothing but an adventitious relation to appropriate outward acts and objects.

How then may we apply these notions to the case of our

religious attitudes? Plainly we shall be following the natural trends of unreflective speech if we say that religious attitudes presume *superiority* in their objects, and such superiority, moreover, as reduces us, who feel the attitudes, to comparative nothingness. For having described a worshipful attitude as one in which we feel disposed to bend the knee before some object, to defer to it wholly, and the like, we find it natural to say that such an attitude can only be fitting where the object reverenced *exceeds* us very vastly, whether in power or wisdom or in other valued qualities. And while it is certainly possible to worship stocks and stones and articles of common use, one does so usually on the assumption that they aren't merely stocks and stones and ordinary articles, but the temporary seats of 'indwelling presences' or centres of extraordinary powers and virtues. And if one realizes clearly that such things *are* merely stocks and stones or articles of common use, one can't help suffering a total vanishing or grave abatement of religious ardour. To feel religiously is therefore to presume surpassing greatness in some object: so much characterizes the attitudes in which we bow and bend the knee, and enters into the ordinary meaning of the word 'religious'. But now we advance further —in company with a large number of theologians and philosophers, who have added new touches to the portrait of deity, pleading various theoretical necessities, but really concerned to make their object worthier of our worship— and ask whether it isn't wholly anomalous to worship anything *limited* in any thinkable manner. For all limited superiorities are tainted with an obvious relativity, and can be dwarfed in thought by still mightier superiorities, in which process of being dwarfed they lose their claim upon our worshipful attitudes. And hence we are led on irresistibly to demand that our religious object should have an *unsurpassable* supremacy along all avenues, that it should tower *infinitely* above all other objects. And not only are we led to demand for it such merely quantitative superiority: we also ask that it shouldn't stand surrounded by a world of *alien* objects, which owe it no allegiance, or set limits to its influence. The proper object of religious reverence must in some manner be *all-comprehensive*: there mustn't be anything capable of existing, or of displaying any virtue, without owing all of these absolutely to this single source. All these, certainly, are difficult requirements, involving not only the obscurities and doubtful significance of the infinite, but also all the well-worn antagonisms of the immanent and trans-cendent, of finite sinfulness and divine perfection and pre-ordination, which centuries of theological brooding have failed to dissipate. But we are also led on irresistibly to a yet more stringent demand, which raises difficulties which make the difficulties we have mentioned seem wholly inconsider-able: we can't help feeling that the worthy object of our worship can never be a thing that merely *happens* to exist, nor one on which all other objects merely *happen* to depend. The true object of religious reverence must not be one, merely, to which no *actual* independent realities stand opposed: it must be one to which such opposition is totally *inconceivable*. God mustn't merely cover the territory of the actual, but also, with equal comprehensiveness, the territory of the possible. And not only must the existence of *other* things be unthinkable without him, but his own non-existence must be wholly unthinkable in any circumstances. There must, in short, be no conceivable alternative to an existence properly termed 'divine': God must be wholly inescapable, as we remarked previously, whether for thought or reality. And so we are led on insensibly to the barely intelligible notion of a Being in whom Essence and Existence lose their separateness. And all that the great medieval thinkers really did was to carry such a development to its logical limit.

We may, however, approach the matter from a slightly different angle. Not only is it contrary to the demands and claims inherent in religious attitudes that their object should *exist* 'accidentally': it is also contrary to those demands that it should *possess its various excellences* in some merely adventitious or contingent manner. It would be quite unsatisfactory from the religious standpoint, if an object merely *happened* to be wise, good, powerful and so forth, even to a superlative degree, and if other beings had, *as a mere matter of fact*, derived their excellences from this single source. An object of this sort would doubtless deserve respect and admiration, and other quasi-religious attitudes, but it would not deserve the utter self-abandonment peculiar to the religious frame of mind. It would deserve the δουλεία canonically accorded to the saints, but not the λατρεία that we properly owe to God. We might respect this object as the crowning instance of most excellent qualities, but we should incline our head before the qualities and not before the person. And wherever such qualities were manifested, though perhaps less eminently, we should always be ready to perform an essentially similar obeisance. For though such qualities might be intimately characteristic of the Supreme Being, they still wouldn't be in any sense inalienably his own. And even if other beings had, in fact, derived such qualities from this sovereign source, they still would be *their own* qualities, possessed by them in their own right. And we should have no better reason to *adore* the author of such virtues, than sons have reason to adore superior parents, or pupils to adore superior teachers. For while these latter may deserve deep deference, the fact that we are coming to *participate* in their excellences renders them unworthy of our *worship*. Plainly a being that possesses and imparts desirable qualities—which other things might nevertheless have manifested though this source were totally absent—has all the utter inadequacy as a religious object which is expressed by saying that it would be *idolatrous* to worship it. Wisdom, kindness and other excellences deserve respect wherever they are manifested, but no being can appropriate them as its personal perquisites, even if it does possess them in a superlative degree. And so we are led on irresistibly, by the demands inherent in religious reverence, to hold that an adequate object of our worship must possess its various qualities *in some necessary manner*. These qualities must be intrinsically incapable of belonging to anything except in so far as they belong primarily to the object of our worship. Again we are led on to a queer and barely intelligible Scholastic doctrine, that God isn't merely good, but is in some manner indistinguishable from his own (and anything else's) goodness.

What, however, are the consequences of these requirements upon the possibility of God's existence? Plainly, (for all who share a contemporary outlook), they entail not only that there isn't a God, but that the Divine Existence is either senseless[3] or impossible. The modern mind feels not the faintest axiomatic force in principles which trace contingent things back to some necessarily existent source, nor does it find it hard to conceive that things should display various excellent qualities without deriving them from a source which manifests them supremely. Those who believe in necessary truths which aren't merely tautological, think that such truths merely connect the *possible* instances of various characteristics with each other: they don't expect such truths to tell them whether there *will* be instances of any characteristics. This is the outcome of the whole medieval and Kantian criticism of the Ontological Proof. And, on a yet more modern view of the matter, necessity in propositions merely reflects our use of words, the arbitrary conventions of our language. On such a view the Divine Existence could only be a necessary matter if we had made up our minds to speak theistically *whatever the empirical circumstances might turn out to be*. This, doubtless, would suffice for some, who speak theistically, much as Spinoza spoke monistically, merely to give expression to a particular way of looking at things, or of feeling about them. And it would also suffice for those who make use of the term 'God' to cover whatever tendencies towards righteousness and beauty are actually included in the make-up of our world. But it wouldn't suffice for the full-blooded worshipper, who can't help finding our actual world anything but edifying, and its half-formed tendencies towards righteousness and beauty very far from adorable. The religious frame of mind seems, in fact, to be in a quandary; it seems invincibly determined both to eat its cake

---

[3] I have included this alternative, of which I am not fond, merely because so many modern thinkers make use of it in this sort of connection.

and have it. It desires the Divine Existence both to have that inescapable character which can, on modern views, only be found where truth reflects an arbitrary convention, and also the character of 'making a real difference' which is only possible where truth doesn't have this merely linguistic basis. We may accordingly deny that modern approaches allow us to remain agnostically poised in regard to God: they force us to come down on the atheistic side. For if God is to satisfy religious claims and needs, he must be a being in every way inescapable, One whose existence and whose possession of certain excellences we cannot possibly conceive away. And modern views make it self-evidently absurd (if they don't make it ungrammatical) to speak of such a Being and attribute existence to him. It was indeed an ill day for Anselm when he hit upon his famous proof. For on that day he not only laid bare something that is of the essence of an adequate religious object, but also something that entails its necessary non-existence.[4]

The force of our argument must not, however, be exaggerated. We haven't proved that there aren't beings of all degrees of excellence and greatness, who may deserve attitudes approximating indefinitely to religious reverence. But such beings will at best be instances of valued qualities which we too may come to exemplify, though in lesser degree. And not only would it be idolatrous for us to worship them, but it would also be monstrous for them to exact worship, or to care for it. The attitude of such beings to our reverence would necessarily be deprecating: they would prefer co-operative atheists to adoring zealots. And they would probably hide themselves like royal personages from the anthems of their worshippers, and perhaps the fact that there are so few positive signs of their presence is itself a feeble evidence of their real existence. But whether such beings exist or not, they are not divine, and can never satisfy the demands inherent in religious reverence. And the effect of our argument will further be to discredit generally such forms of religion as attach a uniquely sacred meaning to

4 Or 'non-significance', if this alternative is preferred.

existent things, whether these things be men or acts or institutions or writings.

But there are other frames of mind, to which we shouldn't deny the name 'religious', which acquiesce quite readily in the non-existence of their objects. (This non-existence might, in fact, be taken to be the 'real meaning' of saying that religious objects and realities are 'not of this world'.) In such frames of mind we give ourselves over unconditionally and gladly to the task of indefinite approach toward a certain imaginary focus[5] where nothing actually is, and we find this task sufficiently inspiring and satisfying without demanding (absurdly) that there should be something actual at that limit. And the atheistic religious attitude we have mentioned has also undergone reflective elaboration by such philosophers as Fichte and Erigena and Alexander. There is, then, a religious atheism which takes full stock of our arguments, and we may be glad that this is so. For since the religious spirit is one of reverence before things greater than ourselves, we should be gravely impoverished and arrested if this spirit ceased to be operative in our personal and social life. And it would certainly be better that this spirit should survive, with all its fallacious existential trimmings, than that we should cast it forth merely in order to be rid of such irrelevances.

King's College
LONDON

B

G. E. HUGHES

Professor Findlay offers what he regards as a conclusive disproof of the existence of God. I do not intend here to state or restate any positive arguments for God's existence;

[5] To use a Kantian comparison.

indeed I am doubtful whether any such arguments are completely cogent (in the sense of showing conclusively that certain propositions which any sensible man would accept as true entail that God exists). But I am quite certain that Professor Findlay's disproof is invalid, and I want to show why.

Before I do so, however, I want to point out one great merit which he has compared with many other atheists whom one encounters, in that he has a much better idea than they have of what is involved in theism. Many arguments against the existence of God are such that the theist can gaily rebut them with the remark, 'But that is not at all the kind of being in whose existence I believe'. Not so with Professor Findlay's argument. He devotes the major part of his article to a clarification of some of the things which must be meant by 'God' if that term is to be used in an adequate religious sense. And he singles out (rightly, it seems to me) as crucial in the traditional Christian philosophical conception of God the notion that God is a being who both exists and possesses the various attributes he does possess 'in some necessary manner'. Any being of which this were not true, he says, might 'deserve the δουλεία canonically accorded to the saints, but not the λατρεία that we properly owe to God': it would be *idolatrous* to worship it. All this seems to me perfectly true; it is not, of course (as Professor Findlay would doubtless admit) a full exposition of theism, but it does express one essential element in the conception of God. Many theists might prefer an alternative formulation, and many might contend that there are more important things than this to be said about God; but unless a person believes at least that there exists a being describable in terms not essentially different from these then it would be better in the interests of clarity if of nothing else that he should cease to call himself a theist. This is not to say that I accept Professor Findlay's account of the motives which have led Christian philosophers to expound this conception of God, or that I should acquiesce in what I take to be the imputation of dishonesty involved in accusing them of 'pleading various theoretical necessities,

57

but really concerned to make their object worthier of our worship', but it is not necessary to take up this point here. What I hope I have made clear is that what I am quarrelling with in Professor Findlay's argument is not his account of the meaning of 'God' but his contention that this account entails that there is no God. This is what he argues towards the end of his paper, the crucial paragraph being that on pp. 54–5.

The argument here is, however, open to several serious objections.

(1) Firstly, a minor, though I think a highly symptomatic point: 'These requirements' (viz. that if God exists he must exist necessarily, and so forth), Professor Findlay writes, 'plainly (for all who share a contemporary outlook) entail not only that there isn't a God, but that the Divine Existence is either senseless or impossible.' Now, in the ordinary sense of 'contemporary', this just isn't true. All that could be maintained, on any definition of 'contemporary' which has the faintest claim to objectivity, is that the adherents of certain flourishing contemporary schools of thought would agree (or ought, on their own premises, to agree) that the entailment in question holds; there are in fact plenty of other present-day philosophers (e.g. the Neo-Scholastics) who would not at all agree. What then does Professor Findlay mean by 'contemporary'? Either, I think, he intends it as mere bluster—i.e. he is trying to say, 'If you don't see this, you're just a stick-in-the-mud'; or else he is using it simply as a label for a certain well-known view. Now admittedly we all have to baptize our own and other people's philosophical children, but we ought to be careful in our choice of names; the claiming of a royal title at the font does not automatically confer sovereignty. To refer to what is in fact only one among many modern philosophical views in terms which suggest that it is the *only* one, or at least that it is the only one which any sensible man can now hold, is simply to throw a spurious cloak of authoritativeness over something which is still *sub judice*. Whether even a complete unanimity among present-day philosophers would guarantee the entailment is of course

another question; but at least I don't think the theist need be intimidated by all this talk about 'a contemporary outlook' and 'the modern mind'.

(2) But this is the least of the complaints I have to make against Professor Findlay's argument. 'The modern mind', he continues, 'feels not the slightest force in principles which trace contingent things back to some necessarily existing source.' This, as I have remarked, is true only in a tendentious sense of 'modern', but even accepting that the 'modern mind' is correct on this issue, all that this amounts to is a denial of the validity of one of the traditional arguments for God's existence (viz. the argument *e contingentia mundi*, the so-called Third Way of Aquinas), and of course the invalidity of an argument does not entail the falsity of its conclusion.

(3) This is not, however, the nerve of Professor Findlay's argument. He does not wish merely to deny the validity of this traditional argument; he wishes further to assert that it follows from the contemporary outlook which he has in mind that God, defined as he defines him, *necessarily does not exist*. Any religiously adequate conception of God, he urges, must portray him as a necessary being, and 'modern views make it self-evidently absurd (if they don't make it ungrammatical) to speak of such a being and attribute existence to him'. Now admittedly most modern philosophers have a distaste for phrases like 'necessary being' and 'contingent being' (and this is a distaste which I share); most of those who are still content to use the terms 'necessary' and 'contingent' would wish to restrict their application to *propositions*. This, however, is a requirement we can easily comply with. Instead of saying 'God is a necessary being' we can say 'The proposition "God exists" is necessary, or necessarily true'; and I readily grant that this reformulation has great advantages. Professor Findlay's contention is, I take it, that it is self-evidently absurd to hold that 'God exists' is a necessary proposition; and, unless I am much mistaken, he contends this because he thinks that certain modern philosophical investigations of which he approves have shown that all existential propositions are necessarily contingent and all necessary propositions

are necessarily non-existential. As an instance of a view which he appears to consider modern *in excelsis* he mentions the theory that 'necessity in propositions merely reflects our use of words, the arbitrary conventions of our language'; (in fact, in the later part of the paragraph we are examining, this conventionalist view seems alone to be recognized as 'modern', whereas earlier in the same paragraph others were explicitly admitted to this favoured catagory—but I forbear to press the point). Now this conventionalist view is a theory about the nature of the necessary propositions of *logic and mathematics*; it owes all the plausibility it possesses to its ability to analyse the propositions of these two classes (or this one class, if that is preferred); and it does not in the least follow that there may not be other classes of necessary propositions which are incapable of such an analysis. Similarly the complementary theory that all existential propositions are contingent is, properly under-stood, a theory about *empirical* propositions; and it does not in the slightest follow from the view that all empirical exis-tential propositions are contingent that there may not be some other class of existential propositions which are not to be given such an analysis. Now those who maintain that 'God exists' is a necessary proposition usually maintain that it is the *only* necessary existential proposition; it is no part of their case that any empirical existential propositions are necessary, and they would not be in the slightest disconcerted by the view that these are all contingent; (indeed, to refer again to Aquinas, it is clear that if any necessary empirical existential proposition could be found the argument *e contingentia mundi* would immediately collapse). Nor, of course, would they hold that 'God exists' is a logical or mathematical proposition, and so a theory about such propositions seems scarcely relevant either. The attempt in fact is being made to present us with the dilemma: either 'God exists' is a verbal tautology, in which case it is non-existential (and therefore, of course, nonsensical); or it is not a tautology, in which case it is contingent (and therefore not about God). But this simply begs the central question at issue, viz. whether there can be any necessary non-tautological propositions. Professor Findlay has certainly not shown that there cannot; admittedly it is understandable and perfectly legitimate that in a short paper he should not attempt a full-dress argument for the philosophical basis of the views he holds, but it is, I think, sufficiently clear that he thinks that the conventionalist view has shown the impossibility of such propositions. In fact, however, even admitting (as Professor Findlay too easily, I think, assumes) that the conventionalist view has been established, the most that it shows is that *certain classes of necessary propositions* 'merely reflect the arbitrary conventions of our language'; and there is a wide gulf between maintaining this and maintaining that *only* such conventionally based propositions can be necessary. The technique of analysing statements into their empirical and non-empirical elements and then displaying the empirical elements as contingent and the non-empirical as non-existential, possibly even as tautologies, and of examining the often intricate and curious ways in which these elements can be combined in one statement—this, I should be the last to deny, has proved a most valuable device in that it often throws a flood of light on the ways in which we describe the world. What I protest against is its extension—or worse still, the conviction that it *must* be extended—beyond its natural, legitimate sphere, which is that of scientific and everyday statements about the 'natural world', to a sphere which it was never devised to cope with.

(4) Professor Findlay, I think (though I am not quite sure), employs a further argument which may be stated thus: 'If God exists, then he must exist *necessarily*, i.e. his existence must be "inescapable and necessary, whether for thought or reality". (p. 48); but some thinkers (the "contemporary" ones) do not find God's existence inescapable for their thought, they find it perfectly possible to conceive that there is no God; therefore God's existence is not inescapable for thought; therefore God does not exist.' My reason for thinking that he does wish to argue in this way (and even that this is perhaps his central argument) is partly that this

seems to be the plain implication of the following passage on p. 48, in which he indicates in advance the main line of his discussion: 'We shall try to show that the Divine Existence can only be conceived, in a religiously satisfactory manner, if we also conceive it as something inescapable and necessary, whether for thought or reality. From which it follows that our modern denial of necessity or rational evidence for such an existence amounts to a demonstration that there cannot be a God'; and partly that otherwise I cannot see the point in his criticism of the argument *e contingentia mundi* (to which I have already referred), which in itself proves nothing to the point but which seen as a stage in this argument does have relevance. My reason for doubting whether he *is* using this argument, however, is that in the paragraph on pp. 54–5, which as I have said contains the nerve of his argument for atheism, he seems to think that his argument depends on an acceptance of 'modern' philosophical views; whereas the argument I am tentatively attributing to him, if it is valid at all, does *not* depend on this but only on the much weaker (and indeed indisputable) premiss that some thinkers at some times have not found God's existence inescapable for their thought. But in case he does wish to use this argument, or in case anyone else wishes to, even if he does not, I want to point out that it rests on a confusion between a proposition's being necessary and its being *seen* or *known* to be necessary. That there is such a distinction and that it is important needs, I suppose, no elaboration. We often find ourselves confused and doubtful about whether a certain proposition is or is not necessary; we constantly meet people who use necessary propositions as if they were contingent, or contingent propositions as if they were necessary, or propositions which on one interpretation are necessary but on another contingent, without being clear in which sense they are using them. This is why the phrase 'inescapable for thought' is so dangerously ambiguous. If a proposition is necessary, then certainly we may say that anyone who thinks clearly and who thoroughly understands the subject-matter involved will find himself forced to accept it; and we can if we wish use the phrase 'inescapable for thought' to indicate simply this fact about a proposition. But it is by no means the case—as we all know—that *everyone* who considers such a proposition does find himself driven to accept it; and we might use the term 'inescapable for thought' in such a way that a proposition would be said to be inescapable for thought only if everyone who thought about it did in fact find himself forced to accept it. Now, if 'God exists' is to be a necessary proposition it only needs to be inescapable for thought in the first of these two senses; but if the argument we are examining is to hold it must be inescapable for thought in the second (and much stronger) sense.

Now no one, as far as I know, has maintained that God's existence is inescapable in the second sense; but it is worth while to point out that even in the first sense the phrase is still ambiguous. (*a*) A proposition might be inescapable in the sense that it is self-evident, that its truth or validity could be grasped by someone who thought clearly and thoroughly understood the terms involved, without the necessity of deducing it from other propositions. Of course, as I have remarked, it would not follow that any given person who considered such a proposition would be convinced of its truth, since he might not think clearly enough or have a sufficient understanding of its terms. It would not even follow that anyone at all could be found who grasped its self-evidence, since no one might in fact fulfil the conditions I have mentioned. It would not even follow, so far as I can see, that even human reason at its best could grasp its self-evidence, since there might be some limitations to human powers of reasoning and understanding which made it impossible that any conceivable human being could fulfil the conditions. We can therefore draw a distinction which we can express as that between a proposition's being (i) self-evident in itself; (ii) self-evident to certain actual human beings; (iii) self-evident to human reason at its best. (*b*) A proposition might be inescapable only in the sense that it is entailed by some other proposition or propositions which we have sound evidence for believing to be true. It does not, of course, follow that a proposition which is inescapable in this sense is a necessary proposition (since one contingent proposition can entail another and we seem to have sound reasons for believing some contingent propositions to be true), but it might be one. We can then draw distinctions under this heading corresponding to those under (*a*).

Perhaps it may be useful in this connection to illustrate the point of these distinctions by expressing in terms of them the disagreement about the proposition 'God exists' between Anselm who accepted and Aquinas who rejected the Ontological Argument. Both agreed that the proposition 'God exists' is self-evident in itself. Anselm held that it was also self-evident to certain actual human beings (of whom he himself was one), and *a fortiori* that it was self-evident to human reason at its best. Aquinas, however, denied that it was self-evident even to human reason at its best, and *a fortiori* to any actual human beings; he held, however, that it was inescapable in sense (*b*) to certain actual human beings (of whom *he* was one) and that it would be so to any human being who accepted certain empirical premises and clearly understood the argument from them.

For the above reasons I think it is safe to proclaim the failure of what I cannot resist calling Professor Findlay's Ontological Disproof of God's existence. By an 'Ontological Disproof' I mean an argument from the analysis of a concept to non-existence, just as the 'Ontological Proof' is an argument from the analysis of a concept to existence. Now an ontological disproof can certainly be valid, but only on one condition, viz. that the concept shall be shown to be self-contradictory; thus the proposition 'there is a round square in the next room' could be refuted by an ontological disproof. What I think Professor Findlay requires to show is that there is a contradiction of this kind involved in the notion of a 'necessary being', or if you prefer, in the statement ' "x exists" is a necessary proposition'. This he has not shown; the nearest he offers to an argument for it is the contention that all necessary propositions are tautologies and no tautology can be existential; but if I have been correct in pointing out that this, if it has been shown at all, has been shown to hold only of the necessary propositions of logic and mathematics, then what we have here is simply the old sad story of a useful but limited technique over-reaching itself—and over-reaching itself by an assumption it can do nothing to justify.

There is just one other point I want to add. It seems to me that the most plausible form of the Ontological Disproof would run as follows: 'If we define (or partially define) "God" as a "necessary being"—as we must—then this means that the proposition "God exists" becomes a tautology. Now no tautology can possibly be existential. Therefore "God exists" cannot possibly assert that God exists. Which is absurd.' I think this is a trickier argument to refute than any of Professor Findlay's, and it has, moreover, the advantage that it does not presuppose that only tautological propositions can be necessary. I think, however, that a reply can be made out along the following lines, though I admit I am less confident about this than about what I have said in my previous paragraphs. The theist had better not try to dispute the statement that no tautology can be existential; (indeed, perhaps one way of stating the fallacy in the traditional Ontological Argument is to say that it tries to make 'God exists' a tautology without realizing that no tautology can be existential). What he must do is to maintain that defining God as a necessary being does not involve regarding 'God exists' as a tautology. Admittedly if 'blue', e.g. were part of the definition of 'x', the 'x is blue' *would* be a tautology; but, as we all know so well, 'existence is not a predicate' and the matter is different here. Professor Findlay has said (and I have agreed with him) that an entity x would not rightly be called 'God' unless 'x exists' were a necessary proposition; (this is my terminology, not his, but I hope he would agree). Now every theist would, I think, wish to assert more about God than merely that he exists necessarily, and even that he strictly *means* more by the term 'God' than this; he wishes to assert that God has certain characteristics, and that no entity which did not possess these characteristics would be entitled to be called 'God', even though it did exist necessarily. Let us call these characteristics, whatever they may be, $a \ldots n$; they will not, of course, include existence or necessary existence, since existence is not a predicate. Then consider the proposition, 'An entity possessing characteristics $a \ldots n$ exists', which we shall call p. Now p may be either necessary, contingent and true, contingent and false, or impossible; and the point of the statement that a being which did not exist necessarily would not be God may be expressed by saying that only if p is a necessary proposition should we correctly call the 'entity possessing characteristics $a \ldots n$' God; if p turned out to be merely contingent and true, the entity would not be God—it would not deserve λατρεία. Now p is clearly not tautological, nor is it impossible unless there is a formal contradiction between some of the characteristics $a \ldots n$, which Professor Findlay does not contend (indeed, if I understand his second last paragraph rightly, he entertains the possibility that p may be contingent and *true*). Clearly, too, if $a \ldots n$ were any combination of empirical characteristics, p could not be necessary. But what the theist has to maintain is that *in this special case p* is necessary without being tautological; he need not maintain that this necessity can actually be seen by inspection of p, though in that case (if he is concerned to convince his opponent and not merely to rebut the charge of logical inconsistency) he would presumably have to maintain that there are other reasons for holding that p is necessary. And what the Ontological Atheist (i.e. the person who maintains that theism can be seen to be logically impossible by mere analysis of the concept of 'God') must show is that it is logically impossible for p to be a necessary proposition.

There may be other arguments for this ontological atheism than those advanced by Professor Findlay; if so I should be extremely interested to know what they are. Only they must not proceed, if they are to avoid begging the whole question at issue, simply by presenting us with the distinction between tautologies and empirical existential propositions and asking us to choose whether we will eat our cake or have it. The most that 'modern' views about such propositions can tell us about the contention that 'God exists' is a necessary proposition is that if it is we cannot here be using the term 'necessary' in quite the same sense as that in which we say that logico-mathematical propositions are necessary, and that we cannot be using the term 'exists' in quite the same way as when we say that tables and chairs exist. But these are statements with which the theist need have no quarrel.

Victoria University College
   Wellington
   NEW ZEALAND

C

A. C. A. RAINER (WINDSOR)

The affirmative answer which Professor Findlay gives to his question in his article is implied, so he argues, by the position of all those philosophers who maintain that 'necessity' can belong only to entailments or to linguistic rules, and not to propositions which assert existence (pp. 54–5). Now, the religious believer is committed, according to his analysis (pp. 50–5), to asserting God's existence as a 'necessary truth'. Therefore the believer is committed to assertions about an existent which are 'either senseless or impossible' (p. 54). If by God we mean an *ens necessarium* or a Being that exists with 'necessity' (and, according to Findlay, the religious believer *must* mean this), then 'modern views make it self-evidently absurd (if they don't make it ungrammatical) to speak of such a Being and attribute existence to him' (p. 55).

This argument lies open, I submit, to two main objections: (i) It depends on an ambiguity in the meaning and the application of the words 'necessity' and 'necessary'. (ii) The conclusion that it is 'self-evidently absurd' to speak about a Necessary Being is inconsistent with Findlay's own analysis of the religious attitude and its object in the earlier part of his article. Findlay, it is true, is not forced to attribute *existence* to the object which he assigns to the religious attitude. But he has chosen to describe the attitude of the believer in metaphysical terms which his conclusion, if correct, divests of significance.

(i) The necessity of God's existence is not the same as the necessity of a logical implication. It means, for those who believe in it, God's complete actuality, indestructibility, *aseitas* or independence of limiting conditions. It is a property ascribed to God, not a property of our assertions about God. To maintain that the ascription of such a property is logically absurd is to confuse the necessity of God's Being with the necessity of our thinking about it. That is to commit the converse fallacy of Anselm's ontological argument, namely, to say that a Perfect Being cannot exist necessarily, because we cannot necessarily assert its existence. Our assertion of God's existence may be contingent, although God's existence is necessary in the sense of being indestructible or eternal.

Findlay has argued further (pp. 52–4), that religious belief also implies the assertion that God possesses his properties in a necessary manner. Is this assertion logically absurd? Since it is an implicative or co-implicative proposition the absurdity cannot lie in attributing logical necessity to an existent, or in claiming logical necessity for an existential proposition. The admitted peculiarity of theological descriptions lies rather in their referring to a 'necessity' which cannot be established demonstratively. Religious belief does indeed imply that relations between God's attributes are the foundations of necessary truths, but of truths which are necessary *for God*, who alone can apprehend his essence, and not for us, whose descriptions of the Divine Nature are, owing to our limited capacity, analogical and not intuitive. The 'necessity' of assertions about God's nature and of the connection between his nature and his existence is relative to God's omniscience and not to human reason or experience. If at some level of mystical experience we could participate in God's own vision of his nature, then such assertions might become 'necessary truths' for us. But even without such participation we can assert significantly that a Being exists which possesses its properties in a necessary manner, and that for Divine Knowledge the relations between its nature and its existence are eternally and necessarily true.

For us, both the assertion of God's necessary existence and the assertion of his necessary possession of the properties of a Perfect Being are contingent. But they are verifiable in relation to moral and mystical experience and they are subject to the test of coherence with experience of our selves and of the world. I submit that it is a sufficient reply to Findlay's reasoning to maintain that the absurdity on modern logical principles of assertions of God's existence attaches only to those which (like Anselm's ontological proof), claim necessity for themselves as assertions, and not to those which assert the necessity of God's existence and nature.

(ii) If it is 'absurd' and 'ungrammatical' to talk about God's nature and existence, how are we to distinguish religion from day-dreaming, or artistic imagination or moral aspiration? Must we conclude that Findlay's discussion of religion and its object (on pp. 50–5) is 'self-evidently absurd'? If that discussion is to have a meaning, can it be 'self-evidently absurd' to speak about a Perfect Being? In the course of this psychological discussion the term 'God' has acquired a sufficiently determinate meaning to distinguish its denotation from the class of good and incompletely powerful beings and the classes of evil and ethically neutral beings. It is surprising and even disconcerting to find Findlay dismissing the term 'God' as non-significant in a single page of philosophical analysis, after showing so carefully in his psychological account that it is the focus of the religious attitude. The point is too complex to discuss adequately here. I must limit myself to suggesting that if the term 'God' is really non-significant, Findlay's earlier description of the religious attitude should be translated into emotive or projectional terms. There is a discrepancy between his psychological and philosophical analyses of religion. That, and not the self-stultification of religious belief is what his account of the matter shows.

It is true that, in the last paragraph of his article, Findlay tells us that frames of mind which 'acquiesce . . . in the non-existence of their objects' may be called 'religious'. But he is here using the term 'religious' in quite a different sense from the sense in which it is asserted on p. 52 that it is 'contrary to the demands and claims inherent in religious attitudes that their objects should *exist* accidentally'; and it is the earlier discussion, so a believer would maintain, and not the final paragraph of the article, which describes the religious attitude correctly. Moral aspiration is not religion; and religion is not day-dreaming. For a religious believer the assumption of the existence of the object of his belief is (to use Findlay's own expression on p. 52) 'wholly inescapable'.[6]

It may be worth while to point out in conclusion that there does not appear to be any agreement among the contemporary thinkers whose logical position is adopted by Findlay about the necessity of atheism. Lord Russell has stated on more than one occasion that his own secularist beliefs are based on empirical and not on logical grounds. Broad has always been careful to avoid committing himself to any rashly negative speculative conclusions.[7] There is nothing which definitely implies the *absurdity* of religious terms in Wittgenstein's *Tractatus*, though he makes clear that religion on his assumptions belongs to the sphere of the *inexpressible*. Carnap and his school would accept the absurdity of asserting God's existence, but on epistemological, not on strictly logical grounds. Whitehead did not accept the orthodox view of God's existence and nature; but he did not reject it for logical reasons.

But supposing that there were a consensus of contemporary thinkers about the theological implications of their inter-

6 Findlay forgets too, does he not, that belief in God, according to the testimony of believers, rests on faith, and not on logical insight? All that the believer claims is that belief in God, like belief in the existence of other persons, is a *reasonable* faith, not a necessary truth.

7 In his address to the Joint Session of the Mind Association and Aristotelian Society in 1947 he indicated that a synthesis in terms of values is, in his opinion, a tenable alternative in speculative philosophy 'Some Methods of Speculative Philosophy', *P.A.S.* Supp. Vol. XXI, pp. 26–7.

pretation of logic, or that the negative implications for theology of this interpretation had been demonstrated, what should the believer do? Accept the result without demur, and apply to a psycho-analyst for help in adjusting himself emotionally to a godless world? Not if he were a philosophical believer. It would be his responsibility, rather, to direct discussion on to the adequacy of the interpretation of logic assumed by contemporary thinkers. Precisely what form this interpretation should take is, and will continue to be, a matter for debate on purely logical and epistemological grounds. A critical examination of the presuppositions of thought and communication will help to clarify theological as well as scientific and philosophical thought. But do religious existentialists and intuitionalists alone among contemporary thinkers deserve to be ignored when they urge that the experience of moral and spiritual 'commitment' is relevant in testing a philosophical interpretation?

King's College
  Newcastle-upon-Tyne
  ENGLAND

D
J. N. FINDLAY

I am grateful to the able articles of Professor Hughes and Mr Rainer, which have forced me to restate and re-examine some of the points raised in my article on the non-existence of God. I anticipated the general line of their criticisms, and I entirely welcome them. For there can be nothing really 'clinching' in philosophy: 'proofs' and 'disproofs' hold only for those who adopt certain premisses, who are willing to follow certain rules of argument, and who use their terms in certain definite ways. And every proof or disproof can be readily evaded, if one questions the truth of its premisses, or the validity of its type of inference, or if one finds new senses in which its terms may be used. And it is quite proper, and one's logical duty, to evade an argument in this manner, if it leads to preposterous consequences. And Hughes and Rainer are within their rights in thinking my conclusions preposterous: only I don't agree with them. I may say further, that I only brought in references to a 'contemporary outlook', 'modern approaches' and so on, because I wanted to be frank and modest, and not because I thought such descriptions honorific. I merely wished to indicate for *what* classes of person I hoped that my argument would hold water, instead of claiming (absurdly) that it would hold for all persons, whatever they might assume, and however they might choose to use their terms.

I think, however, that my article will be better understood, if I mention the circumstances in which I first conceived it. Its central idea occurred to me as long ago as 1932, when I was not at all strongly influenced by 'verificationism' or 'logical empiricism'. The main point of my article can be simply stated as a development of the Kantian treatment of the Ontological Proof, which I was considering at the time: I am surprised, in fact, that it hasn't occurred to other persons. And it is strange that Kant, who found so many antinomies in our notion of the 'World', found none at all in our notion of God. For Kant said that it couldn't be necessary that there should ever *be* anything of any description whatsoever, and that *if* we included 'existence' in the definition of something—Kant, of course, didn't think we *should* so include it, as existence 'wasn't a predicate'—we could only say, *hypothetically*, that *if* something of a certain sort existed, then it *would* exist necessarily, but not, categorically, that it actually existed. And he also said that if one were willing to deny the existence of God, one couldn't be compelled to assert any property of him, no matter how intimately such a property formed part of his 'nature'. Now, Kant, of course, didn't make existence (or necessary existence) part of God's nature,[8] but I have argued that one *ought* to do so, if God is to be the adequate object of our religious attitudes. So that for

[8] Perhaps he does, however. See *Kritik der reinen Vernunft*, p. 676.

72

all those who are willing to accept *my* account of an adequate religious object, and also Kant's doctrine of the hypothetical character of necessary predications, it must follow inevitably that there cannot be an adequate object for our religious attitudes.

Now I admit to the full that my argument *doesn't* hold for those who have no desire to say that God exists in some necessary and inescapable manner. And hence Rainer is saying nothing to the point when he remarks that Broad and Russell (mentioned as typical modern thinkers) have not thought there was anything *impossible* in the existence of God. For neither Broad nor Russell thought of God as something whose non-existence *should* be inconceivable. And my argument also *doesn't* hold for those who regard the Ontological Proof (or some other *a priori* proof) as a valid argument. Nor will it hold for those who are willing to say, with Rainer, that one might *come* to perceive the necessity of God's existence in some higher mystical state, nor for those who say, with Hughes and St. Thomas, that God himself can perceive the 'necessity' of his own 'existence', though both this 'existence' and this 'necessity' are something totally different from anything that we understand by these terms. I should indeed be naïve if I thought I could trap the analogical eel[9] in my dialectical net. But my argument holds for all those thinkers—who may properly be called 'modern' in no narrow or 'tendentious' sense—who accept Kant's view that there aren't any necessary facts of existence and who also can be persuaded to hold that a God who is 'worth his salt' must either exist necessarily (in the same sense of 'necessary') or not at all. The force of my argument doesn't depend, moreover, on any recent analysis of necessity in terms of tautology: it holds on *any* account of the necessary that can be squared with the above conditions.

My argument is, however, exposed to much more serious difficulties than those raised by Rainer and Hughes. For the 'really modern philosopher' might doubt whether there was any genuine difference between my sort of atheism

9 This term isn't used disrespectfully: I approve of eels.

and the analogical theism of my opponents. And my argument has certainly suggested that there *was* some important difference between the two positions. For my opponents would admit, as I do, that one can never hope to have the Divine 'fully before one', so as to be able to say 'Lo here!' of it, in the same way that one says this of one's friend Jones or the Eiffel Tower. They would say with me, that one can't ever hope to meet with more than 'expressions', 'approximations' or 'analogies' of the Divine, that it is in the nature of the Divine to outsoar and elude one. And I, for my part, should be willing to accord to my *focus imaginarius* that same attitude of unquestioning reverence, that my critics accord to their existent God: it is, in fact, *because* I think so highly of certain ideals, that I also think it unworthy to identify them with anything existent. And there is nothing absurd in having any number of emotional or other attitudes to objects that one thinks of as imaginary. The 'god' of the atheist will indeed be slightly different from the God of the theist—Rainer has taught me this—but he will only be so by an addition of 'brackets'. And the atheist might also admit the existence of something that I should describe (with great trepidation) as a 'god-ward trend' in things: certainly there are *some* facts in our experience which are (one might say) *as if* there were a God. And when theists say that their God exists in some sense quite different from created objects, there seems but a hairsbreadth between them and such atheists as place their ideal, with Plato and Plotinus, ἐπέκεινα τῆς οὐσίας.

In reply to *such* criticisms (if anyone were to raise them) I could give no better reason for preferring *my* atheistic formulations, than that they suited me from a *moral* and *religious* standpoint. For I am by temperament a Protestant, and I tend towards atheism as the purest form of Protestantism. By 'Protestantism' I mean the conviction—resting, as it seems to me, on elementary truisms—that it isn't *essential* in order to be a sound or 'saved' person, that one should pay deference to institutions, persons, books, ceremonies and so forth, or do anything more than develop those qualities in which being a sound or 'saved' person consists. (Not that I think meanly of ceremonies, books, persons and so forth, if *not* regarded as essential.) Now I don't doubt that theism *can* be so held as not to involve any idolatrous implications, but I think it *hard* to be a theist without falling into idolatry, with all its attendant evils of intolerance and persecution. And this is particularly the case in a religion like Christianity where the Divine is *identified* with a particular historical person, who existed in no analogical manner, but precisely as you and I do. I am not, however, a religious genius, nor do I know how to replace the existential formulations of our present religion, with non-existential formulations that would prove equally effective, whether in stimulating endeavour or in damming up the tide of cruelty and injustice. For these reasons I am not at all keen to shake faiths or overturn altars (if indeed I were able to do so).

King's College
   LONDON

V

A RELIGIOUS WAY OF
KNOWING

C. B. MARTIN

I

Some theologians support their claim to knowledge of the existence of God on the basis of direct experience of God. I shall attempt to point out some of the eccentricities of this alleged way of knowing. The two main sources which I shall use are Professor J. Baillie's *Our Knowledge of God* and Professor H. H. Farmer's *Towards Belief in God*.

We are rejecting logical argument of any kind as the first chapter of our theology or as representing the process by which God comes to be known. We are holding that our knowledge of God rests rather on the revelation of His personal Presence as Father, Son, and Holy Spirit. . . . Of such a Presence it must be true that to those who have never been confronted with it argument is useless, while to those who have it is superfluous.

BAILLIE, p. 132.

It is not as the result of an inference of any kind, whether explicit or implicit, whether laboriously excogitated or swiftly intuited, that the knowledge of God's reality comes to us. It comes rather through our direct, personal encounter with Him in the Person of Jesus Christ His Son our Lord.

Ibid., p. 143.

If now we ask how we would expect such a reality (God) to disclose itself to us, the answer can only be that we can have no expectancy about the matter at all; for in the nature of the case there are no parallels, no analogies on

76

which expectancy may be based. The divine reality is, by definition, unique. Or, in other words, we would expect that if we know the reality of God in respect of this fundamental aspect of His being at all, we shall just know that we are dealing with God, the ultimate source and disposer of all things, including ourselves, and there will be nothing more to be said. It will not be possible to describe the compelling touch of God otherwise than as the compelling touch of God. To anyone who has no such awareness of God, leading as it does to the typically religious attitudes of obeisance and worship, it will be quite impossible to indicate what is meant; one can only hope to evoke it, on the assumption that the capacity to become aware of God is part of normal human nature like the capacity to see light or to hear sound.

FARMER, p. 40.

The arguments of the theologians quoted have been taken out of context. I do not want to suggest that the quotations give a faithful or complete impression of their total argument. The following quotations from Professor Farmer indicate two further lines of argument which cannot be discussed here.

Reflection

For what we have now in mind is no demonstrative proofs *from* the world, but rather confirmatory considerations which present themselves to us when we bring belief in God with us *to* the world. It is a matter of the coherence of the belief with other facts. If we find that the religious intuition which has arisen from other sources provides the mind with a thought in terms of which much else can without forcing be construed, then that is an intellectual satisfaction, and a legitimate confirmation of belief, which it would be absurd to despise.

FARMER, p. 113.

Pragmatic Element

We shall first speak in general terms of what may be called the human situation and need, and thereafter we shall try to show how belief in God, as particularized in its Christian form (though still broadly set forth), fits on to this situation and need.

Ibid., p. 62.

II

The alleged theological way of knowing may be described as follows:

'I have direct experience (knowledge, acquaintance, apprehension) of God, therefore I have valid reason to believe that God exists.'

A. By this it may be meant that the statement 'I have had direct experience of God, but God does not exist' is contradictory. Thus, the assertion that 'I have had direct experience of God' commits one to the assertion that God exists. From this it follows that 'I have had direct experience of God' is more than a psychological statement, because it claims more than the fact that I have certain sensations—it claims that God exists. Thus as it stands this is a correct form of deductive argument. The assertion 'I have direct experience of God' includes the assertion 'God exists' thus, the conclusion 'therefore, God exists' follows tautologically.

B. Unfortunately, this deduction is useless. The addition of the existential claim 'God exists' to the psychological claim of having religious experiences must be shown to be warrantable. It cannot be shown to be warrantable by any deductive argument, because psychological statements of the form:

(1) I feel as if an unseen person were interested in (willed) my welfare.

(2) I feel an elation quite unlike any I have ever felt before.

(3) I have feelings of guilt and shame at my sinfulness.

(4) I feel as if I were committed to bending all of my efforts to living in a certain way,
    etc., etc.

can make the claim only that I have these complex feelings and sensations. Nothing else follows deductively. No matter what the existential statement might be that is added to the psychological statement, it is always logically possible for future psychological statements to call this existential claim in doubt. The only thing that I can establish beyond correction on the basis of having certain feelings and sensations is that I have these feelings and sensations. No matter how unique an experience may be claimed to be, it cannot do the impossible.

There is an influential and subtle group of religious thinkers who would not insist upon any existential claim. My remarks are largely irrelevant to this group. It would be hasty to describe their religious belief as 'psychological' or employ any other such general descriptive term. For example, the 'call', in even the most liberal and 'subjective' Quaker sects, could not be reduced to feeling statements, etc. The 'call', among other things, implies a mission or intricate programme of behaviour. The non-subjective element of the 'call' is evident because in so far as one failed to live in accordance with a mission just so far would the genuineness of the 'call' be questioned. It will be seen that this verification procedure is necessarily not available in the religious way of knowing to be examined.

C. Neither is the addition of the existential claim 'God exists' to the psychological claim made good by any inductive argument. There are no tests agreed upon to establish genuine experience of God and distinguish it decisively from the ungenuine. Indeed, many theologians deny the possibility of any such test or set of tests. Nor is there any increased capacity for prediction produced in the Christian believer which we cannot explain on a secular basis. However, just such a capacity is implied by those who talk of religious experience as if it were due to some kind of sixth sense.

(1) The believer may persuade us that something extraordinary has happened by saying, 'I am a changed man since 6.37 p.m., 6th May, 1939'. This is a straightforward empirical statement. We can test this by noticing whether or not he has given up bad habits, etc. We may allow the truth of the statement, even if he has not given up bad habits, etc.

because we may find evidence of bad conscience, self-searchings and remorse that had not been present before that date.

(2) However, if the believer says, 'I had a direct experience of God at 6.37 p.m., 6th May, 1939', this is not an empirical statement in the way that the other statement is. The checking procedure is very far from clear. No matter how much or how little his subsequent behaviour such as giving up bad habits, etc., is affected, it could never prove or disprove his statement.

An important point to note is that the theologian discourages any detailed description of the required experience ('apprehension of God'). The more naturalistic and detailed the description of the required experience became, the easier would it become to deny the existential claim. One could say, 'Yes, I had those very experiences, but they certainly did not convince me of God's existence'. The only sure defence here would be for the theologian to make the claim analytic—'You *couldn't* have those experiences and at the same time sincerely deny God's existence'.

D. The way in which many theologians talk would seem to show that they think of knowing God as something requiring a kind of sixth sense.

(1) The Divine Light is not merely of a colour usually visible only to eagles and the Voice of God is not merely of a pitch usually audible only to dogs. No matter how much more keen our senses became, we should be no better off than before. This sixth sense, therefore, must be very different from the other five.

(*a*) This supposed religious sense has no vocabulary of its own, but depends upon metaphors drawn from the other senses. There are no terms which apply to it and it alone. There is a vocabulary for what is sensed but not for the sense. We 'see' the Holy, the Numinous, the Divine, etc. This linguistic predicament may be compared with the similar one of the intuitionists when they talk of 'seeing' a logical connection. It also may be compared with 'hearing' the Voice of Conscience.

(*b*) The intuitionists seldom differ from the rest of us in the number of facts referred to in describing how we come to understand logical statements and their relations. The intuitionist, however, emphasizes the fact that often we come to understand the point of an argument or problem in logic very suddenly. We mark this occurrence by such phrases as 'the light dawned', 'understood it in a flash'. Such events are usually described in terms of a complete assurance that one's interpretation is correct and a confidence that one will tend to be able to reproduce or recognize the argument or problem in various contexts in the future. A vitally important distinction between this 'seeing' and the religious 'seeing' is that there is a checking procedure for the former, but not for the latter. If the intuitionist finds that his boasted insight was wrong, then he says, 'I couldn't really have "seen" it'. No matter how passionate his claim he cannot have 'seen' that $2+2=5$.

III

The religious way of knowing is described as being unique.

A. No one can deny the existence of feelings and experiences which the believer calls 'religious' and no one can deny their power. Because of this and because the way of knowing by direct experience is neither inductive nor deductive, theologians have tried to give this way of knowing a special status. One way in which this has been done has been to claim that religious experience is unique and incommunicable. There is a sense in which this is true. This sense may be brought out by a list such as the following:

(1) You don't know what the experience of God is until you have had it.

(2) You don't know what a blue sky is until you have been to Naples.

(3) You don't know what poverty is until you have been poor.

(4) 'We can only know a person by the direct communion of sympathetic intercourse.' (William Temple).

Professor Baillie, in likening our knowledge of God to our knowledge of other minds, says that it is

> like our knowledge of tridimensional space and all other primary modes of knowledge, something that cannot be imagined by one who does not already possess it, since it cannot be described to him in terms of anything else than itself.
>
> BAILLIE, p. 217.

What Professor Baillie does not see is that according to his criteria anything can qualify as a primary mode of knowledge. Each one of the statements in the above list is unique and incommunicable in just this way. You must go to Naples and not just to Venice. A postcard is no substitute.

B. That this sort of uniqueness is not to the point in supporting the existential claim 'God exists' can be seen by examining the following two samples :

(1) You don't know what the experience of God is until you have had it.

(2) You don't know what the colour blue is until you have seen it.

Professor Farmer says,

> All the basic elements in our experience are incommunicable. Who could describe light and colour to one who has known nothing but darkness ?
>
> FARMER, p. 41.

Just in so far as the experience of God is unique and incommunicable in this way, then just so far is it not to the point in supporting the existential claim 'God exists'.

All that this proves is that a description of one group of sensations A in terms of another set of sensations B is never sufficient for knowing group A. According to this definition of 'know', in order to know one must have those sensations. Thus, all that is proved is that in order to know what religious experience is one must have a religious experience. This helps in no way at all to prove that such experience is direct apprehension of God and helps in no way to support the existential claim 'God exists'.

C. Professor Farmer makes the point that describing the experience of God to an unbeliever is like describing colour to a blind man. So it is, in the sense that the believer has usually had experiences which the unbeliever has not. However, it is also very much unlike. The analogy breaks down at some vital points.

(1) The blind man may have genuine though incomplete knowledge of colour. He may have an instrument for detecting wave lengths, etc. Indeed, he may even increase our knowledge of colour. More important still, the blind man may realize the differences in powers of prediction between himself and the man of normal eyesight. He is well aware of the fact that, unlike himself, the man of normal eyesight does not have to wait to hear the rush of the bull in order to be warned.

(2) This point is connected with the problem of how we are to know when someone has the direct experience of God or even when we ourselves have the direct experience of God. It was shown above how the situation is easier in the case of the blind man. It is easy also, in the case of knowing a blue sky in Naples. One can look at street signs and maps in order to be sure that this is the really blue sky in question. It is only when one comes to such a case as knowing God that the society of tests and check-up procedures that surround other instances of knowing, completely vanishes. What is put in the place of these tests and checking procedures is an immediacy of knowledge that is supposed to carry its own guarantee. This feature will be examined later.

D. It is true that the man of normal vision has a way of knowing colour which the blind man does not have. Namely, he can see coloured objects. However, as we have seen, it would be wrong to insist that this is the only way of knowing colour and that the blind man has *no* way of knowing colour. There is a tendency to deny this and to maintain that having colour sensations is *the* way of knowing colour. Perhaps Professor Farmer has this in mind when he tries to make an analogy between the incommunicability of the believer's direct knowledge of God to the unbeliever and the incommunicability of the normal man's knowledge of colour to the blind man. The analogy is justified if 'knowing colour' is made synonymous with 'having colour sensations'.

(1) On this account, no matter how good his hearing and reliable his colour-detecting instruments, etc., the blind man could not know colour and the man of normal vision could not communicate to him just what this knowledge would be like.

(2) The believer has had certain unusual experiences which, presumably, the unbeliever has not had. If 'having direct experience of God' is made synonymous with 'having certain religious experiences', and the believer has had these and the unbeliever has not, then we may say that the believer's knowledge is incommunicable to the unbeliever in that it has already been legislated that in order to know what the direct experience of God is one must have had certain religious experiences.

> To anyone who has no such awareness of God, leading as it does to the typically religious attitudes of obeisance and worship, it will be quite impossible to indicate what is meant; one can only hope to evoke it. . . .
>
> FARMER, p. 40.

Reading theological text-books and watching the behaviour of believers is not sufficient.

E. The theologian has made the above analogy hold at the cost of endangering the existential claim about God which he hoped to establish.

(1) If 'knowing colour' is made synonymous with 'having colour sensations' and 'having direct experience of God' is made synonymous with 'having certain religious experiences', then it is certainly true that a blind man cannot 'know colour' and that a non-religious man cannot 'have direct experience of God'. By definition, also, it is true that the blind man and the non-religious man cannot know the meaning of the phrases 'knowing colour' and 'having direct experience of God', because it has been previously legislated

84

that one cannot know their meaning without having the relevant experiences.

(2) If this analogy is kept then the phrases 'knowing colour' and 'having direct experience of God' seem to make no claim beyond the psychological claims about one's colour sensations and religious feelings.

(3) If this analogy is not kept then there is no sense in the comparison between the incommunicability between the man of normal vision and the blind man and the incommunicability between the believer and the unbeliever.

(4) If 'knowing colour' is to be shaken loose from its purely psychological implications and made to have an existential reference concerning certain features of the world then a whole society of tests and check-up procedures which would be wholly irrelevant to the support of the psychological claim about one's own colour sensations become relevant. E.g. what other people see and the existence of light waves and the description of their characteristics needing the testimony of research workers and scientific instruments.

F. Because 'having direct experience of God' does not admit the relevance of a society of tests and checking procedures it places itself in the company of the other ways of knowing which preserve their self-sufficiency, 'uniqueness' and 'incommunicability' by making a psychological and not an existential claim. E.g. 'I seem to see a blue piece of paper'. This statement requires no further test or checking procedure in order to be considered true. Indeed, if A makes the statement 'I seem to see a blue piece of paper', then not only does A need no further corroboration, but there could be no disproof of his statement for him, for, if B says to A, 'It does not seem to me as if I were now seeing a blue piece of paper', then B's statement does *not* call A's statement in doubt for A though it does for B. However, if A makes the statement, 'I see a piece of blue paper', and B says in the same place and at the same time, 'I do not see a piece of blue paper', then B's statement *does* call A's statement in doubt for A. Further investigation will then be proper and if no piece of paper can be felt and other investigators cannot see or feel the paper and photographs reveal nothing, then A's statement will be shown to have been false. A's only refuge will be to say, 'Well, I certainly seem to see a piece of blue paper'. This is a perfect refuge because no one can prove him wrong, but its unassailability has been bought at the price of making no claim about the world beyond the claim about his own state of mind.

G. Another way of bringing out the closeness of the religious statement to the psychological statement is the following.

(1) When A wishes to support the assertion that a certain physical object exists, the tests and checking procedures made by A himself are not the only things relevant to the truth of his assertion. Testimony of what B, C, D, etc. see, hear, etc. is also relevant. That is, if A wanted to know whether it was really a star that he saw, he could not only take photographs, look through a telescope, etc., but also ask others if they saw the star. If a large proportion of a large number of people denied seeing the star, A's claim about the star's existence would be weakened. Of course, he might still trust his telescope. However, let us now imagine that A does not make use of the tests and checking procedures (photographs and telescopes) but is left with the testimony of what he sees and the testimony of others concerning what they see. In this case, it is so much to the point if a large number of people deny seeing the star, that A will be considered irrational or mad if he goes on asserting its existence. His only irrefutable position is to reduce his physical object claim to an announcement concerning his own sensations. Then the testimony of men and angels cannot disturb his certitude. These sensations of the moment he knows directly and immediately and the indirect and non-immediate testimony of men and angels is irrelevant. Absolute confidence, and absolute indifference to the majority judgment, is bought at the price of reducing the existential to the psychological.

(2) The religious claim is similar to, though not identical with, the above case in certain important features. We have seen that there are no tests or checking procedures open to

the believer to support his existential claim about God. Thus, he is left with the testimony of his own experience and the similar testimony of the experience of others. And, of course, he is not left wanting for such testimony, for religious communities seem to fulfil just this sort of need.

(3) Let us imagine a case comparable to the one concerning the existence of a physical object. In this case A is a professor of Divinity and he believes that he has come to know of the existence of God through direct experience of God. In order to understand the intricate character of what Professor A is asserting we must imagine a highly unusual situation. The other members of the faculty and the members of Professor A's religious community suddenly begin sincerely to deny his and what has been their assertion. Perhaps they still attend church services and pray as often as they used to do, and perhaps they claim to have the same sort of experiences as they had when they were believers, but they refuse to accept the conclusion that God exists. Whether they give a Freudian explanation or some other explanation or no explanation of their experiences, they are agreed in refusing to accept the existential claim (about God) made by Professor A. How does this affect Professor A and his claim? It may affect Professor A very deeply— indeed, he may die of broken-hearted disappointment at the loss of his fellow-believers. However, the loss of fellow-believers may not weaken his confidence in the truth of his assertion or in the testimony of his experience. In this matter his experience may be all that ultimately counts for him in establishing his confidence in the truth of his claim about the existence of God. It has been said that religious experience carries its own guarantee and perhaps the above account describes what is meant by this.

H. It is quite obvious from the examples given above that the religious statement ('I have direct experience of God') is of a different status from the physical object statement ('I can see a star') and shows a distressing similarity to the psychological statement ('I seem to see a star'). The bulk of this paper has been devoted to showing some of the many forms this similarity takes. Does this mean then that the religious statement and its existential claim concerning God amount to no more than a reference to the complex feelings and sensations of the believer?

I. Perhaps the best way to answer this last question is to take a typical psychological statement and see if there is anything which must be said of it and all other psychological statements which cannot be said of the religious statement.

(1) One way of differentiating a physical object statement from a psychological statement is by means of prefixing the phrase 'I seem . . .'. For instance, the statement 'I can see a star' may be transformed from a statement concerning the existence of a certain physical object to a statement concerning my sensations by translating it into the form 'I seem to see a star.' The first statement involves a claim about the existence of an object as well as an announcement concerning my sensations and therefore subjects itself to the risk of being wrong concerning that further claim. Being wrong in this case is determined by a society of tests and checking procedures such as taking photographs and looking through telescopes, and by the testimony of others that they see or do not see a star. The second statement involves no claim about the existence of an object and so requires no such tests and no testimony of others; indeed, the sole judge of the truth of the statement is the person making it. If no existential claim is lost by the addition of this phrase to a statement then the statement is psychological. For instance, the statement 'I feel pain' loses nothing by the addition 'I seem to feel pain.'

(2) In the case of the religious statement 'I have direct experience of God' the addition of the phrase is fatal to all that the believer wants to assert. 'I seem to be having direct experience of God' is a statement concerning my feelings and sensations of the moment and as such it makes no claim about the existence of God. Thus, the original statement 'I have direct experience of God' is not a psychological statement. This should not surprise us. We should have known it all along, for isn't it an assertion that one comes to know some-

thing, namely God, by means of one's feelings and sensations and this something is not reducible to them? The statement is not a psychological one just because it is used to assert the existence of something. Whether this assertion is warranted and what exactly it amounts to is quite another question.

We are tempted to think that the religious statement *must* be of one sort or another. The truth is that *per impossibile* it is both at once. The theologian must use it in both ways and which way he is to emphasize at a particular time depends upon the circumstances of its use; and most particularly upon the direction of our probings.

(3) The statement 'I seem to be having direct experience of God' is an eccentric one. It is eccentric not only because introspective announcements are unusual and because statements about God have a peculiar obscurity, but for a further and more important reason. This peculiarity may be brought out by comparing this statement with others having the same form. A first formulation of this may be put in the following way. In reference to things other than our sensations of the moment knowledge is prior to seeming as if.

The statement 'I seem to be looking directly at a chair' has a meaning only in so far as I already *know* what it is like to look directly at a chair. The statement 'I seem to be listening to a choir' has a meaning only in so far as I already *know* what it is like to be listening to a choir. The assumption of knowledge in both of these cases is one which all normal people are expected to be able to make and do in fact make.

The statement 'I seem to be having direct experience of God' does not lend itself so easily to the criterion for meaning exemplified in the above, because if this statement has meaning only in so far as one already *knows* what it is like to have direct experience of God, then the assumption of such knowledge is certainly not one which all normal people may be expected to be able to make or do in fact make.

However, it may be said that the assumption of such knowledge as knowledge of what it is like see a gorgon may not be assumed of all normal people and, therefore, the case of religious knowledge is in no peculiar position.

The answer to this objection and the discovery of the peculiarity of the religious statement may come about by asking the question 'How do we come to learn what it would be like to look directly at a chair, hear a choir, see a gorgon, have direct experience of God?'

It is not that there are no answers to the question concerning how we come to learn what it would be like to have direct experience of God. We are not left completely in the dark. Instead, the point is that the answers to this question are quite different from those referring to the questions concerning how we come to learn what it would be like to look directly at a chair, hear a choir, and see a gorgon.

No one has ever seen a gorgon, yet there certainly are people who, by means of their specialized knowledge of mythical literature, may claim in a perfectly meaningful manner that it now seems to them as if they were seeing a gorgon.

Let us imagine a society in which there are no chairs and no one knows anything at all about chairs. If we were to try to teach one of the members of this society what it would be like to see a chair and if we were not allowed to construct a chair, what sort of thing might we do? We might look around at the furniture and say, 'A chair is a kind of narrow settee. It is used to sit on'. This would be a beginning. Then we might compare different settees as to which are more chair-like. We might draw pictures of chairs, make gestures with our hands showing the general shape and size of different sorts of chairs. If, on the following day, he said, 'I had a most unusual dream last night. I seemed to be looking directly at a chair', we should admit that his statement was closer in meaning to a similar one which we who have seen chairs might make than it would be to a similar one which another member might make who had no information or instruction or experience of chairs. We would insist that we had better knowledge of what it is to see a chair than does the instructed member of society who has still actually to see a chair. However, to know pictures of chairs is to know chairs in a legitimate sense.

But let us now imagine a utopian society in which none of the members has ever been in the least sad or unhappy. If we were to try to teach one of the members of this society what it would be like to feel sad, how would we go about it? It can be said that giving definitions, no matter how ingenious, would be no help, drawing pictures of unhappy faces, no matter how well drawn, would be no help, so long as these measures failed to evoke a feeling of sadness in this person. Comparing the emotion of sadness with other emotions would be no help, because no matter how like other emotions (weariness, etc.) are to sadness they fail just because they are not sadness. No, sadness is unique and incomparable.

To anyone who has no such awareness of sadness, leading as it does to the typically unhappy behaviour of tears and drawn faces, it will be quite impossible to indicate what is meant, one can only hope to evoke it, on the assumption that the capacity to become aware of sadness is part of normal human nature like the capacity to see light or to hear sound.

This last paragraph is a play upon a quotation given at the very beginning of the paper. The following is the original version.

To anyone who has no such awareness of God, leading as it does to the typically religious attitudes of obeisance and worship, it will be quite impossible to indicate what is meant; one can only hope to evoke it, on the assumption that the capacity to become aware of God is part of normal human nature like the capacity to see light or to hear sound.

FARMER, p. 40.

(4)

'We are rejecting logical argument of any kind as the first chapter of our epistemology of aesthetics, or as representing the process by which beauty comes to be known. . . .

'It is not as the result of an inference of any kind, whether explicit or implicit, whether laboriously excogitated or swiftly intuited, that the knowledge of beauty comes to us.

'. . . to those who have never been confronted with the experience of seeing the beauty of something, argument is useless.'

As these statements stand they are plainly false. Professors of aesthetics and professional art critics often do help us to come to 'knowledge of beauty' by all kinds of inference and arguments. They may, and often do, help us to come to a finer appreciation of beautiful things. Knowledge of the rules of perspective and understanding of an artist's departure from them is relevant to an aesthetic appreciation of his work.

However, it is possible to interpret these statements as true and this is more important for our purpose.

There is sense in saying that an art critic, who has vastly increased our aesthetic sensitivity and whose books of art criticism are the very best, may never have known beauty. If there are no signs of this critic ever having been stirred by any work of art, then no matter how subtle his analyses, there is sense in claiming that he has never been confronted with the experience of seeing the beauty of something. This sense just is that we are determined not to say that a person has seen the beauty of something or has knowledge of beauty if he does not at some time have certain complex emotions and feelings which are typically associated with looking at paintings, hearing music and reading poetry. To 'know beauty' or to 'see the beauty of something' means, among other things, to have certain sorts of emotions and feelings.

The quotation given above was a play on a quotation given at the beginning of the paper. The following is the original version with the appropriate cuts.

'We are rejecting logical argument of any kind as the first chapter of our theology or as representing the process by which God comes to be known. . . .

'It is not as the result of an inference of any kind, whether explicit or implicit, whether laboriously excogitated or swiftly intuited, that the knowledge of God comes to us.

'...to those who have never been confronted with it [direct, personal encounter with God] argument is useless.'

As these statements stand they are plainly false. Professors of divinity and clergymen are expected to do what Professor Baillie claims cannot be done.

However, it is possible to interpret these statements as true and this is more important for our purpose.

There is sense in saying that a theologian (who has vastly increased our religious sensitivity and whose books of theology are the very best) may never have known God. If there are no signs of this theologian ever having been stirred by any religious ritual or act of worship, then no matter how subtle his analyses, there is sense in claiming that he has never been confronted with God's personal Presence. This sense just *is* that we are determined not to say that a person has knowledge of God if he does not at some time have certain complex emotions and feelings which are associated with attending religious services, praying and reading the Bible. To 'know God' or to be confronted with God's 'personal Presence' means, of necessity, having certain sorts of emotions and feelings.

(5) The analogy suggested above between aesthetic experience and religious experience and between aesthetic knowledge and religious knowledge cannot be examined further in this paper. However, certain preliminary suggestions may be made. The following quotations set the problem.

> In it [art] also there is an awareness, however unformulated and inarticulate, of a world of beauty which can be grasped and actualized in creative activity, yet it will never be possible fully to grasp it and actualize it in all its infinite reach and depth. In the appreciation of beauty in artistic products something of the same sense of an 'infinite beyond' disclosing itself through, yet transcending, what is contemplated and enjoyed, is present. It is precisely this that marks the difference between, say, a

Beethoven symphony and a shallow and 'tinny' jazz-dance.

FARMER, *Towards Belief in God*, p. 56.

After quoting Santayana's remark, 'Religions are better or worse, never true or false', Professor Farmer says:

It is sufficient answer to this suggestion to say that it is utterly false both to art and to religion. It is a central element in the artistic consciousness that it is, in its work, seeking to grasp and express an ideal world which in spite of its ideality is real and in some sense stands objectively over against the artist; it is never apprehended as merely a source of internal satisfaction and delights. Without this neither the work of artistic production nor its product would internally satisfy or delight. This is even more obviously true of religion. In religion the reality-interest is paramount. Once persuade the religious man that the reality with which he supposes himself to be dealing is not 'there' in the sense in which he supposes it to be 'there' and his religion vanishes away.

FARMER, *Towards Belief in God*, p. 176.

One may select a group of statements to compare and analyse. The following would be samples of such statements.

'The Believer experiences God.'
'The Sensitive Listener experiences Beauty in the music.'
'The Believer experiences something of the infinite goodness of God.'
'The Sensitive Listener experiences the subtlety, sadness, colour, etc., of the music as part of what is the Beauty in the music.'
'One may hear God through prayer.'
'One may hear the Beautiful above or in the voices of the actors and the instruments of the orchestra.'
'What the artist experiences and knows, namely Beauty, is ultimately incommunicable.'
'What the Believer experiences and knows, namely God, is ultimately incommunicable.'
'One may learn to come to know God.'

94

'One may learn to come to know Beauty.'

'One may learn to come to know one's wife.'

Going over the complex uses of such statements may help one to discover something of the intricate logic of certain kinds of religious statements.

In this paper the analogy between seeing blue and experiencing God has been examined and found to be misleading. The suggested analogy between experiencing the Beautiful and experiencing God has further complexities and requires another examination which, among other things, would show how religious experience is and is not another experience in the way in which seeing red may be said to be another experience to seeing blue or hearing a nightingale.

Another important subject with which this paper has not dealt is the connection between what the believer expects from immortality and his religious belief. This peculiar kind of test or verification has special difficulties which cannot be treated here.

IV

Conclusion

It must be made clear in conclusion that the lack of tests and checking procedures which has been noted is not merely an unfortunate result of human frailty. It is necessarily the nature of the case. If tests and checking procedures were devised they would not, could not, support the claim of the believer. They may do for the detection of saints and perhaps even angels, but never of God. Of course, in a way theologians know this.

This paper has been an attempt to indicate how statements concerning a certain alleged religious way of knowing betray a logic extraordinarily like that of statements concerning introspective and subjective ways of knowing. It is not my wish to go from a correct suggestion that the logic is *very*, *very* like to an incorrect suggestion that the logic is *just* like.

University of Adelaide
AUSTRALIA

95

VI

THEOLOGY AND FALSIFICATION

(i) From the *University* Discussion

A

ANTONY FLEW

Let us begin with a parable. It is a parable developed from a tale told by John Wisdom in his haunting and revelatory article 'Gods'.[1] Once upon a time two explorers came upon a clearing in the jungle. In the clearing were growing many flowers and many weeds. One explorer says, 'Some gardener must tend this plot'. The other disagrees, 'There is no gardener'. So they pitch their tents and set a watch. No gardener is ever seen. 'But perhaps he is an invisible gardener.' So they set up a barbed-wire fence. They electrify it. They patrol with bloodhounds. (For they remember how H. G. Wells's *The Invisible Man* could be both smelt and touched though he could not be seen.) But no shrieks ever suggest that some intruder has received a shock. No movements of the wire ever betray an invisible climber. The bloodhounds never give cry. Yet still the Believer is not convinced. 'But there is a gardener, invisible, intangible, insensible to electric shocks, a gardener who has no scent and makes no sound, a gardener who comes secretly to look after the garden which he loves.' At last the Sceptic despairs, 'But what remains of your original assertion? Just how does what you call an invisible, intangible, eternally elusive gardener differ from an imaginary gardener or even from no gardener at all?' *It differs for me!* "*Indeed? But ? C.S.*

[1] *P.A.S.*, 1944–5, reprinted as Ch. X of *Logic and Language*, Vol I (Blackwell, 1951), and in his *Philosophy and Psychoanalysis* (Blackwell, 1953).

In this parable we can see how what starts as an assertion, that something exists or that there is some analogy between certain complexes of phenomena, may be reduced step by step to an altogether different status, to an expression perhaps of a 'picture preference'.[2] The Sceptic says there is no gardener. The Believer says there is a gardener (but invisible, etc.). One man talks about sexual behaviour. Another man prefers to talk of Aphrodite (but knows that there is not really a superhuman person additional to, and somehow responsible for, all sexual phenomena).[3] The process of qualification may be checked at any point before the original assertion is completely withdrawn and something of that first assertion will remain (Tautology). Mr. Wells's invisible man could not, admittedly, be seen, but in all other respects he was a man like the rest of us. But though the process of qualification may be, and of course usually is, checked in time, it is not always judiciously so halted. Someone may dissipate his assertion completely without noticing that he has done so. A fine brash hypothesis may thus be killed by inches, the death by a thousand qualifications.

And in this, it seems to me, lies the peculiar danger, the endemic evil, of theological utterance. Take such utterances as 'God has a plan', 'God created the world', 'God loves us as a father loves his children'. They look at first sight very much like assertions, vast cosmological assertions. Of course, this is no sure sign that they either are, or are intended to be, assertions. But let us confine ourselves to the cases where those who utter such sentences intend them to express assertions. (Merely remarking parenthetically that those who intend or interpret such utterances as crypto-commands, expressions of wishes, disguised ejaculations, concealed

---

[2] Cf. J. Wisdom, 'Other Minds', *Mind*, 1940; reprinted in his *Other Minds* (Blackwell, 1952).

[3] Cf. Lucretius, *De Rerum Natura*, II, 655-60,

> Hic siquis mare Neptunum Cereremque vocare
> Constituet fruges et Bacchi nomine abuti
> Mavolat quam laticis proprium proferre vocamen
> Concedamus ut hic terrarum dictitet orbem
> Esse deum matrem dum vera re tamen ipse
> Religione animum turpi contingere parcat.

97

ethics, or as anything else but assertions, are unlikely to succeed in making them either properly orthodox or practically effective).

Now to assert that such and such is the case is necessarily equivalent to denying that such and such is not the case.[4] Suppose then that we are in doubt as to what someone who gives vent to an utterance is asserting, or suppose that, more radically, we are sceptical as to whether he is really asserting anything at all, one way of trying to understand (or perhaps it will be to expose) his utterance is to attempt to find what he would regard as counting against, or as being incompatible with, its truth. For if the utterance is indeed an assertion, it will necessarily be equivalent to a denial of the negation of that assertion. And anything which would count against the assertion, or which would induce the speaker to withdraw it and to admit that it had been mistaken, must be part of (or the whole of) the meaning of the negation of that assertion. And to know the meaning of the negation of an assertion, is as near as makes no matter, to know the meaning of that assertion.[5] And if there is nothing which a putative assertion denies then there is nothing which it asserts either: and so it is not really an assertion. When the Sceptic in the parable asked the Believer, 'Just how does what you call an invisible, intangible, eternally elusive gardener differ from an imaginary gardener or even from no gardener at all?' he was suggesting that the Believer's earlier statement had been so eroded by qualification that it was no longer an assertion at all.

Now it often seems to people who are not religious as if there was no conceivable event or series of events the occurrence of which would be admitted by sophisticated religious people to be a sufficient reason for conceding 'There wasn't a God after all' or 'God does not really love us then'. Someone tells us that God loves us as a father loves his children. We are reassured. But then we see a child dying of inoperable cancer of the throat. His earthly father is driven

[4] For those who prefer symbolism: $p \equiv \sim\sim p$.

[5] For by simply negating $\sim p$ we get $p : \sim\sim p \equiv p$.

frantic in his efforts to help, but his Heavenly Father reveals no obvious sign of concern. Some qualification is made— God's love is 'not a merely human love' or it is 'an inscrutable love', perhaps—and we realize that such sufferings are quite compatible with the truth of the assertion that 'God loves us as a father (but, of course, . . .)'. We are reassured again. But then perhaps we ask: what is this assurance of God's (appropriately qualified) love worth, what is this apparent guarantee really a guarantee against? Just what would have to happen not merely (morally and wrongly) to tempt but also (logically and rightly) to entitle us to say 'God does not love us' or even 'God does not exist'? I therefore put to the succeeding symposiasts the simple central questions, 'What would have to occur or to have occurred to constitute for you a disproof of the love of, or of the existence of, God?'

University College of North Staffordshire
ENGLAND

B[6]
R. M. HARE

I wish to make it clear that I shall not try to defend Christianity in particular, but religion in general—not because I do not believe in Christianity, but because you cannot understand what Christianity is, until you have understood what religion is.

I must begin by confessing that, on the ground marked out by Flew, he seems to me to be completely victorious. I therefore shift my ground by relating another parable. A certain lunatic is convinced that all dons want to murder him. His friends introduce him to all the mildest and most respectable dons that they can find, and after each of them has retired, they say, 'You see, he doesn't really want to murder you; he spoke to you in a most cordial manner;

6 Some references to intervening discussion have been excised—Editors.

surely you are convinced now?' But the lunatic replies 'Yes, but that was only his diabolical cunning; he's really plotting against me the whole time, like the rest of them; I know it I tell you'. However many kindly dons are produced, the reaction is still the same.

Now we say that such a person is deluded. But what is he deluded about? About the truth or falsity of an assertion? Let us apply Flew's test to him. There is no behaviour of dons that can be enacted which he will accept as counting against his theory; and therefore his theory, on this test, asserts nothing. But it does not follow that there is no difference between what he thinks about dons and what most of us think about them—otherwise we should not call him a lunatic and ourselves sane, and dons would have no reason to feel uneasy about his presence in Oxford.

Let us call that in which we differ from this lunatic, our respective *bliks*. He has an insane *blik* about dons; we have a sane one. It is important to realize that we have a sane one, not no *blik* at all; for there must be two sides to any argument—if he has a wrong *blik*, then those who are right about dons must have a right one. Flew has shown that a *blik* does not consist in an assertion or system of them; but nevertheless it is very important to have the right *blik*.

Let us try to imagine what it would be like to have different *bliks* about other things than dons. When I am driving my car, it sometimes occurs to me to wonder whether my movements of the steering-wheel will always continue to be followed by corresponding alterations in the direction of the car. I have never had a steering failure, though I have had skids, which must be similar. Moreover, I know enough about how the steering of my car is made, to know the sort of thing that would have to go wrong for the steering to fail —steel joints would have to part, or steel rods break, or something—but how do I know that this won't happen? The truth is, I don't know; I just have a *blik* about steel and its properties, so that normally I trust the steering of my car; but I find it not at all difficult to imagine what it would be like to lose this *blik* and acquire the opposite one. People would say I was silly about steel; but there would be no mistaking the reality of the difference between our respective *bliks*—for example, I should never go in a motor-car. Yet I should hesitate to say that the difference between us was the difference between contradictory assertions. No amount of safe arrivals or bench-tests will remove my *blik* and restore the normal one; for my *blik* is compatible with any finite number of such tests.

It was Hume who taught us that our whole commerce with the world depends upon our *blik* about the world; and that differences between *bliks* about the world cannot be settled by observation of what happens in the world. That was why, having performed the interesting experiment of doubting the ordinary man's *blik* about the world, and showing that no proof could be given to make us adopt one *blik* rather than another, he turned to backgammon to take his mind off the problem. It seems, indeed, to be impossible even to formulate as an assertion the normal *blik* about the world which makes me put my confidence in the future reliability of steel joints, in the continued ability of the road to support my car, and not gape beneath it revealing nothing below; in the general non-homicidal tendencies of dons; in my own continued well-being (in some sense of that word that I may not now fully understand) if I continue to do what is right according to my lights; in the general likelihood of people like Hitler coming to a bad end. But perhaps a formulation less inadequate than most is to be found in the Psalms: 'The earth is weak and all the inhabiters thereof: I bear up the pillars of it'.

The mistake of the position which Flew selects for attack is to regard this kind of talk as some sort of *explanation*, as scientists are accustomed to use the word. As such, it would obviously be ludicrous. We no longer believe in God as an Atlas—*nous n'avons pas besoin de cette hypothèse*. But it is nevertheless true to say that, as Hume saw, without a *blik* there can be no explanation; for it is by our *bliks* that we decide what is and what is not an explanation. Suppose we believed that everything that happened, happened by pure chance. This *nor is the unfalsifiability criterion, as such, an assertion —*

would not of course be an assertion; for it is compatible with anything happening or not happening, and so, incidentally, is its contradictory. But if we had this belief, we should not be able to explain or predict or plan anything. Thus, although we should not be *asserting* anything different from those of a more normal belief, there would be a great difference between us; and this is the sort of difference that there is between those who really believe in God and those who really disbelieve in him.

The word 'really' is important, and may excite suspicion. I put it in, because when people have had a good Christian upbringing, as have most of those who now profess not to believe in any sort of religion, it is very hard to discover what they really believe. The reason why they find it so easy to think that they are not religious, is that they have never got into the frame of mind of one who suffers from the doubts to which religion is the answer. Not for them the terrors of the primitive jungle. Having abandoned some of the more picturesque fringes of religion, they think that they have abandoned the whole thing—whereas in fact they still have got, and could not live without, a religion of a comfortably substantial, albeit highly sophisticated, kind, which differs from that of many 'religious people' in little more than this, that 'religious people' like to sing Psalms about theirs—a very natural and proper thing to do. But nevertheless there may be a big difference lying behind—the difference between two people who, though side by side, are walking in different directions. I do not know in what direction Flew is walking; perhaps he does not know either. But we have had some examples recently of various ways in which one can walk away from Christianity, and there are any number of possibilities. After all, man has not changed biologically since primitive times; it is his religion that has changed, and it can easily change again. And if you do not think that such changes make a difference, get acquainted with some Sikhs and some Mussulmans of the same Punjabi stock; you will find them quite different sorts of people.

There is an important difference between Flew's parable

and my own which we have not yet noticed. The explorers do not *mind* about their garden; they discuss it with interest, but not with concern. But my lunatic, poor fellow, minds about dons; and I mind about the steering of my car; it often has people in it that I care for. It is because I mind very much about what goes on in the garden in which I find myself, that I am unable to share the explorers' detachment.

Balliol College
OXFORD

C

BASIL MITCHELL

Flew's article is searching and perceptive, but there is, I think, something odd about his conduct of the theologian's case. The theologian surely would not deny that the fact of pain counts against the assertion that God loves men. This very incompatibility generates the most intractable of theological problems—the problem of evil. So the theologian *does* recognize the fact of pain as counting against Christian doctrine. But it is true that he will not allow it—or anything —to count decisively against it; for he is committed by his faith to trust in God. His attitude is not that of the detached observer, but of the believer.

Perhaps this can be brought out by yet another parable. In time of war in an occupied country, a member of the resistance meets one night a stranger who deeply impresses him. They spend that night together in conversation. The Stranger tells the partisan that he himself is on the side of the resistance—indeed that he is in command of it, and urges the partisan to have faith in him no matter what happens. The partisan is utterly convinced at that meeting of the Stranger's sincerity and constancy and undertakes to trust him.

They never meet in conditions of intimacy again. But sometimes the Stranger is seen helping members of the resistance, and the partisan is grateful and says to his friends, 'He is on our side'.

Sometimes he is seen in the uniform of the police handing over patriots to the occupying power. On these occasions his friends murmur against him: but the partisan still says, 'He is on our side'. He still believes that, in spite of appearances, the Stranger did not deceive him. Sometimes he asks the Stranger for help and receives it. He is then thankful. Sometimes he asks and does not receive it. Then he says, 'The Stranger knows best'. Sometimes his friends, in exasperation, say 'Well, what *would* he have to do for you to admit that you were wrong and that he is not on our side?' But the partisan refuses to answer. He will not consent to put the Stranger to the test. And sometimes his friends complain, 'Well, if *that's* what you mean by his being on our side, the sooner he goes over to the other side the better'.

The partisan of the parable does not allow anything to count decisively against the proposition 'The Stranger is on our side'. This is because he has committed himself to trust the Stranger. But he of course recognizes that the Stranger's ambiguous behaviour *does* count against what he believes about him. It is precisely this situation which constitutes the trial of his faith.

When the partisan asks for help and doesn't get it, what can he do? He can (*a*) conclude that the stranger is not on our side or; (*b*) maintain that he is on our side, but that he has reasons for withholding help.

The first he will refuse to do. How long can he uphold the second position without its becoming just silly?

I don't think one can say in advance. It will depend on the nature of the impression created by the Stranger in the first place. It will depend, too, on the manner in which he takes the Stranger's behaviour. If he blandly dismisses it as of no consequence, as having no bearing upon his belief, it will be assumed that he is thoughtless or insane. And it quite obviously won't do for him to say easily, 'Oh, when used of the Stranger the phrase "is on our side" *means* ambiguous behaviour of this sort'. In that case he would be like the religious man who says blandly of a terrible disaster 'It is God's will'. No, he will only be regarded as sane and reasonable in his belief, if he experiences in himself the full force of the conflict.

It is here that my parable differs from Hare's. The partisan admits that many things may and do count against his belief: whereas Hare's lunatic who has a *blik* about dons doesn't admit that anything counts against his *blik*. Nothing *can* count against *bliks*. Also the partisan has a reason for having in the first instance committed himself, viz. the character of the Stranger; whereas the lunatic has no reason for his *blik* about dons—because, of course, you can't have reasons for *bliks*.

This means that I agree with Flew that theological utterances must be assertions. The partisan is making an assertion when he says, 'The Stranger is on our side'.

Do I want to say that the partisan's belief about the Stranger is, in any sense, an explanation? I think I do. It explains and makes sense of the Stranger's behaviour: it helps to explain also the resistance movement in the context of which he appears. In each case it differs from the interpretation which the others put upon the same facts.

'God loves men' resembles 'the Stranger is on our side' (and many other significant statements, e.g. historical ones) in not being conclusively falsifiable. They can both be treated in at least three different ways: (1) As provisional hypotheses to be discarded if experience tells against them; (2) As significant articles of faith; (3) As vacuous formulae (expressing, perhaps, a desire for reassurance) to which experience makes no difference and which make no difference to life.

The Christian, once he has committed himself, is precluded by his faith from taking up the first attitude: 'Thou shalt not tempt the Lord thy God'. He is in constant danger, as Flew has observed, of slipping into the third. But he need not; and, if he does, it is a failure in faith as well as in logic.

Keble College
OXFORD

D

ANTONY FLEW

It has been a good discussion: and I am glad to have helped to provoke it. But now—at least in *University*—it must come to an end: and the Editors of *University* have asked me to make some concluding remarks. Since it is impossible to deal with all the issues raised or to comment separately upon each contribution, I will concentrate on Mitchell and Hare, as representative of two very different kinds of response to the challenge made in 'Theology and Falsification'.

The challenge, it will be remembered, ran like this. Some theological utterances seem to, and are intended to, provide explanations or express assertions. Now an assertion, to be an assertion at all, must claim that things stand thus and thus; *and not otherwise*. Similarly an explanation, to be an explanation at all, must explain why this particular thing occurs; *and not something else*. Those last clauses are crucial. And yet sophisticated religious people—or so it seemed to me—are apt to overlook this, and tend to refuse to allow, not merely that anything actually does occur, but that anything conceivably could occur, which would count against their theological assertions and explanations. But in so far as they do this their supposed explanations are actually bogus, and their seeming assertions are really vacuous.

Mitchell's response to this challenge is admirably direct, straightforward, and understanding. He agrees 'that theological utterances must be assertions'. He agrees that if they are to be assertions, there must be something that would count against their truth. He agrees, too, that believers are in constant danger of transforming their would-be assertions into 'vacuous formulae'. But he takes me to task for an oddity in my 'conduct of the theologian's case. The theologian surely would not deny that the fact of pain counts against the assertion that God loves men. This very incompatibility generates the most intractable of theological problems, the problem of evil'. I think he is right. I should have made a distinction between two very different ways of dealing with what looks like evidence against the love of God: the way I stressed was the expedient of qualifying the original assertion; the way the theologian usually takes, at first, is to admit that it looks bad but to insist that there is—there must be—some explanation which will show that, in spite of appearances, there really is a God who loves us. His difficulty, it seems to me, is that he has given God attributes which rule out all possible saving explanations. In Mitchell's parable of the Stranger it is easy for the believer to find plausible excuses for ambiguous behaviour: for the Stranger is a man. But suppose the Stranger is God. We cannot say that he would like to help but cannot: God is omnipotent. We cannot say that he would help if he only knew: God is omniscient. We cannot say that he is not responsible for the wickedness of others: God creates those others. Indeed an omnipotent, omniscient God must be an accessory before (and during) the fact to every human misdeed; as well as being responsible for every non-moral defect in the universe. So, though I entirely concede that Mitchell was absolutely right to insist against me that the theologian's first move is to look for an *explanation*, I still think that in the end, if relentlessly pursued, he will have to resort to the avoiding action of *qualification*. And there lies the danger of that death by a thousand qualifications, which would, I agree, constitute 'a failure in faith as well as in logic'.

Hare's approach is fresh and bold. He confesses that 'on the ground marked out by Flew, he seems to me to be completely victorious'. He therefore introduces the concept of *blik*. But while I think that there is room for some such concept in philosophy, and that philosophers should be grateful to Hare for his invention, I nevertheless want to insist that any attempt to analyse Christian religious utterances as expressions or affirmations of a *blik* rather than as (at least would-be) assertions about the cosmos is fundamentally misguided. *First,* because thus interpreted they would be entirely unorthodox. If Hare's religion really is a *blik,* involving no cosmological assertions about the nature and activities of a supposed personal creator, then surely he is not a Christian at all? *Second,* because thus interpreted, they could scarcely do the job they do. If they were not even intended as assertions then many religious activities would become fradulent, or merely silly. If 'You ought *because* it is God's will' asserts no more than 'You ought', then the person who prefers the former phraseology is not really giving a reason, but a fraudulent substitute for one, a dialectical dud cheque. If 'My soul must be immortal *because* God loves his children, etc.' asserts no more than 'My soul must be immortal', then the man who reassures himself with theological arguments for immortality is being as silly as the man who tries to clear his overdraft by writing his bank a cheque on the same account. (Of course neither of these utterances would be distinctively Christian: but this discussion never pretended to be so confined.) Religious utterances may indeed express false or even bogus assertions: but I simply do not believe that they are not both intended and interpreted to be or at any rate to presuppose assertions, at least in the context of religious practice; whatever shifts may be demanded, in another context, by the exigencies of theological apologetic.

One final suggestion. The philosophers of religion might well draw upon George Orwell's last appalling nightmare *1984* for the concept of *doublethink.* '*Doublethink* means the power of holding two contradictory beliefs simultaneously, and accepting both of them. The party intellectual knows that he is playing tricks with reality, but by the exercise of *doublethink* he also satisfies himself that reality is not violated' (*1984,* p. 220). Perhaps religious intellectuals too are sometimes driven to doublethink in order to retain their faith in a loving God in face of the reality of a heartless and indifferent world. But of this more another time, perhaps.

University College of North Staffordshire
ENGLAND

(ii) Arising from the *University* Discussion [7]

I. M. CROMBIE

There are some who hold that religious statements cannot be fully meaningful, on the ground that those who use them allow nothing to count decisively against them, treat them, that is, as incapable of falsification. This paper is an attempted answer to this view; and in composing it I have had particularly in mind an article by Antony Flew (Ch. VI A above), and an unpublished paper read by A. M. Quinton to the Aquinas Society of Oxford. I shall offer only a very short, and doubtless tendentious, summary of my opponents' views.

Briefly, then, it is contended that there are utterances made from time to time by Christians and others, which are said by those who make them to be statements, but which are thought by our opponents to lack some of the properties which anything must have before it deserves to be called a statement. 'There is a God', 'God loves us as a father loves his children', 'He shall come again with glory ...' are examples of such utterances. *Prima facie* such utterances are neither exhortations, nor questions, nor expressions of wishes; *prima facie* they appear to assert the actuality of some state of affairs; and yet (and this is the objection) they are allowed to be compatible with any and every state of affairs. If they are compatible with any and every state of affairs, they cannot mark out some one state of affairs (or group of states of affairs); and if they do not mark out some one state of affairs, how can they be statements? In the case of any ordinary statement, such as 'It is raining', there is at least one situation (the absence of falling water) which is held to

---

7 This paper was composed to be read to a non-philosophical audience. In composing it I have also filched shamelessly (and shamefully no doubt distorted) some unpublished utterances of Dr. A. M. Farrer's.

be incompatible with the statement, and it is the incompatibility of the situation with the statement which gives the statement its meaning. If, then, religious 'statements' are compatible with anything and everything, how can they be statements? How can the honest inquirer find out what they mean, if nobody will tell him what they are incompatible with? Are they not much more like such exhortations as 'Keep smiling', whose confessed purpose is to go on being in point whatever occurs? Furthermore, is it not true that they only appear to be statements to those of us who use them, because we deceive ourselves by a sort of conjuring trick, oscillating backwards and forwards between a literal interpretation of what we say when we say it, and a scornful rejection of such anthropomorphism when anybody challenges us? When we *say*: 'He shall come again with glory . . .', do we not picture real angels sitting on real clouds; when asked whether we really mean the clouds, we hedge; offer perhaps another picture, which again we refuse to take literally; and so on indefinitely. Whatever symbolism we offer, we always insist that only a crude man would take it literally, and yet we never offer him anything but symbolism; deceived by our imagery into supposing that we have something in mind, in fact there is nothing on which we are prepared to take our stand.

This is the position I am to try to criticize. It is, I think, less novel than its clothes; but none the less it is important. I turn to criticism.

Let us begin by dismissing from our inquiry the troublesome statement 'There is a God' or 'God exists'. As every student of logic knows, all statements asserting the existence of something offer difficulties of their own, with which we need not complicate our embarrassment.

That being dismissed, I shall want to say of statements about God that they consist of two parts. Call them, if you like, subject and predicate. Whatever you call them, there is that which is said, and that which it is said about—namely God. It is important to make this distinction, for different problems arise about the different parts. As a first approximation towards isolating the difference, we may notice that the predicate is normally composed of ordinary words, put to un-ordinary uses, whereas the subject-word is 'God', which has no other use. In the expression 'God loves us', the word 'God' is playing, so to speak, on its Home Ground, the phrase 'loves us' is playing Away. Now there is one set of questions which deal with the problem of why we say, and what we mean by saying, that God loves us, rather than hates us, and there is another set of questions concerned with the problem of what it is that this statement is being made about.

To approach the matter from an angle which seems to me to afford a good view of it, I shall make a few observations about the epistemological nature of religious belief. Let me caution the reader that, in doing so, I am not attempting to describe how religious belief in fact arises.

Theoretically, then, not in how it arises, but in its logical structure, religious belief has two parents; and it also has a nurse. Its logical mother is what one might call *undifferentiated theism*, its logical father is particular events or occasions interpreted as theophanic, and the extra-parental nurture is provided by religious activity.

A word, first, about the logical mother. It is in fact the case that there are elements in our experience which lead people to a certain sort of belief, which we call a belief in God. (We could, if we wished, call it rather an attitude than a belief, so long as we were careful not to call it an attitude to life; for it is of the essence of the attitude to hold that nothing whatever in life may be identified with that towards which it is taken up.) Among the elements in experience which provoke this belief or attitude, perhaps the most powerful is what I shall call a sense of contingency. Others are moral experience, and the beauty and order of nature. Others may be actual abnormal experience of the type called religious or mystical. There are those to whom conscience appears in the form of an unconditional demand; to whom the obligation to one's neighbour seems to be something imposed on him and on me by a third party who is set over us both. There are those to whom the beauty and order of nature appears as the intrusion into nature of a realm of beauty and order beyond it. There are those who believe themselves or others to be enriched by moments of direct access to the divine. Now there are two things that must be said about these various theistic interpretations of our experience. The first is that those who so interpret need not be so inexpert in logic as to suppose that there is anything of the nature of a deductive or inductive argument which leads from a premiss asserting the existence of the area of experience in question to a conclusion expressing belief in God. Nobody who takes seriously the so-called moral argument need suppose that the *prima facie* authority of conscience cannot be naturalistically explained. He can quite well acknowledge that the imperativeness which so impresses him could be a mere reflection of his jealousy of his father, or a vestigial survival of tribal taboo. The mystic can quite well acknowledge that there is nothing which logically forbids the interpretation of the experience which he enjoys in terms of the condition of his liver or the rate of his respirations. If, being acquainted with the alternative explanations, he persists in rejecting them, it need not be, though of course it sometimes is, because he is seized with a fallacious refutation of their validity. All that is necessary is that he should be honestly convinced that, in interpreting them, as he does, theistically, he is in some sense facing them more honestly, bringing out more of what they contain or involve than could be done by interpreting them in any other way. The one interpretation is preferred to the other, not because the latter is thought to be refutable on paper, but because it is judged to be unconvincing in the light of familiarity with the facts. There is a partial parallel to this in historical judgment. Where you and I differ in our interpretation of a series of events, there is nothing outside the events in question which can over-rule either of us, so that each man must accept the interpretation which seems, on fair and critical scrutiny, the most convincing to him. The parallel is only partial, however, for in historical (and literary) interpretation there is something which to some extent controls one's interpretation, and that is one's general knowledge of human nature; and in metaphysical interpretation there is nothing analogous to this. That, then, is my first comment on theistic interpretations; for all that these journeys of the mind are often recorded in quasi-argumentative form, they are not in any ordinary sense arguments, and their validity cannot be assessed by asking whether they conform to the laws either of logic or of scientific method. My second comment upon them is, that, in stating them, we find ourselves saying things which we cannot literally mean. Thus the man of conscience uses some such concept as the juridical concept of authority, and locates his authority outside nature; the man of beauty and order speaks of an intrusion from another realm; the mystic speaks of experiencing God. In every case such language lays the user open to devastating criticism, to which he can only retort by pleading that such language, while it is not to be taken strictly, seems to him to be the natural language to use.

To bring these points into a somewhat stronger light, let me say something about the sense of contingency, the conviction which people have, it may be in blinding moments, or it may be in a permanent disposition of a man's mind, that we, and the whole world in which we live, derive our being from something outside us. The first thing I want to say about this is that such a conviction is to no extent like the conclusion of an argument; the sense of dependence feels not at all like being persuaded by arguments, but like seeing, seeing, as it were, through a gap in the rolling mists of argument, which alone, one feels, could conceal the obvious truth. One is not *persuaded* to believe that one is contingent; rather one feels that it is only by persuasion that one could ever believe anything else. The second thing I want to say about this conviction of contingency is that in expressing it, as Quinton has admirably shewn, we turn the word 'contingent' to work which is not its normal employment, and which it cannot properly do.

For the distinction between necessity and contingency is

not a distinction between different sorts of entities, but between different sorts of statement. A necessary statement is one whose denial involves a breach of the laws of logic, and a contingent statement is one in which this is not the case. (I do not, of course, assert that this is the only way in which these terms have been used in the history of philosophy; but I do assert that this is the only use of them which does not give rise to impossible difficulties. I have no space to demonstrate this here; and indeed I do not think that it is any longer in need of demonstration.) But in this, the only coherent, sense of 'contingent', the existence of the world may be contingent fact, but so unfortunately is that of God. For *all* existential statements are contingent; that is to say, it is never true that we can involve ourselves in a breach of the laws of logic by merely denying of something that it exists. We cannot therefore in this sense contrast the contingent existence of the world with the necessary existence of God.

It follows that if a man persists in speaking of the contingency of the world, he must be using the term in a new or transferred sense. It must be that he is borrowing[8] a word from the logician and putting it to work which it cannot properly do. Why does he do this, and how can he make clear what precisely this new use is? For it is no good saying that when we are talking about God we do not use words in their ordinary senses unless we are prepared to say in what senses it is that we do use them. And yet how can we explain to the honest inquirer what is the new sense in which the word 'contingent' is being used when we use it of the world? For if it is proper to use it, in this sense, of everything with which we are acquainted, and improper to use it only of God, with whom we are not acquainted, how can the new use be learnt? For we normally learn the correct use of a word by noticing the differences between the situations in which it may be applied and those in which it may not; but the word

---

[8] It might be argued that, historically, the borrowing was the other way round. To decide that we should have to decide where the frontier between logic and metaphysics really comes in the work of those whose doctrine on the relationship between these disciplines is unsatisfactory.

'contingent' is applicable in all the situations in which we ever find ourselves. If I said that everything but God was flexible, not of course in the ordinary sense, but in some other, how could you discover what the new sense was?

The answer must be that when we speak of the world as contingent, dependent, an effect or product, and so contrast it with a necessary, self-existent being, a first cause or a creator, we say something which on analysis will not do at all (for devastating criticisms can be brought against all these formulations), but which seems to us to be the fittest sort of language for our purpose. Why we find such language appropriate, and how, therefore, it is to be interpreted, is not at all an easy question; that it does in some way, it may be in some logically anomalous way, convey the meaning of those who use it, seems however to be an evident fact. How it is that the trick is worked, how it is that this sort of distortion of language enables believers to give expression to their beliefs, this it is the true business of the natural theologian to discuss. Farrer, for example, in *Finite and Infinite*, has done much to elucidate what it is that one is striving to express when one speaks of the contingency of the world, and so to enlighten the honest inquirer who wishes to know how the word 'contingent' is here being used.

What I have said about contingency and necessity applies also to obligation and its transcendent ground (or goodness and its transcendent goal), to design and its transcendent designer, to religious experience and its transcendent object. In all these cases we use language which on analysis will not do, but which seems to us to be appropriate for the expression of our beliefs; and in all these the question can be, and is, discussed, why such language is chosen, and how it is to be understood.

That then is the logical mother of religious belief; call her natural theism, or what you will, she is a response, not precisely logical, and yet in no sense emotional or evaluative, to certain elements in our experience, whose characteristic is that they induce us, not to make straightforward statements about the world, but to strain and distort our media of communication in order to express what we make of them. In herself she is an honest woman; and if she is sometimes bedizened in logical trappings, and put out on the streets as an inductive argument, the fault is hardly hers. Her function is, not to prove to us that God exists, but to provide us with a 'meaning' for the word 'God'. Without her we should not know whither statements concerning the word were to be referred; the subject in theological utterances would be unattached. All that we should know of them is that they were not to be referred to anything with which we are or could hope to be acquainted; that, and also that they were to be understood in terms of whatever it is that people suppose themselves to be doing when they build churches and kneel down in them. And that is not entirely satisfactory; for while there is much to be said in practice for advising the honest inquirer into the reference of the word 'God' to pursue his inquiry by familiarizing himself with the concrete activity of religion, it remains true that the range and variety of possible delusions which could induce such behaviour is theoretically boundless, and, as visitors to the Pacific coast of the United States can testify, in practice very large.

The logical father of religious belief, that which might bring us on from the condition of merely possessing the category of the divine, into the condition of active belief in God, this consists, in Christianity (and if there is nothing analogous in other religions, so much the worse for them), in the interpretation of certain objects or events as a manifestation of the divine. It is, in other words, because we find, that, in thinking of certain events in terms of the category of the divine, we can give what seems to us the most convincing account of them, that we can assure ourselves that the notion of God is not just an empty aspiration. Without the notion of God we could interpret nothing as divine, and without concrete events which we felt impelled to interpret as divine we could not know that the notion of divinity had any application to reality. Why it is that as Christians we find ourselves impelled to interpret the history of Israel, the life and death of Christ, and the experience of his Church as relevatory of God, I shall not here attempt to say; it is an oft-told tale, and I shall content myself with saying that we can hardly expect to feel such an impulsion so long as our knowledge of these matters is superficial and altogether from without. Whyever we feel such an impulsion, it is not, of course, a logical impulsion; that is, we may resist it (or fail to feel it) without thereby contravening the laws of logic, or the rules of any pragmatically accredited inductive procedure. On the anthropological level the history of Israel, Old and New, is certainly the history of a religious development from its tribal origins. We may decide, or we may not, that it is something more, something beyond the wit of man to invent, something which seems to us to be a real and coherent communication from a real and coherent, though superhuman, mind. We may decide, or we may not; neither decision breaks the rules, for in such a unique matter there are no rules to conform to or to break. The judgment is our own; and in the language of the New Testament it judges us; that is, it reveals what, up to the moment of our decision, the Spirit of God has done in us—but that, of course, is to argue in a circle.

Belief, thus begotten, is nurtured by the practice of the Christian life—by the conviction so aroused (or, of course, not aroused; but then it is starvation and not nurture) that the Christian warfare is a real warfare. Something will have to be said about this later on, but for the moment I propose to dismiss it, and to return to the consideration of the significance of religious utterances in the light of the dual parentage of religious belief.

I have argued that unless certain things seem to us to be signs of divine activity, then we may hope that there is a God, but we cannot properly believe that there is. It follows from this that religious belief must properly involve treating something as revelatory of God; and that is to say that it must involve an element of authority (for to treat something as divine revelation is to invest it with authority). That what we say about God is said on authority (and, in particular, on the authority of Christ) is of the first importance in considering the significance of these statements. In what way this is so, I shall hope to make clear as we go along.

If we remember that our statements about God rest on the authority of Christ, whom we call his Word, we can see what seems to me the essential clue to the interpretation of the logical nature of such utterances, and that is, in a word, the notion of parable. To elucidate what I mean by 'parable' (for I am using the word in an extended sense) let us consider Christ's action on Palm Sunday, when he rode into Jerusalem on an ass. This action was an act of teaching. For it had been said to Jerusalem that her king would come to her riding upon an ass. Whoever, therefore, deliberately chose this method of entry, was saying in effect: 'What you are about to witness (namely my Passion, Death and Resurrection) is the coming of the Messianic King to claim his kingdom'. The prophecy of Messiah's kingdom was to be interpreted, not in the ordinary sense, but in the sense of the royal kingship of the Crucified. To interpret in this way is to teach by violent paradox, indeed, but none the less it is to teach. Part of the lesson is that it is only the kings of the Gentiles that lord it over their subjects; if any man will be a king in Israel (God's chosen people), he must humble himself as a servant; part of it is that the Crucifixion is to be seen as Messianic, that is as God's salvation of his chosen people. Now the logical structure which is involved here is something like this:—You are told a story (Behold, thy king cometh, meek and lowly, and riding upon an ass). You will not know just what the reality to which the story refers will be like until it happens. If you take the story at its face value (an ordinary, though humble, king, bringing an ordinary political salvation), you will get it all wrong. If you bring to bear upon its interpretation all that the Law and the Prophets have taught you about God's purposes for his people, though you will still not know just what it will be like until it happens, none the less you will not go wrong by believing it; for then you will know that Christ ought to have suffered these things, and to enter into his glory, and so you will learn what the story has to tell you of God's purposes for man, and something therefore, indirectly, of God. If you remember what Isaiah says about humility and sacrifice, you will see that what is being forecast is that God's purposes will be accomplished by a man who fulfils the Law and the Prophets in humble obedience.

This story is that one that can be fairly fully interpreted. There are others that cannot. There is, for example, Hosea's parable in which he likens himself to God, and Israel to his unfaithful wife, and expresses his grief at his wife's unfaithfulness. If, now, you ask for this to be fully interpreted, if you ask Hosea to tell you what he supposes it is like for the Holy One of Israel, of whom no similitude may be made, to be grieved, demanding to know, not what would happen in such a case to the unfaithful sinner who had provoked the divine wrath, but what was the condition of the divine mind in itself, then no doubt he would have regarded the very question as blasphemous. As an inspired prophet, he felt himself entitled to say that God was grieved, without presuming to imagine what such a situation was like, other than in its effects. What he said was said on authority; it was not his own invention, and therefore he could rely on its truth, without supposing himself to understand its full meaning. In so far as Hosea's parable is 'interpreted', the interpretation is confined to identifying the *dramatis personae* (Hosea=God, his wife=Israel). It is noteworthy that the interpretation which is sometimes given to the parables of the New Testament is usually of the same sketchy kind (The reapers are the angels). In Plato's famous parable of prisoners in a cave, it is quite possible to describe the situation which the parable seeks to illuminate. One can describe how a man can begin by being content to establish rough laws concerning what follows what in nature, how he may proceed from such a condition to desire explanations of the regularities which are forced on his attention, rising thus to more abstract and mathematical generalizations, and then, through the study of mathematics, to completely abstract speculation. One cannot similarly describe the situation which the parable of the Prodigal Son is intended to illustrate (or rather one can only describe the human end of it); and no attempt is ever made to do so.

I make no apology for these paragraphs about the Bible; after all the Bible is the source of Christian belief, and it cannot but illuminate the logical nature of the latter to consider the communicational methods of the former. But we must turn back to more general considerations. It is, then, characteristic of a parable that the words which are used in it are used in their ordinary senses. Elsewhere this is not always so. If you speak of the virtues of a certain sort of car, the word 'virtue', being applied to a car, comes to mean something different from what it means in application to human beings. If you speak of hot temper, the word 'hot' does not mean what it means in the ordinary way. Now many people suppose that something of the latter sort is happening in religious utterances. When God is said to be jealous, or active in history, it is felt that the word 'jealous' or 'active' must be being used here in a transferred sense. But if it is being used in a transferred sense, some means or other must be supplied whereby the new sense can be taken. The activity of God is presumably not like the activity of men (it does not make him hot or tired); to say then that God is active must involve modifying the meaning of the word. But, if the word is undergoing modification, it is essential that we should know in what direction. In the case of ordinary transfers, how do we know what sort of modification is involved? This is a large question, but roughly, I think, the answer is, in two ways. Firstly there is normally a certain appropriateness, like the appropriateness of 'hot' in 'hot temper'; and secondly we can notice the circumstances in which the word gets used and withheld in its transferred sense. If I hear the phrase 'Baroque music', the meaning of the word 'Baroque' in its normal architectural employment may set me looking in a certain direction; and I can clinch the matter by asking for examples, 'Bach? Buxtehude? Beethoven?' But for either of these ways to be of any use to me, I must know something about *both* ends of the transfer. I must know something about Baroque architecture, *and* I must be able to run through musical styles in my head, to look for the musical analogue of Baroque features. If I cannot stumble on your meaning without assistance, I can still do so by eliciting from you that Bach and Buxtehude are, Handel and Mozart are not, examples of the sort of music you have in mind. This is informative to me if and only if I know something of Buxtehude and Bach, Handel and Mozart.

Now we all know what it is like for a man to be active. We can quote examples, decide correctly, and so forth. But what about divine activity? Surely we cannot have it both ways. Either God can be moderately like a man, so that the word 'active', used of him, can set us looking in the right direction; or he can be quite unlike a man, in which case it cannot. Nor can we be helped by the giving of examples, unless it is legitimate to point to examples of divine activity —to say, 'Now here God is being active, but not there.' This constitutes the force of Flew's demand that we should tell him how statements about God can be falsified. In essence Flew is saying: 'When you speak about God, the words which occur in the predicate part of your statements are not being used in the ordinary sense; you make so great a difference between God and man, that I cannot even find that the words you use set me looking in anything that might perhaps be the right direction. You speak of God as being outside time; and when I think what I mean by "activity", I find that that word, as used about a timeless being, suggests to me nothing whatsoever. There is only one resort left; give me examples of when one of your statements is, and is not, applicable. If, as no doubt you will say, that is an unfair demand, since they are always applicable (e.g. God is always active, so that there are no cases of his inactivity to be pointed to), I will not insist on actual examples; make them up if you like. But do not point to *everything* and say, " *That* is what I mean"; for *everything* is not *that*, but this and this and this and many other mutual incompatibles; and black and white and red and green and kind and cruel and coal and ink and everything else together cannot possibly elucidate to me the meaning of a word.'

As I have said, the answer must be that when we speak about God, the words we use are intended in their ordinary sense (for we cannot make a transfer, failing familiarity with both ends of it), although we do not suppose that in their ordinary interpretation they can be strictly true of him. We do not even know how much of them applies. To some extent it may be possible to take a word like 'activity' and whittle away that in it which most obviously does not apply. It is, however, an exaggeration, at the least, to suppose that this process of whittling away leaves us in the end with a kernel about which we can say that we know that it does apply. A traditional procedure is to compose a scale on which inanimate matter is at the bottom, the characteristically human activities, such as thinking and personal relationship, at the top, and to suppose that the scale is pointing towards God; and so on this assumption the first thing to do is to pare away from the notion of human activity whatever in it is common to what stands below it on the scale—for example actual physical moving about. Taking the human residue, we try to decide what in it is positive, and what is negative, mere limitation. The tenuous ghost of a concept remaining we suppose to be the essential structure of activity (that structure which is common to running and thinking) and so to be realized also in divine activity. Perhaps this is how we imagine our language to be related to the divine realities about which we use it; but such ghostly and evacuated concepts are clearly too tenuous and elusive to be called the meanings of the words we use. To think of God thus is to think of him not in our own image, but in the rarefied ghost of our own image; and so we think of him in our own image, but do not suppose that in so thinking of him we begin to do him justice. What we do, then, is in essence to think of God in parables. The things we say about God are said on the authority of the words and acts of Christ, who spoke in human language, using parable; and so we too speak of God in parable—authoritative parable, authorized parable; knowing that the truth is not literally that which our parables represent, knowing therefore that now we see in a glass darkly, but trusting, because we trust the source of the parables, that in believing them and interpreting them in the light of each other, we shall not be misled, that we shall have such knowledge as we need to possess for the foundation of the religious life.

So far so good. But it is only the predicates of theological utterances which are parabolic; it is only in what is *said about* God that words are put to other than customary employment. When we say 'God is merciful', it is 'merciful' that is in strange company—deprived of its usual escort of human sentiments. But the word 'God' only occurs in statements about God. Our grasp of this word, therefore, cannot be derived from our grasp of it in ordinary human contexts, for it is not used in such contexts. How then is our grasp of it to be accounted for? In other words, if I have given some account of how, and in what sense, we understand the meaning of the things we say about God, I have still to give some account of how, and in what sense, we know what it is that we are saying them about.

In thus turning back from the predicate to the subject of religious utterances, we are turning from revealed theology to natural theology, from the logical father to the logical mother of religious belief. And the answer to the question: 'What grasp have we of the meaning of the word "God"?' must be dealt with along the following lines. Revelation is important to the believer not for what it is in itself (the biography of a Jew, and the history of his forerunners and followers), nor because it is revelation of nothing in particular, but because it is revelation of God. In treating it as something important, something commanding our allegiance, we are bringing to bear upon it the category of the transcendent, of the divine. Of the nature of that category I have already spoken. In other words, there must exist within a man's mind the contrast between the contingent and the necessary, the derivative and the underivative, the finite and the infinite, the perfect and the imperfect, if anything is to be for him a revelation of God. Given that contrast, we are given also that to which the parables or stories are referred. What is thus given is certainly not knowledge of the object to which they apply; it is something much more like a direction. We do not, that is, know to what to refer our parables; we know merely that we are to refer them out of experience, and out of it *in which direction*. The expression 'God' is to refer to that object, whatever it is, and if there be one, which is such that the knowledge of it would be to us knowledge of the unfamiliar term in the contrast between finite and infinite.

Statements about God, then, are in effect parables, which are referred, by means of the proper name 'God', out of our experience in a certain direction. We may, if we like, by the process of whittling away, which I have mentioned, try to tell ourselves what part of the meaning of our statements applies reasonably well, what part outrageously badly; but the fact remains that, in one important sense, when we speak about God, we do not know what we mean (that is, we do not know what that which we are talking about is like), and do not need to know, because we accept the images, which we employ, on authority. Because our concern with God is religious and not speculative (it is contemplative in part, but that is another matter), because our need is, not to know what God is like, but to enter into relation with him, the authorized images serve our purpose. They belong to a type of discourse—parable—with which we are familiar, and therefore they have communication value, although in a sense they lack descriptive value.

If this is so, how do we stand with regard to verification and falsification? Must we, to preserve our claim to be making assertions, be prepared to say what would count against them? Let us see how far we can do so. Does anything count against the assertion that God is merciful? Yes, suffering. Does anything count decisively against it? No, we reply, because it is true. Could anything count decisively against it? Yes, suffering which was utterly, eternally and irredeemably pointless. Can we then design a crucial experiment? No, because we can never see all of the picture. Two things at least are hidden from us; what goes on in the recesses of the personality of the sufferer, and what shall happen hereafter.

Well, then, the statement that God is merciful is not testable; it is compatible with any and every tract of experience which we are in fact capable of witnessing. It cannot be verified; does this matter?

To answer this, we must make up our minds why the demand for verification or falsification is legitimate. On this large matter I shall be summary and dogmatic, as follows. (1) The demand that a statement of fact should be verifiable is a conflation of two demands (2) The *first* point is that all statements of fact must be verifiable in the sense that there must not exist a *rule of language* which precludes testing the statement. That is to say, the way the statement is to be taken must not be such that to try to test it is to show that you do not understand it. If I say that it is wrong to kill, and you challenge my statement and adduce as evidence against it that thugs and headhunters do so out of religious duty, then you have not understood my statement. My statement was not a statement of fact, but a moral judgment, and your statement that it should be tested by anthropological investigations shows that you did not understand it. But so long as there exists no *logical* (or we might say *interpretational*) ban on looking around for verification, the existence of a *factual* ban on verification does not matter. 'Caesar had mutton before he crossed the Rubicon' cannot in fact be tested, but by trying to devise ways of testing it you do not show that you have not understood it; you are merely wasting your time. (3) The *second* point is that, *for me, fully* to understand a statement, *I* must know what a test of it would be like. If I have no idea how to test whether somebody had mutton, then I do not know what 'having mutton' means. This stipulation is concerned, not with the logical nature of the expression, but with its communication value for me. (4) There are then two stipulations, and they are different. The first is a logical stipulation, and it is to the effect that nothing can be a statement of fact if it is untestable in the sense that the notion of testing it is precluded by correctly interpreting it. The second is a communicational stipulation, and it is to the effect that nobody can fully understand a statement, unless he has a fair idea how a situation about which it was true would differ from a situation about which it was false.

Now with regard to these two stipulations, how do religious utterances fare? With regard to the first, there is no language rule implicit in a correct understanding of them which precludes putting them to the test (there may be a rule of faith, but that is another matter). If a man says, 'How can God be loving, and allow pain?' he does *not* show that he has misunderstood the statement that God is loving. There *is* a *prima facie* incompatibility between the love of God, and pain and suffering. The Christian maintains that it is *prima facie* only; others maintain that it is not. They may argue about it, and the issue cannot be decided; but it cannot be decided, not because (as in the case of e.g. moral or mathematical judgments) the appeal to facts is *logically* the wrong way of trying to decide the issue, and shows that you have not understood the judgment; *but* because, since our experience is limited in the way it is, we cannot get into position to decide it, any more than we can get into position to decide what Julius Caesar had for breakfast before he crossed the Rubicon. For the Christian the operation of getting into position to decide it is called dying; and, though we can all do that, we cannot return to report what we find. By this test, then, religious utterances can be called statements of fact; that is their *logical* classification.

With regard to the second stipulation, the case is a little complicated, for here we are concerned with communication value, and there are the two levels, the one on which we remain within the parable, and the other on which we try to step outside it. Now, on the first level we know well enough how to test a statement like 'God loves us'; it is, for example, like testing 'My father loves me'. In fact, of course, since with parents and schoolmasters severity is notoriously a way of displaying affection, the decisive testing of such a statement is not easy; but there is a point beyond which it is foolish to continue to have doubts. Now, within the parable, we are supposing 'God loves us' to be a statement like 'My father loves me', 'God' to be a subject similar to 'My father', 'God loves us' being thus related to 'My father loves me' as the latter is related to 'Aristotle's father loved him'. We do not suppose that we can actually test 'God loves us', for reasons already given (any more than we can test the one about Aristotle); but the communication value of the statement whose subject is 'God' is derived from the communication value of the same statement with a different proper name as subject. If we try to step outside the parable, then we must admit that we do not know what the situation about which our parable is being told is like; we should only know if we could know God, and know even as also we have been known; see, that is, the unfolding of the divine purposes in their entirety. Such ignorance is what we ought to expect. We do not know how what we call the divine wrath differs from the divine mercy (because we do not know how they respectively resemble human wrath and mercy); but we do know how what *we mean* when we talk about the wrath of God differs from what *we mean* when we talk about his mercy, because then we are within the parable, talking within the framework of admitted ignorance, in language which we accept because we trust its source. We know what is meant *in* the parable, when the father of the Prodigal sees him coming a great way off and runs to meet him, and we can therefore think in terms of this image. We know that we are here promised that whenever we come to ourselves and return to God, he will come to meet us. This is enough to encourage us to return, and to make us alert to catch the signs of the divine response; but it does not lead us to presume to an understanding of the mind and heart of God. In talking we remain within the parable, and so our statements communicate; we do not know how the parable applies, but we believe that it does apply, and that we shall one day see how. (Some even believe, perhaps rightly, that in our earthly condition we may by direct illumination of our minds be enabled to know progressively more about the realities to which our parables apply, and in consequence about the manner of their application).

Much of what I have said agrees very closely with what the atheist says about religious belief, except that I have tried to make it sound better. The atheist alleges that the religious man supposes himself to know what he means by his statements only because, until challenged, he interprets them anthropomorphically; when challenged, however, he retreats rapidly backwards towards complete agnosticism. I agree with this, with two provisos. The first is that the religious man does not suppose himself to know what he means by his statements (for what religious man supposes himself to be the Holy Ghost?); he knows what his statements mean within the parable, and believes that they are the right statements to use. (Theology is not a science; it is a sort of art of enlightened ignorance.) The second proviso is that the agnosticism is not complete; for the Christian, under attack, falls back not in any direction, but in one direction; he falls back upon the person of Christ, and the concrete realities of the Christian life.

Let us consider this for a moment with regard to the divine love. I could be attacked in this sort of way:—'You have contended', my opponent might argue, 'that when we say that God loves us the communication value of the statement is determined by the communication value of a similar statement about a human subject; and that we know the statement to be the right statement, but cannot know *how* it is the right statement, that is, what the divine love is like. But this will not do. Loving is an activity with two poles, the lover and the loved. We may not know the lover, in the case of God, but we *are*, and therefore *must know*, the loved. Now, to say that the image or parable of human love is the right image to use about God must imply that there is some similarity or analogy between human and divine love. Father's love may be superficially very unlike mother's, but, unless there is some similarity of structure between them, we cannot use the same word of both. But we cannot believe that there is any similarity between the love of God and human love, unless we can detect some similarity between being loved by God and being loved by man. But if being loved by God is what we experience all the time, then it is not like being loved by man; it is like being let down right and left. And in the face of so great a discrepancy, we cannot believe that God loves us, if that is supposed to be in any sense a statement of sober fact.'

I cannot attempt to answer this objection; it involves the whole problem of religion. But there is something I want to say about it, which is that the Christian does not attempt to evade it either by helter-skelter flight, or by impudent bluff. He has his prepared positions on to which he retreats; and he knows that if these positions are taken, then he must surrender. He does not believe that they can be taken, but that is another matter. There are three main fortresses behind which he goes. For, *first*, he looks for the resurrection of the dead, and the life of the world to come; he believes, that is, that we do not see all of the picture, and that the parts which we do not see are precisely the parts which determine the design of the whole. He admits that if this hope be vain then we are of all men the most miserable. *Second*, he claims that he sees in Christ the verification, and to some extent also the specification, of the divine love. That is to say, he finds in Christ not only convincing evidence of God's concern for us, but also what sort of love the divine love is, what sort of benefits God is concerned to give us. He sees that, on the New Testament scale of values, it is better for a man to lose the whole world if he can thereby save his soul (which means his relationship to God); and that for that hope it is reasonable to sacrifice all that he has, and to undergo the death of the body and the mortification of the spirit. *Third*, he claims that in the religious life, of others, if not as yet in his own, the divine love may be encountered, that the promise 'I will not fail thee nor forsake thee' is, if rightly understood, confirmed there. If, of course, this promise is interpreted as involving immunity from bodily suffering, it will be refuted; but no reader of the New Testament has any right so to interpret it. It is less glaringly, but as decisively, wrong to interpret it as involving immunity from spiritual suffering; for in the New Testament only the undergoing of death (which means the abdication of control over one's destiny) can be the beginning of life. What then does it promise? It promises that to the man who begins on the way of the Christian life, on the way that is of seeking life through death, of seeking relationship with God through the abdication of the self-sovereignty claimed by Adam, that to him the fight will be hard but not impossible, progress often indiscernible, but real, progress which is towards the paring away of self-hood, and which is therefore often given through defeat and humiliation, but a defeat and humiliation which are not final, which leave it possible to continue. This is the extra-parental nurture of religious belief of which I spoke earlier, and it is the third of the prepared positions on to which the Christian retreats, claiming that the image and reflection of the love of God may be seen not only hereafter, not only in Christ, but also, if dimly, in the concrete process of living the Christian life.

One final word. Religion has indeed its problems; but it is useless to consider them outside their religious context. Seen as a whole religion makes rough sense, though it does not make limpidity.

Wadham College
  OXFORD

VII

RELIGION AS THE INEXPRESSIBLE

THOMAS McPHERSON

People sometimes say that certain Christian beliefs are nonsensical. How, for example, can God be One Person yet Three Persons? Or Three Persons *in* One Person? Is God One Person yet Three Persons in the way that an actress playing Miss Hardcastle in *She Stoops to Conquer* is one person (herself) yet three persons (herself, Miss Hardcastle, and Miss Hardcastle pretending to be the barmaid)? Or in the way in which I may simultaneously be one (affectionate) person to my wife and children, a 'totally different' (bad-tempered) person to my subordinates in the office, and all the time a third person as well (the 'real me' whom nobody understands—the person I think I am when I am 'dramatizing myself' as we say, or 'being inscrutable' as James Thurber says, or being Existentialist)? Or in the way in which a man may be three different persons in succession: in early youth a profligate, in late youth reformed and a leader of men, in middle age dully respectable and unadventurous? And is God Three Persons *in* One Person in the way that Pooh Bah was a great many persons in one, or the editor of a very small country newspaper may be three persons in one (reporter, editor and sub-editor)? Or is he Three Persons in One in the way that Siamese triplets would be three persons in one?

God is 'wholly other', yet God is 'in us'. Christ died, yet lives. Man is made in the image of God, yet God has no form that any mirror could image. Christ said both 'I and my father are one' and 'My father is greater than I'. Christ is the Son of God and God is his Father, and God is also the Father of all of us, yet not in the same way. We are commanded to work out our *own* salvation *for* it is God which worketh in us. The service of God is perfect freedom—these are the kinds of things that are pointed to as hardly good sense.

Now what do such beliefs mean? How are we to understand them? Or is it wrong to try to 'understand' them? Are they absurd or nonsensical? If they are not, then why not? If they are, then how exactly is it that they are absurd or nonsensical? Is it because they do not make 'literal' sense? But do they then have some 'deeper meaning' which is not their literal meaning; do they make sense on a different 'level' from that of literal meaning? And, if so, what is this level, and how is it different from the level of literal meaning?

All these questions indicate a *worry*. It is a worry that we may feel not only with theological statements but with other sorts of statements as well. But we feel it particularly with theological statements because they are (rightly) thought to be asserting something very important. Not everyone has this worry over theological statements, but some do. Of those who have it, some are not Christians mainly because they have it. Others who have it and who *are* Christians, are not altogether sure whether their worry needs to be reconciled with their Christianity, and if it does how they are to accomplish this. (There is a difference between 'direct' statements of religious belief—some familiar quotations from the Bible are clearly of this kind—and statements of a more sophisticated sort constructed by theologians. Sometimes the latter are not so much expressions of the worry as themselves attempts to settle it. But for our purposes we can ignore this distinction.)

Now there is a certain way out of this worry—a way on which I wish to comment. It is this: There are some things that just cannot be said. As long as no one tries to say them there is no trouble. But if anyone does try to say them he must take the consequences. We ought not to try to express the inexpressible. The things that theologians try to say (or some of them) belong to the class of things that just cannot be said. The way out of the worry is retreat into silence. This way is taken not usually by theologians (though it is, of course, taken by some important religious persons who are not theologians) but by philosophers—and philosophers of a kind that theologians commonly regard as their enemies.

Before I go on there is this to be said. It may be felt that the worry I am writing about is one that no sensible person ought to have. In particular, persons who have had a training in theology may feel that the worry arises from altogether too naïve a way of looking at things. Of course, it will be said, there are Christian beliefs which, when written down in cold ink, look nonsensical if judged by ordinary tests of sense and nonsense. But that is just where we can easily go wrong. The tests by which these statements look nonsensical are all very well when applied to some other statements, but such tests are out of place here. The statements of Christian theologians are not intended to be statements like these others. So we cannot try them by such tests.

Now it is true that there are different kinds of nonsense. To see this we need only compare ''Twas brillig, and the slithy toves Did gyre and gimble in the wabe', and 'This book is red and green all over', and 'All only every but', and 'Socrates is numerous'. Each of these utterances is nonsensical for a different reason. (And there are more kinds of nonsense than these).

It is also true that the tests for one kind of nonsense will not be the tests for another. A single test for nonsense applied indiscriminately to all statements will result in some statements being classed as nonsense-statements where without such single-mindedness we might prefer to call them, for example, 'strikingly-expressed'. But sometimes people do want to say: 'God is both One Person and Three Persons, and this is not just a way of speaking: I mean that he *really is* both One Person and Three Persons.' Then we have to ask,

'What exactly does this mean?', and we are surely entitled to begin by taking it perfectly literally.[1]

The way out of the worry that I am commenting on here may be called the positivistic way. I have expressed it above in a very general manner. Variations and refinements I am deliberately not taking into account.

Other ways out of the worry have been discussed frequently enough.[2] The positivistic way is often rejected without examination. Theologians do not see it as an admissible answer to the worry. (Occasionally the philosophical view from which it springs is picked upon by some theologian with philosophical training but developed in an unwise and mistaken manner. I shall return to this at the end.) I am not arguing for anything. All I want to do is to clear the ground and show what is involved in the positivistic way. I am neither adopting nor rejecting it: I want to see what it is. What to the Jews was a stumbling-block and to the Greeks foolishness is to logical positivists nonsense. There is more to be learnt from this than has yet, I think, been realized by most theologians.

Rudolf Otto can take us some distance towards an understanding of the positivistic way. A reminder of some of his views may not be out of place. Otto holds[3] that what is most distinctive in religion cannot be put into words. This is the 'non-rational' part of religion; 'non-rational' he equates with 'not capable of being conceptualized'. The distinctive (non-rational) thing in religion is a certain sort of experience —the numinous experience; and this is partly a feeling—a feeling of creatureliness or creaturehood—and partly consciousness of 'something outside' us, consciousness of the Numen (or the Numinous), the Wholly Other.

---

[1] I am aware that the Christian use of 'person' in 'God is Three Persons in One' is not altogether unsophisticated. A detailed discussion of that statement would need to include a consideration of 'God is three *personae* in one *substantia*'.

[2] For instance, the Neo-Thomist way, which tries to settle the worry by offering a theory of analogical predication, or the way of the Theology of Paradox in which nonsense is positively welcomed (though it is called not 'nonsense' but 'paradox').

[3] R. Otto, *The Idea of the Holy*.

Christianity is a highly conceptualized religion, Otto says. He seems to mean by this that Christianity is full of words: hymns, sermons, theological books, the Bible itself. The conceptualized part of religion—the part that is put into words—is very important. But we, with our highly conceptualized religion, must not forget that there is something else which cannot be put into words; there is a non-rational element in religion—the experience of the numinous.

This is one interpretation of what Otto means, and on the whole I think it is the right one, but there are passages which suggest a different, milder, view.

Otto shifts between two uses of 'concept' and 'conceptualize'. Sometimes he seems to mean by 'concept' something like the concepts of spirit, reason, purpose,[4] and by 'conceptualize' something like 'express in terms of such concepts'. So to say that Christianity is a conceptualized (or a highly conceptualized) religion is like saying that Christianity is expressed in rather an 'abstract' way; it uses too many hard words, is not expressed in 'concrete' terms, is too 'philosophical'. But Otto at other times seems to mean something much wider than this by 'concept'. He says: '*All* language, in so far as it consists of words, purports to convey ideas or concepts—that is what language *means*—and the more clearly and unequivocally it does so, the better the language. And hence expositions of religious truth in language *inevitably* tend to stress the "rational" attributes of God.'[5]

According to this wider interpretation, religion is conceptualized merely by being put into words—any words. It is not conceptualized only because it is put into hard words or 'abstract' words. And it is this wider view that I think Otto on the whole wants to hold.

Now, Otto is writing about the non-rational element in religion, but he writes about it very rationally. His approach is thoroughly matter-of-fact and reasoned. He is writing about a special sort of feeling which he says cannot be clearly

[4] *Op. cit.*, p. 1.
[5] *Ibid.*, p. 2. My italics.

135

and accurately described, yet it is obvious that the aim of his book is clarity and accuracy. His English translator— Professor Harvey—renders Otto's title *Das Heilige* as *The Idea of the Holy*. It is indeed the *idea*—or *concept*—of 'the holy' (whose essence is the numinous) that Otto is writing about; even though the point that he most wants to make about it is that the essence of the holy is not capable of being conceptualized. Otto is writing about that part of religion that cannot, he thinks, be reduced to language, but naturally he has to use language in order to write about it, and it is noticeable how well he uses language; and, furthermore, it is noticeable that he uses language descriptively. In writing of emotions he does not use language in the way that itself arouses emotion: he writes in an 'objective', 'scientific' way.

Otto, then, uses language in order to explain what cannot be said in language. You cannot define the concept of the holy in a completely satisfactory way: you cannot satisfactorily tell others in words what it is: but what you can do in words is tell them about, or remind them of, feelings which are like the numinous feeling (but different from it, too, for the numinous feeling is a unique feeling, and not to be confused with any other no matter how similar to it it may be). You can talk round and round the subject, never quite hitting it exactly (for it is impossible to hit it with words), until you bring your hearer or reader to the point where he sees for himself what the numinous experience is.

Otto, in fact, is writing about the non-rational in a supremely rational way. But he thinks that rationality is not good enough for religion; and it takes a very rational man to see that. He does not want to say that it is wrong for a religion to be highly rational (highly conceptualized). What he wants to say is that we must not be bewitched into overlooking the fact that at the core of religion is a non-rational element—a part that eludes conceptualization. His reaction to the worry might be expressed, for him, like this: 'I agree with you that there is much nonsense in Christian doctrine.' And he would not content himself with agreeing; he would produce illustrations of his own[6] to show just how much nonsense there is in Christian doctrine. Then he would say: 'There are some things that cannot be said; so let us not try to say them.'

Some of what I have just put into Otto's mouth is invention or embroidery. What Otto explicitly says cannot be conceptualized is the numinous experience.[7] As I have just interpreted him I have made him say more than this. But from what he says about 'concept' and 'conceptualize' (on the wider view) this is not an unreasonable interpretation. (Perhaps if Otto had realized that he had laid himself open to be interpreted in this way he would have wished to retreat to his narrower use of 'concept' and 'conceptualize').

But we need not press Otto too far. It is enough if we interpret him as saying only that the numinous experience is what cannot be put into words: for this is, in Otto's view, the distinctive thing in religion. We can find out what more we need to know about the positivistic way from others. Let us try Ludwig Wittgenstein.

It is interesting to compare with Otto's *The Idea of the Holy* the closing pages of Wittgenstein's *Tractatus Logico-Philosophicus*. Wittgenstein speaks there of 'the mystical' (*das Mystische*). For example, he says: 'The feeling of the world as a limited whole is the mystical feeling.'[8] This has clear affinities with Otto's 'creature-feeling'.[9] The interesting thing in this part of the *Tractatus*, for our purposes, is the view there put forward of religion ('the mystical'). The sort of questions about the world that can be asked and answered, according to the *Tractatus*, are questions about *how* the world is. (That is, roughly, questions about 'how the world *works*'). And these are questions of natural science. But the sort of questions

---

6 See *The Idea of the Holy*, p. 205, on the Christian use of 'person'. And cf. Otto's *Religious Essays*, pp. 85–6 and 97.

7 In so far as the numinous experience is an emotion it is no different from other emotions in this. No emotion can be defined in words, or even described —'directly' described—in words.

8 *Tractatus Logico-Philosophicus*, 6.45.

9 *The Idea of the Holy*, pp. 10, 52. It has even more affinities with current interpretations of the Cosmological Argument: see, e.g. E. L. Mascall, *Existence and Analogy*.

that religious people ask are questions about the fact that there is a world at all. ('Why is there a world anyway?').

As Wittgenstein says: 'Not *how* the world is, is the mystical, but *that* it is.'[10]

But the trouble about this sort of question, he holds, is that it cannot be answered. (At the least, we may say, if it appears to be answered, there will not be agreement that any suggested answer is the right answer.) Questions about how the world works can be asked, and answered. But questions about why there is a world at all are quite different: they cannot be answered; that is to say, their answer cannot be an answer in words. Because they cannot be answered in words neither can they be asked in words. 'For an answer which cannot be expressed the question too cannot be expressed.'[11] (It follows, Wittgenstein holds, that scepticism about religious matters is senseless. The questions and answers of religion are not capable of being expressed, and it is absurd to have doubts about the answer to a question that is not capable of being expressed. 'For doubt can only exist where there is a question; a question only where there is an answer, and this only where something *can* be *said*.'[12])

Men cannot help feeling that even if all the 'how' questions had been answered the 'that' question would remain. The problems of life ('the riddle') men feel are not touched on in the answers to the 'how' questions. The way out of this, Wittgenstein says, is found when we see that our feeling that the problems of life have not been touched on comes from the desire to ask questions that cannot be significantly asked. If all 'how' questions are answered there are no other questions left that can be answered (and therefore none that can properly be asked).

It is at this point that Wittgenstein and Otto would part

---

[10] *Op. cit.*, 6.44.

[11] *Ibid.*, 6.5. Cf. Otto, *Religious Essays*, pp. 90–1: 'For the unspeakable is unspeakably beatifying, it is *fascinans*. So rich is its content of blessedness that all other values are shed. But the nature of its content can only be felt, not expressed: therefore "let him who is wise attempt to add no word".' And Wittgenstein again: 'There is indeed the inexpressible. This *shows* itself; it is the mystical' (*Tractatus*, 6.522).

[12] *Ibid.*, 6.51.

company. Wittgenstein goes on to say that the 'solution' of 'the problem of life' (the desire to ask 'that' questions) comes when it is seen that such questions cannot (sensibly) be asked; the solution takes the form of a vanishing of the sense that there is a problem of life. Otto's direction from this point would be different. Where Wittgenstein ends he begins. For Wittgenstein, perhaps, to see that in religion we are asking questions that cannot be answered is, in a way, to see the pointlessness of religion. For Otto, to see that in religion we are asking questions that cannot be answered is to see its point; we do not lose the sense that there is a problem of life, or a 'meaning' to life; but we perhaps realize that the question 'What is the meaning of life?' is not one that can be clearly answered in words, and so not one that can be properly asked.

Now positivistic philosophy is commonly held to be an enemy of religion. But a branding of religious assertions as 'nonsense' need not be anti-religious. It can be interpreted as an attack on those who in the name of religion are perverting religion. It can be interpreted as a return to the truth about religion. Otto conceived himself in *The Idea of the Holy* to be recovering the essential element in religion—which had been in danger of being lost under a cloud of rationalizing. What is essential about religion is its non-rational side, the part that cannot be 'conceptualized'—that is, the part that cannot be put into words. Otto travels the same road as Wittgenstein. Are we to call Otto an enemy of religion? Why not call Wittgenstein its friend?

Modern positivistic philosophy has been developed by men of a scientific and not a religious turn of mind. (Perhaps this is not true of Wittgenstein himself.) The interest of the original logical positivists (The Vienna Circle) seems to have been mainly in science, and for them the task of the philosopher was to be the helper of the scientist. The observation statements of science were their model for sense,[13] and

13 Scientific *laws* should be held to be 'nonsense' as much as theological statements, for they are not verifiable by sense experience.

because the scientist's observation statements are empirically verifiable the test for sense becomes 'amenability to verification by sense experience', and whatever is not so verifiable accordingly is 'non-sense'. (An exception is made of 'analytic' statements, which are also found in science in the form of mathematical statements; but the only theological statement that has any obvious claim to be regarded as analytic is 'God exists', and the grave difficulties that arise if one does regard this as analytic have been pointed out by both St. Thomas Aquinas and Kant.)[14] Theological statements are not (most of them, anyway) verifiable by sense experience, so they are nonsense. 'Nonsense' is a pejorative word, and people do not like being told that they are talking nonsense.[15] Theologians like it as little as anyone else. People who insult one are one's enemies. So the positivists are enemies of religion.

I want to say that this opinion may be a mistaken one. Positivistic philosophers have certainly not thought of themselves as supporters of religion. But that could be because they have mistaken what is important about religion. Theologians have thought of positivistic philosophers as the enemies of religion. But that could be because theologians have mistakenly thought that what the positivists very properly pointed out strikes at what is most important in religion, whereas what it strikes at is what is least important, something concentration on which has led to a mistaken emphasis in accounts of what religion is. Perhaps positivistic philosophy has done a service to religion. By showing, in their own way, the absurdity of what theologians try to utter,

[14] Analytic statements are generally nowadays defined as those whose truth is guaranteed by their form, e.g. 'Either some ants are parasitic or none are' (an example of Professor A. J. Ayer's). It is generally said (somewhat misleadingly) that an analytic statement gains certainty at the expense of informativeness: it says nothing about states of affairs in the real world but merely 'juggles with words'. The relevance of this to the treatment of the statement 'God exists' as analytic (as, for instance, by St. Anselm or Descartes) is obvious.

[15] Nor do they like being told that what they are saying is 'non-significant', which suggests that it is insignificant, i.e. unimportant. But 'non-significant' and 'nonsensical', mean for the positivist only 'not amenable to verification by sense experience'.

positivists have helped to suggest that religion belongs to the sphere of the unutterable. And this may be true. And it is what Otto, too, in his way, wanted to point out.[16] Positivists may be the enemies of theology, but the friends of religion.

I have in the preceding paragraph been trying to make a point in a very general way. But it will be obvious that there is an ambiguity in what I have been saying. There is, as I pointed out earlier, more than one kind of nonsense. I have myself been using 'nonsense' in two ways. There is nonsense in the usual sense in which the theological statements I began by listing have been held to be nonsense—i.e., perhaps, 'literally' absurd. And there is nonsense in the positivists' sense—i.e. where 'nonsensical' means 'not verifiable by sense experience'. And surely these are different senses of 'nonsense'. And if they are different senses of 'nonsense' then to praise the positivists for pointing out that theological statements are 'nonsensical' (in their sense) is not to have said anything that bears on the opening part of this article; for there it was pointed out that people may have a certain worry because they feel some theological statements to be nonsensical—but 'nonsensical' in a different sense of 'nonsensical'.

But there is an important connection. That theological statements are nonsense in one sense of 'nonsense' gives rise to a worry. One way out of the worry (the positivistic way) can be found when it is seen that theological statements are nonsense in another sense of 'nonsense'. Put Wittgenstein and the Vienna Circle together, and join both with Otto, and we have what I am calling the positivistic way: a way that is not a turning of one's back on the worry, not a 'resolving' of it (in the sense of overcoming a neurotic feeling, though Wittgenstein taken alone might to some suggest something of this sort), not an anti-religious reaction (for we have Otto to give it religious respectability).

16 In M. Buber's *I and Thou* there is a similar view. Buber wants to say that the distinctive thing in religion is the 'I-Thou relation'. But if you try to analyse this relation, or to talk about it, it will vanish, and you will find yourself talking about *I* and *It*. It follows that theologians are bound to fail should they seek to say what religion is.

Religion belongs to the sphere of the unsayable, so it is not to be wondered at that in theology there is much nonsense (i.e. many absurdities); this is the natural result of trying to put into words—and to discuss—various kinds of inexpressible 'experiences', and of trying to say things about God. Also, theological statements are held to be non-sense (i.e. not amenable to verification by sense experience) by the philosophers of the Vienna Circle and their followers; and the reason why they are non-sense is that they are attempts to say the unsayable. It is not to be expected that the result of attempts to say the unsayable should be statements that are amenable to verification by sense experience. (Notice that this is the reason why and not just another way of saying the same thing.)

I have discussed the positivistic way out of the worry as a serious contribution to philosophy of religion because that is what I think it is. To regard it as anti-religious is wrong; to think of it as by-passing the worry is wrong; not to take the worry itself seriously is wrong. The positivistic way is important both because it helps to pinpoint the worry and because it shows a way out of it.

Is it the right way? There is no answer to this question, for there is no one right way out of the worry. Worries are not like that. But the positivistic way is one kind of answer; and an answer that is so often not seen, or rather not seen for what it is, that it deserves to be looked at. There certainly seems to be this wrong with it, that it may exclude too much: in throwing out the water of theology we may be also throwing out the baby of 'direct', 'first-order' religious assertions; and this we may well not want to do.

One point to end. If it is foolish for theologians to refuse to learn from positivistic philosophy it is disastrous for them to mistake the lesson. Another, and a preposterous, kind of linking of positivism and theology is possible, and has even been tried.[17] This linking takes the form of an acceptance of the verification principle of the Vienna Circle—that a statement (unless it is analytic) 'has sense', 'is significant',

17 See on this my 'The Existence of God' (*Mind*, October 1950).

'is meaningful', only if it is amenable to verification by sense experience—and issues in an attempt to bludgeon theological statements to make them meet this prescription. This is a forlorn hope, and it is a dangerous thing to do. The proper linkage consists in an accommodation of positivism to theology, not of theology to positivism. Theology does not gain by being reduced to the terms of any school of philosophy.

University College of North Wales
   Bangor
   WALES

VIII

DIVINE OMNIPOTENCE AND HUMAN FREEDOM[1]

ANTONY FLEW

Either God cannot abolish evil or he will not: if he cannot then he is not all-powerful; if he will not then he is not all-good.

The dilemma is much older than this, St. Augustine's formulation of it. Perhaps the most powerful of all sceptical arguments, it has appealed especially to the clearest and most direct minds, striking straight and decisively to the heart of the matter. It was, for instance, central to J. S. Mill's rejection of Christianity and he returns to it repeatedly and often angrily throughout his *Three Essays on Religion*:[2] e.g.

> ... the impossible problem of reconciling infinite benevolence and justice with infinite power in the Creator of

[1] This is a lengthened version of a paper originally read to the Oxford University Socratic Club in October 1954: a shortened version was published in the *Hibbert Journal* for January, 1955. Professor J. L. Mackie of the University of Otago, New Zealand, has since published in *Mind* a paper which runs parallel to this one in many parts, I wish to point out that our papers were entirely independent, and his was in fact completed before mine.

[2] Longman's, 1874. This is a powerful and lucid book, original particularly in that Mill, though rejecting the Christian revelation and consequently not 'incumbered with the necessity of admitting the omnipotence of the Creator' (p. 186), was still, in spite of Hume and Darwin, sufficiently impressed with the argument to design to explore at length the idea of a finite God, allowing 'a large balance of probability in favour of creation by intelligence' (p. 174). Though this book made a considerable contemporary impact it seems to have been curiously neglected since: for it has never been reprinted (the R.P.A. to note); and even such a philosophical scholar as Professor A. N. Prior overlooked the essay on 'Nature', which is centrally relevant to the theme of his *Logic and the Basis of Ethics* (O.U.P., 1949).

such a world as this. The attempt to do so not only involves absolute contradiction in an intellectual point of view but exhibits to excess the revolting spectacle of a jesuitical defence of moral enormities (pp. 186–7).

These are robust words, but not quite final.

(1) Several determined attempts have been made to escape from the dilemma. One favourite—which might be dubbed the Free-will Defence—runs like this. The first move is to point out: 'Nothing which implies contradiction falls under the omnipotence of God'[3]; that is, Even God cannot do what is *logically* impossible; that is, If you make up a self-contradictory, a nonsense, sentence it won't miraculously become sense just because you have put the word 'God' as its subject. The third formulation is greatly superior to the other two, because it brings out the nature of *logical* impossibility. It should appeal to theologians, as being free of the unwanted and of course entirely incorrect[4] suggestion that 'being unable to do the logically impossible' is some sort of limitation on or weakness in Omnipotence, whereas the only limitation lies in men who contradict themselves and talk nonsense about God.[5] The second move in this defence is to claim: 'God gave men free-will'; and this necessarily implies the possibility of doing evil as well as good, that is to say that there would be a contradiction in speaking, it would be nonsense to speak, of creatures with freedom to choose good or evil but not able to choose evil. (Which, no blame to him, is what his creatures men have done). This may be followed by a third rather less common move: to point out that certain good things, viz. certain virtues, logically presuppose: not merely beings with freedom of choice (which

[3] Aquinas *Summa Theologica*, I, Q. XXV, Art. 4.
[4] Which misled a philosopher of the calibre of M'Taggart: see his *Some Dogmas of Religion* (Arnold, 1906 and 1930), §166, where he attacks and rejects the whole notion of omnipotence on these misguided grounds.
[5] Professor C. S. Lewis is one of the very few theologians to have made the point in this superior way, using the 'formal mode of speech' (*The Problem of Pain*: Bles, 1940, p. 16). Credit where this is due; especially as we shall later be assailing other parts of the book in successive footnotes.

alone are capable of either virtue or vice), and consequently the possibility of evil; but also the actual occurrence of certain evils. Thus what we might call the second-order goods of sympathetic feeling and action logically could not occur without (at least the appearance of) the first-order evils of suffering or misfortune. And the moral good of forgiveness presupposes the prior occurrence of (at least the appearance of) some lower-order evil to be forgiven. This may be already a second-order moral evil such as callousness, thus making the forgiveness a third-order good. Here one recalls: *O felix culpa quae tantum ac talem meruit habere redemptorem.*

The upshot is that there are certain goods, e.g. moral virtues, which logically presuppose the possibility of correlative evils, and others, e.g. the virtues of forgiveness and sympathetic action, which logically presuppose the actuality (or at least the appearance) of certain evils, in this case the doing of injuries and the suffering of misfortunes. Thus it would not make sense to suggest that God might have chosen to achieve these goods without the possibility in the one case, the actuality in the other, of the correlative and presupposed evils. Unfortunately men have chosen to misuse their freedom by choosing to exploit the possibility of wrongdoing necessarily involved in the possibility of rightdoing. But this is not God's fault: or at any rate it does not show that God *cannot* be both all-powerful and all-good. It is this Free-will Defence we propose to examine.

(2) It is a powerful defence: which has satisfied many believers; and routed or at least rattled many sceptics. The usual counters are. First: to point out that by no means all the evil in the world can be traced back to an origin in human wickedness, nor shown to make possible any higher-order goods. The obvious and least disputable example is animal pain before the emergence of *homo sapiens*; which cannot be the result of human wickedness because it preceded it; and which cannot have made possible any second-order good, because it preceded the arrival of any beings capable of such second-order goods and evils. Second: to note the injustice of the allocation of the first-order non-

moral evils. The unfortunate idiom which talks of 'Man's sin, and its consequences for Man' at least seems to involve a doctrine of the rightness of collective responsibility,[6] and certainly tends complacently to conceal that the worst consequences of the wickedness of a Hitler fall not on him or other conspicuously guilty men but on their victims. Third: to say that a God who is prepared to allow such a volume of evil as there actually is in the world, because this is the necessary price of securing certain special goods which have been and will be achieved, cannot after all possibly be called good. To call such a being, ruthlessly paying an enormous price in evil means to attain his good ends, himself good is mere flattery: 'worthy only of those whose slavish fears make them offer the homage of lies to a Being who, they profess to think, is incapable of being deceived and holds all falsehood in abomination' (Mill, *loc. cit.*, p. 52); and justifying Hobbes' claim that 'in the attributes we give to God, we are not to consider the signification of philosophical truth; but the signification of pious intention, to do him the greatest honour we are able' (*Leviathan*, Ch. XXXI, Everyman, p. 195). Fourth: to warn the religious apologist meticulously to avoid any pretence that God could be limited by the laws of his own Universe. Thus the suggestion that suffering, as a matter of fact, can refine characters as nothing else can is not merely doubtfully true but also, in this context, blasphemous. For the notion of causally necessary means to ends, as opposed to that of logically necessary preconditions, cannot apply to creative omnipotence.[7]

These counter-attacks have not the simple seemingly decisive force of the original dilemma. Against the first it is possible to suggest, and impossible definitively to dispose of, the possibility that whatever evil does not ultimately originate in human wickedness originates in the wickedness

---

6 See, for instance, the strictures on it of Professor H. D. Lewis in his *Morals and The New Theology* (Gollancz, 1947), *passim*, and his *Morals and Revelation* (Allen & Unwin, 1951), Ch. II and V.

7 See Mill, *loc. cit.*, pp. 176–7: where Mill goes on to draw the conclusion that arguments to design square ill with this notion.

of evil spirits beginning before man began.[8] Against the third it is possible to appeal to the fact that no man knows what will be the ultimate sum of good to place in the scales against the absolutely enormous, but perhaps relatively trifling and in any case also unknown, ultimate sum of evil.[9] And the Christian can complain that the epithet 'ruthless' neglects a vital implication of the incarnation doctrine; that God pities and shares the sufferings of his creatures.

There thus seem to be ways out of a dilemma which presented Christianity as a simultaneous belief in two logically incompatibles and to a more defensible position where great

[8] This idea is taken very seriously indeed by C. S. Lewis (*loc. cit.*, pp. 121f.). To make this more than just another desperate *ad hoc* expedient of apologetic it is necessary to produce independent reason for launching such an hypothesis (if 'hypothesis' is not too flattering a term for it). We cannot here embark on the important question of what sort of reason there could be: but for stimulating suggestions see John Wisdom, *Other Minds* (Blackwell, 1952).

[9] See, for instance, I. M. Crombie in Chapter VI (ii) above. C. S. Lewis was again driven to a desperate manœuvre (*loc. cit.*, pp. 103–4): 'We must never make the problem of pain worse than it is by vague talk of "the unimaginable sum of human misery". Suppose that I have a toothache of intensity x: and suppose that you, who are seated beside me, also begin to have a toothache of intensity x. You may if you choose say that the total amount of pain in the room is now $2x$. But you must remember that no one is suffering $2x$: search all time and all space and you will not find that composite pain in anyone's consciousness. There is no such thing as a sum of suffering, for no one suffers it. When we have reached the maximum that a single person can suffer, we have, no doubt, reached something very horrible, but we have reached all the suffering there ever can be in the universe. The addition of a million fellow sufferers adds no more pain.' But this is fantastic. The facts that no one can suffer more than they can, and that the calculus of arithmetic cannot be applied to the field of pain (or pleasure) as fully and precisely as Bentham would have liked, provide not the slightest reason for saying that it makes no sense to use such expressions as 'sum of pain' in the rough-and-ready way in which people do in fact use them. They surely use them: *not* as part of some impossible piece of applied mathematics from which a numerical value for a sum of pains of different people, durations and intensities might be derived (Bentham himself sensibly refrained from such an enterprise: see, e.g. *Principles of Morals and Legislation* Ch. IV); *but* simply to bring out such truisms as that, all other things being equal, it's a worse business if two people have toothache than if one does, and worse still if there is an epidemic. It is thus preposterous for Lewis to maintain that 'the addition of a million fellow sufferers adds no more pain': and monstrous thereby to imply, presumably, that this addition makes no value difference.

faith is still called for, but no longer a faith in what is known to be not merely untrue but an 'absolute contradiction'. The sceptic has apparently been forced to abandon his clear-cut knock-down refutation and to resort to arguing: that there need not have been so much and/or certain kinds of evil to get the good; that if there need, or in any case, it were better not to have had the goods which could only be bought at such a price. Such arguments may still constitute a formidable challenge; but they do leave the believer with some freedom of manœuvre.

(3) This account in terms of move and counter-move is only a crudely stylized cartoon, without the panoply of distinctions and refinements required to do justice to the full complexity of the logical situation. But its purpose is merely to set the stage for the launching of a further, new, or at least unusual, sceptical counter-attack. This is directed at the key position of the whole Free-will Defence: the idea that there is a contradiction involved in saying that God might have made people so that they always in fact *freely* chose the right. If there is no contradiction here then Omnipotence might have made a world inhabited by wholly virtuous people; the Free-will Defence is broken-backed; and we are back again with the original intractable antinomy.

(a) The first phase consists in bringing out what is meant by 'acting freely', 'being free to choose' and so on: particularly that none of these concepts necessarily involve unpredictable or uncaused action. A paradigm case of acting freely, of being free to choose, would be the marriage of two normal young people, when there was no question of the parties 'having to get married', and no social or parental pressure on either of them: a case which happily is scarcely rare. To say that Murdo was free to ask whichever eligible girl of his acquaintance he wanted, and that he chose to ask, was accepted by, and has now married Mairi of his own free will, is not to say that his actions and choices were uncaused or in principle unpredictable: but precisely and only that, being of an age to know his own mind, he did what he did and rejected possible alternative courses of action without being under any pressure to act in this way. Indeed those who know Murdo and Mairi may have known what was going to happen long before the day of the wedding. And if it is the case that one day a team of psychologists and physiologists will be able to predict a person's behaviour far more completely and successfully than even his best friends now can, even up to one hundred per cent completely and successfully: still this will not show that he never acts freely, can never choose between alternatives, deciding for himself on the one which most appeals to him. (Or on the one which is most uncongenial for that matter, if that is what he chooses to do). Unless they produce evidence that there was obstruction or pressure or an absence of alternatives their discoveries will not even be relevant to questions about his freedom of choice: much less a decisive disproof of the manifest fact that sometimes he has complete, sometimes restricted, and sometimes no freedom.

Again: to say that a person could have helped doing something is not to say that what he did was in principle unpredictable nor that there were no causes anywhere which determined that he would as a matter of fact act in this way. It is to say that *if* he had chosen to do otherwise he would have been able to do so; that there were alternatives, within the capacities of one of his physical strength, of his I.Q., with his knowledge, and open to a person in his situation. As before, the meaning of the key phrase 'could have helped it' can be elucidated by looking at simple paradigm cases: such as those in which fastidious language users employ it when the madness of metaphysics is not upon them; such as those by reference to which the expression usually is, and ultimately has always to be, explained.

It is no use saying that such employments of phrases of this sort are *really* 'loose' or 'incorrect'. For these are paradigm cases of what the phrases actually do mean: we are not dealing with some compound descriptive expression correctly formed of words which can and have been given sense independently and which like 'the first man to run a four-minute mile' might or might not ever have found an application (because this feat might or might not ever have been achieved). Now if this sort of argument is sound, then there is no contradiction involved in saying that a particular action or choice was: *both* free, and could have been helped, and so on; *and* predictable, or even foreknown, and explicable in terms of caused causes. Of course, it is not possible here definitively to establish that it *is* sound but it is to the point to mention: That this is the line taken by Hobbes and Hume among the classical philosophers; and which is now being confidently employed with great subtlety through many ramifications by the majority of those contemporary British philosophers who have tackled any of the puzzles about free-will.[10] That it is the doctrine of the Roman Church that God's foreknowledge covers all human behaviour and is not incompatible with man's freedom.[11] That if it is wrong then it will be possible to fit human freedom into the world only in the gaps of scientific ignorance. That if it is wrong then it is hard to see what meaning these expressions have and how if at all they could ever be taught, understood or correctly used. Whereas if we are right then anyone who tells us that science shows or could show us that there is no such thing as acting freely, etc., is: *either* just wrong, because there certainly are cases such as our paradigms; *or* misleadingly using the key expressions in some new sense needing to be explained. And if what he is saying is true then it cannot involve a denial of what we know to be true, that there are plenty of cases in which people, in the ordinary senses of the words, acted or act or will act freely, had or will have a choice, could have helped what they did, and will be able to help what they will do.

10 See, e.g. *Leviathan* Ch. XXI, and pamphlet 'Of Liberty and Necessity'; *Enquiry concerning Human Understanding*, § VIII; *Treatise of Human Nature*, B II, P III, § 1–3; and references in T. S. Gregory (editor), *Dictionary of Philosophy* (Sheed and Ward, forthcoming), article on 'Contemporary British Philosophy', § 11.

11 See for instance, *Concilium Valentinum* (Contra Joannem Scotum) *de praedestinatione*, Can 2 [Denzinger, *Enchiridion Symbolorum*, § 321] also *Concilium Vaticanum*, Sessio III Cap I [*Ibid.* § 1784]. Note especially in the latter 'Omnia enim nuda et aperta sunt oculis eius, *ea etiam quae libera creaturarum actione futura sunt*' (Italics mine).

(*b*) The second phase, once we are clear of misconceptions about the meaning of 'acting freely' and so on, is to argue that: not only is there no necessary conflict between acting freely and behaving predictably and/or as a result of caused causes; but furthermore that Omnipotence might have, could without contradiction be said to have, created people who would always as a matter of fact freely have chosen to do the right thing. Now we have already argued to the effect that there is no contradiction in saying: Murdo chose to marry Mairi of his own free will; and furthermore he would not have chosen to do this if his endocrine glands had not as a matter of fact been in such and such a state, that is, that his glandular condition was one of many causes of his choice. Whether or not it is the case that hypothetical propositions of this sort could be truly asserted of any and every piece of human behaviour; whether or not, that is, every human action, decision and reaction actually has physiological causes; still to say that this is so and to say that people sometimes can help doing what they do, do act freely and so on is not necessarily to contradict oneself.

It might be objected that if Murdo acted because his glands were in such and such a state then he cannot have chosen Mairi because he wanted to be married to her: that the one explanation excludes the other.[12] But this is not so: for the one assigns a cause; gives a, but not presumably the only, precondition the absence of which would have been followed by the absence of Murdo's action. While the other indicates his motive, again perhaps not the only one; and to say that and in what way a piece of behaviour was motivated is not to deny that it was caused.[13] Compare the analogous mistake of thinking that: if I think as I do because of such and such causes or because of such and such motives (i.e. if there are conditions without which I should not think as I do, or if I want to think as I do); then it *cannot* also be the case

Handwritten margin note (left, upper): i.e. to arrange the world at creation so that evil events never emerged

Handwritten margin note (left, lower): But when we say he freely chose her, we are not speaking of a motive

12 Socrates argues on this assumption (*Phaedo*, 98 B 7f.).

13 I have argued various relevant points rather more fully in 'Psychoanalytic Explanation' (*Analysis*, 1949, reprinted with modifications in Miss Margaret Macdonald's *Philosophy and Analysis* (Blackwell, 1955), and in 'Crime or Disease' (*British Journal of Sociology*, March 1954).

that there are and I have sufficient reasons, arguments, grounds, for thinking as I do.[14] The word 'because' is multiply ambiguous: there are many different sorts of explanation, which do not necessarily exclude one another; as many sorts as there are sorts of question.

It might be objected—this is really the same objection differently wrapped—that in the situation described it is not really Murdo or Mairi but their glands which made the decision. But again we appeal to the Argument of the Paradigm Case:[15] If this is not a case of Murdo deciding then what is; then what would be *meant* by 'Murdo deciding'? Again, glands are not people: so it is only a misleading metaphor to speak of glands *deciding* anything. And someone's glands are not *other people* taking decisions out of his hands, railroading him into action against his will, or fixing things irrevocably before he comes along; but *parts of him*, without which he would not be what he is.[16]

Returning to the thesis from these objections: if it really is logically possible for an action to be both freely chosen and yet fully determined by caused causes, then the keystone argument of the Free-will Defence, that there is a contradiction in speaking of God so arranging the laws of nature that all men always as a matter of fact freely choose to do the right, cannot hold. And if this goes the strength of the third possible part of that defence, that certain higher-order goods logically presuppose the occurrence of their appropriate lower-order evils, will be put to the test. Let us proceed to test it.

(*c*) Now even if the sceptic were not equipped with the arguments we have just deployed he could still point out that only some of those higher-order goods which logically presuppose (at least the appearance of) their lower-order evils

---

14 This has been argued at length by Miss G. E. M. Anscombe in *Socratic Digest*, 4 (Blackwell, 1948): in a brilliant paper which would have been reprinted in this volume had not the authoress felt unable to consent to its inclusion in a book in the title of which the word 'theology' appeared.

15 See J. O. Urmson in *Rev. Int. de Philosophie*, 1953, to be reprinted in *Essays in Conceptual Analysis* (ed. Antony Flew: Macmillan forthcoming).

16 Hence the Alice in Wonderland quality of 'I sat down to interview my brains'—John Dalmas in R. Chandler, *Trouble is my Business* (Penguin Books, undated), p. 145.

necessarily require for their display the actual occurrence of the evils in question; that not all the moral goods are second-order (though they all without exception presuppose freedom: see Kant and everybody else); and that at best this move, like the whole Free-will Defence of which it is a part, surely cannot cover all aspects of the problem of evil. For someone could exercise forgiveness when he thought, but mistakenly, that another had done him an injury (though it might be said that even such an appearance of moral evil was bad): while virtues such as honesty and intellectual integrity are surely not in any way parasitical on antecedent evils, moral or non-moral; and the difficulties mentioned in (2) above remain untouched. Furthermore a great deal of that lower-order evil which there actually is in the world which is logically suitable as a basis for higher-order goods is apparently in fact wasted: inasmuch as these goods do not seem in fact to be realized. However, it would be unwise to try to make very much of this appeal to experience: for an ingenious apologist could without too much difficulty show that it is at least logically possible that all actual lower-order evils are being, or will be, exploited as the logically necessary bases of higher-order goods; and thus make room for an exercise of faith in God. (For example: all moral evils provide a possible occasion for divine forgiveness; and even the preservation of the eternally damned may be somehow made out to be a logically necessary condition of the fulness of heaven's joys.)[17]

But if the sceptic accepts our main argument he can urge in addition that, if there is no contradiction in suggesting

[17] Consider: *O felix culpa quae tantum ac talem meruit habere redemptorem* quoted above, a thought which goes back at least as far as St. Augustine; and St. Thomas Aquinas, who after arguing that 'the blessed in glory will have no pity for the damned' maintains not exactly that 'the blessed will rejoice in the punishment of the wicked' but that 'the Divine Justice and their own deliverance will be the direct cause of the joy of the blessed: while the punishment of the damned will cause it indirectly' (*Summa Theologica*, III, Supp. Q. 94)—a view of a sort some might have thought peculiar to such ferocious Fathers as Tertullian. Perhaps in a footnote one may be excused a confession to nausea at the Angelic Doctor's smug contemplation of unspeakable horror.

that Omnipotence might so arrange his creation that all men in fact always would freely choose the right; then there is no need for any vale of soul making; nor for any wastage of souls choosing damnation and the pit. The putative end-product, people who, no matter what the temptations, always would choose the right—thus being not too excessively disqualified to receive the Beatific Vision—logically could have been produced without: *either* the evil involved in the creation of those who wickedly choose damnation; *or* the evil necessary for the actual exercise of those virtues which cannot be exercised without the actual occurrence of the evil logically required to call them forth. Omnipotence could have created creatures who he could have been sure *would* respond to the appropriate challenge by a willing exercise of fortitude: without these creatures having to acquire this character by any *actual* exercise of fortitude. What it could still make no sense to suggest would be that God could have had *actual* displays of, say, fortitude or could himself have *actually* forgiven anyone, without there being the evil of pain to be endured or of sin to be forgiven.[18]

18 C. S. Lewis, *loc. cit.*, pp. 89–90, offers an extraordinary argument to meet the objection 'If God is omniscient he must have known what Abraham would do, without any experiment, why then this needless torture?' (of actually going through with it). 'The reality of Abraham's obedience was the act itself; and what God knew in knowing that Abraham "would obey" was Abraham's actual obedience on that mountain top at that moment. To say that God "need not have tried the experiment" is to say that, because God knows, the thing known by God need not exist.' But this does not do at all. Any plausibility Lewis' argument may have derives from an ambiguity in 'would': for the objector is saying that Omniscience must know how people *would* behave if they *were* to be tested; whereas Lewis is replying that he could not know that they *will* in future so behave unless they *are* in fact going so to behave. The reply is simply irrelevant.

Perhaps he had in the back of his mind one logical and one philosophical doctrine, false and true respectively, which might be urged at this point. First, that subjunctive conditionals are not truly propositions, and hence could not be known: even by God. This is usually derived as an unwelcome paradoxical consequence of the picture theory of meaning and the perception theory of knowledge (see Edna Daitz in *Mind*, 1953, or in *Essays in Conceptual Analysis*, for an account of the former and H. L. A. Hart in *P.A.S.*, Supp., Vol. XXIII, for an examination of the latter). Second, that it makes no sense to attribute actual as opposed to potential possession of virtues to people who have never in fact displayed them. We here can only point (*d*) It will perhaps help if we try to dispose of some possible misconceptions, before moving ahead in our argument.

(i) All that we have to say in this paper is, of course, entirely beside the point for anyone who adopts any variant of the position that infinite creative power is its own sufficient justification, or leaves no room for justification. As Hobbes who wrote: 'And Job, how earnestly does he expostulate with God, for the many afflictions that he suffered, notwithstanding his righteousness. This question in the case of Job is decided by God himself, not by arguments derived from Job's sin, but his own power' (*Leviathan*, Ch. XIII: Everyman, p. 191).[19] Which is perhaps a misinterpretation of *Job*: though it is reminiscent of such

out: first, that the former contradicts the doctrine of Molina and his followers among the late scholastics that there can be *scientia media* (knowledge of hypotheticals) between *scientia visionis* (knowledge of fact) and *scientia simplicis intelligentiae* (knowledge of truths of logic)—to say nothing of common sense. (For my account of Molina I am relying on Ch. X of D. J. B. Hawkins, *The Essentials of Theism*.) Second, that there is a vast gap between the contingent though, doubtless, true proposition that dispositional human characteristics can only be acquired by appropriate action (ἡ δ' ἠθικὴ ἐξ ἔθους περιγίνεται— Aristotle, *Nicomachean Ethics* 1103A,17) and the *a priori* and certainly true one that they cannot be actually possessed by those who have not yet displayed them. Third, that we have in the former a modern instance of the way in which a peculiar logical doctrine may be theologically motivated— compare the thesis of Odo of Tournai that 'whenever a new child comes into being God produces a new property of an already existing substance, not a new substance' (F. C. Copleston, *A History of Philosophy, Vol. II, Augustine to Scotus*, p. 141); which was designed to and seemed to him to be the only way to save the doctrine of Original Sin. I suspect we have other but more deeply buried examples in some contemporary more purely philosophical writing: not that this is relevant to the important questions of truth and validity.

19 I have heard this quoted with approval by a Roman Catholic apologist: who thus virtually admitted Mill's charge, 'It becomes the bowing down to a gigantic image of something not fit for us to imitate. It is the worship of power only' (*loc. cit.*, p. 113). It is sometimes thought that Hobbes here and elsewhere was an atheist being sarcastic. This seems very doubtful. Certainly Hobbes was often called an atheist: but this was a charge which came as easily to the lips of the conventional in the seventeenth century as that of 'communism' does in the U.S.A. today (often with consequences as unfairly disastrous as those which fall on those whose guilt is there thus established by accusation). But the idea that the passage quoted above is ingenuous squares perfectly with Hobbes' political views; and with the fact that he devotes a large part of *Leviathan*, the part which modern students neglect to read, to strenuous Biblical exegesis.

notoriously hard sayings as 'neither hath this man sinned nor his fathers; but that the works of God might be made manifest in him' (John 9.3). Or as one might say that since all things depend absolutely on God there can be no *locus standi* for an independent appraisal. Or as one might say that the Creator has an absolute right to do whatever he likes with his own creatures. Or as those who would *define* all moral notions in terms of God's will: and thereby make it self-contradictory to say that God acted unjustly or did evil. But such positions are uncomfortable, particularly for those who wish also to find in God something straightforwardly deserving praise. Thus it is usual, alternatively or additionally, to insist with Hooker that 'They err ... who think that of the will of God to do this or that there is no reason besides His will' (*Laws*, I, Sec. 2).

(ii) We certainly do not claim to have produced arguments by themselves sufficient to show that a good God (logically) could not have arranged for the occurrence of all actual moral and non-moral evils as being necessarily required for the actual exercise of higher-order virtues.

For it might be said, first, that the value of actual displays of these virtues, as opposed to their mere potential possession (which would be a matter of its being the case that if their exercise *were* to be called for the response *would* not be wanting), in some ways more than compensates for the evils which such displays must necessarily involve. This is a value position which might be held even by people not committed to religious apologetic. And second, that all the evils of the world are the logically necessary preconditions of the actual display, now or in the hidden future, of virtues and other higher-order goods. This second stage does involve a really massive draft on the reserves of faith; which it would surely only be reasonable to make if you had logically compulsive arguments of natural reason, or at least very strong ones of apparent revelation, pointing to the existence of a deity both omnipotent and benevolent. (The former, at any rate, we certainly have not got and could not have: see, for instance, Smart in Ch. III above.)

Alternatively or additionally it might be said that, since the criteria which anything is properly required to satisfy in order to deserve to be appraised as good vary according to the nature of the thing in question[20]; the criteria appropriately applicable to establish the goodness of God must of logical necessity be *very* different from those satisfied by good men.[21] And furthermore that the satisfaction of these appropriately peculiar criteria is logically compatible with being the omnipotent creator of a world containing the manifest evils which we see around us; to say nothing of the others incomparably more appalling, threatened by traditional Christianity.

But these are matters depending largely on personal value decisions, whereas this our main thesis does not do; though in the course of maintaining it we have neither hesitated to express our own value commitments nor to repudiate those made by some others.

(iii) This argument has not, of course, the slightest tendency to show the non-existence of any sort of God: for it pretends to establish only that the favourite attempt to justify the ways of God to man contains a contradiction (whereas those who have made this attempt have usually mistaken the contradiction to lie with their opponents). The temptation to draw such negative existential conclusions from it stems: first, from the wishful thinking which is endemic among and, under suitably solemn disguises, often avowed by those who argue about God; and second, from the more subtle error of failing to distinguish the elements of objective would-be factual content from the elements of valuational appraisal and personal commitment in utterances made about God. As an example of the first consider Kantian-style arguments to God and Immortality on the grounds that things must *ultimately* be as they ought to be if

---

[20] See R. M. Hare, *The Language of Morals*, Pt. II (O.U.P., 1952).

[21] See Mill, *loc. cit.*, *passim*. The irreverent may also recall the story of an argument between two theological students which ended: 'Oh, *I see*: my *Devil* is your *God*.' Disputes between spokesmen of the rival Eastern and Western concepts of democracy can have a similar *dénouement*.

'morality is to make sense'[22] and 'the demands of our moral nature are to be satisfied'. As an example of both together consider how to have discerned the inconceivably terrible, and morally repulsive, aspect of the Hell-filling omnipotent creator God of Roman Catholicism beneath the clouds of praise is not to have provided any sort of reason for believing that things cannot really be as bad as this: and the assumption that it is does little credit to those who are too often eager to accuse believers of wishful thinking. While the fact that *we* personally could not honestly apply such terms of favourable appraisal as 'good', 'just', 'loving' and so forth—terms which are usually, *pace* Hobbes, applied by believers with sincere and straightforward intent—to an omnipotent creator even of this world, much less of Hell, constitutes no sort of reason for denying that as a matter of fact it is created; and that as a matter of fact the creator so arranges things that the lots of individual men will be of this sort or of that according to his arrangements that they act in this way or in that. Indeed the Roman Catholic account of the universe and its Creator would surely gain rather than lose in plausibility as a hypothetical description of all that is if it were presented as far as possible 'aseptically'; in language stripped of all terms of favourable and unfavourable appraisal, of intervention and commitment.

(iv) 'Higher-order', 'lower-order' and 'parasitical' mark here positions in a logical hierarchy, and must not be mistaken to imply superiority or inferiority in any sort of value. But anyone attempting to justify the ways of God to man, and rejecting or refusing to rely on any of the positions of (3) (*d*) (i) above will, I think, have to commit himself to putting most logically higher-order goods like forgiveness or fortitude higher on his scale of values than most logically first-order goods like the simple satisfactions of gardening: the former being mainly, but not entirely, moral; and the latter being

---

22 'Make sense' ≡ 'pay off'? Consider: ' "The parson asks us to accept literally the Day of Judgment." And why not? What possible sense have morals if in the end it doesn't *matter* how we behave?'—Canon H. C. Warner, in a letter in *Picture Post*, Feb. 1, 1954. Is Kant's argument in substance so very different?

mainly, but not entirely, non-moral. Hence the terrible value decision of the Roman Church which

> holds that it were better for the sun and moon to drop from heaven, for the earth to fail, and for all the many millions who are upon it to die . . . in extremest agony . . . than that one soul, I will not say should be lost, but should commit one single venial sin, should tell one wilful untruth . . . or steal one poor farthing without excuse (J. H. Newman, *On Anglican Difficulties*, VIII).

This apologist will also surely (see (3) (*d*) (ii) above) have to put the actual *exercise* of virtues, even at the logically necessary cost of the occurrence of lower-order evils, higher than the potential *possession* of these same virtues: a commitment perhaps less widely realized and accepted.

In sharp value disagreement with any apologetics of this sort many secular people would go far beyond simply rejecting these extreme positions and say that *ultimately* the justification of the exercise of the virtues is that this is the (causally) necessary condition of the attainment of the maximum sum of the non-moral goods of human satisfaction: see, e.g. Mill, *Utilitarianism, passim,* and especially the remarks upon asceticism for its own sake (Everyman, pp. 15–16); remembering that the clue to the appeal of this essay, perennial in spite of the assaults of the logicians, lies in the fact that it seems to codify and express the ethical position, with all its faults, implicit in the attitudes of most secular reformers. But for God there can, of course, be no causally necessary conditions (See (2) above).

(4) We cannot hope here even to begin to meet objections to the theses of (3) based on the rejection of our fundamental idea that freedom and universal causal determinism are not necessarily incompatible. But suppose now that someone accepting it raised the objection that what has been shown is: *not* that there is no "contradiction in speaking of *God* so arranging things that all men would always as a matter of fact freely choose to do the right"; *but* that there is no contradiction in the idea of men always freely doing the right although all their behaviour without exception followed (i.e.

could be subsumed under or fitted into) universal laws of nature, although it was determined by (i.e. completely predictable on the basis of) those laws, and although the notion of caused cause was applicable to it all. The nerve of the distinction lies in the *personality* of God, which makes a crucial difference: in the former case a *quasi-personal* being has *fixed* everything that everyone will do, and choose, and suffer; in the latter case it has not been *fixed*, but it is just the fact that people will make precisely those decisions which they will make and not those alternative decisions which they could have made if they had had the mind to. The former is the doctrine of predestination[23]: the latter of determinism.[24]

Now, the argument would run, whereas the latter is perhaps compatible with human freedom and the fair ascription of responsibility to human agents; the former certainly is not. For consider the phenomenon of post-hypnotic suggestion: described in this quotation from Knight and Knight, *A Modern Introduction to Psychology* (University Tutorial Press, 1948), p. 212:

> A subject is hypnotized, and is told that after a precise time interval . . . he is to carry out some series of actions. . . . When he is awakened from the hypnotic trance he remembers nothing of these instructions. Nevertheless, when the prescribed time is up, he will carry out the programme in every detail. If he is asked why he is behaving in this curious fashion, he will usually produce some highly ingenious rationalization. . . .

Now, it might be said, predestinationism makes out that all of us, all the time, whether we know it or not, *both* when by ordinary standards we are acting freely and could help doing what we choose to do, *and* when we are acting under compulsion, have no choice, or are not acting at all

---

[23] 'God from all eternity did by the most wise and holy counsel of his own will, freely and unchangeably ordain whatsoever comes to pass' (*Westminster Confession*, 1649).

[24] Notice that we have been careful in our choice of phrases above to avoid any of the predestinarian suggestions which are often confusingly incorporated in determinist formulations.

but are asleep or paralysed; all of us are, really and ultimately, as it were acting out the irresistible suggestions of the Great Hypnotist. And this idea surely is incompatible with that of our being free agents, properly accountable for what we do. Hence there is after all 'a contradiction in speaking of God so arranging things that all men always as a matter of fact freely choose to do the right'.

(*a*) This objection is apparently conclusive. Yet it involves a crucial and subtle mistake: the actual logical situation is exceedingly hard to determine categorically; but the uncertainty is not about whether or not sceptical attack can be warded off but about which and how many positions have to be yielded to it.

Now certainly if we were to discover that a person or group of people, whom previously we had thought to be acting freely and therefore to be properly accountable in law and morals for what they misdid, had in fact been acting out the suggestions of some master-hypnotist, then we should need to reconsider all questions of their accountability in the light of this fresh information. It would not prove that they were not in any degree responsible, even if we knew that this hypnotist's suggestions were irresistible.[25] For there would remain the question whether they willingly put themselves in his power knowing what this might involve: here the analogy is with the man who knows that he is 'not responsible for what he does' when he is drunk but who could have helped getting into that state (see Aristotle, *Nicomachean Ethics*, III, v, §8: 1113 B 31ff.). What our information would be sufficient to prove is that there was someone else besides the apparent agent, namely the hypnotist, who is at least as responsible, at least an accessory before the fact: here the analogy is to the boss who sends one of his gang to do a job, or to the man who sets a booby-trap leaving it where his victim will certainly spring it.

But the case of predestination, where the hypnotist would be not a human being but God, is essentially different.

25 It is said that this is not in fact the case with any actual hypnotist: though the evidence is conflicting; and in any case irrelevant to our argument here.

First, because here there is no question of any of us being in any way responsible for allowing ourselves to fall under the spell of this hypnotist. Second, because here it is not a matter of some being divinely hypnotized and some not; or of all being so for part of the time, and part not; but of absolutely everyone from the beginning to the end of time being hypnotized all the time. The first reaction to the idea of God, the Great Hypnotist, is that this would mean that no one ever was or had been or would be *really* responsible, that none of the people whom we should otherwise have been certain could have helped doing things *really* could. And so on. But this is at least very misleading. Certainly it would be monstrous to suggest that anyone, *however truly responsible in the eyes of men*, could fairly be called to account and punished by the God who had rigged his every move. All the bitter words which have ever been written against the wickedness of the God of predestinationism—especially when he is also thought of as filling Hell with all but the elect—are amply justified.[26] But this is not sufficient to show that every use of any of the phrases 'acted freely', 'had a choice', 'made his own decisions' and so forth as applied to any human being must have been wrong, if predestinationism is true. Again remember the Argument of the Paradigm Case. The *meaning* of these phrases has been given in terms of certain familiar human situations, and the differences between these. No new information, not even the supposed item of theological fact that we are created by Omnipotence, can possibly show that such phrases cannot correctly be applied

[26] 'The recognition, for example, of the object of highest worship in a being who could make a Hell; and who could create countless generations of human beings with the certain foreknowledge that he was creating them for this fate. . . . Any other of the outrages to the most ordinary justice and humanity involved in the common Christian conception of the moral character of God sinks into insignificance beside this dreadful idealization of wickedness' (*Three Essays on Religion*, pp. 113–14). Cf. the *Westminster Confession*, 'By the decree of God, for the manifestation of His glory, some men and angels are predestinated unto everlasting life, and others foreordained to everlasting death'. On these issues I can find no difference of substance between Calvinism and Roman Catholicism: Calvin stated with harsh clarity and without equivocation what is implicit in conciliar pronouncements.

to such situations, or that there do not subsist between these situations the differences they were introduced to mark.[27] The position seems to be that: while there is no 'contradiction in speaking of God as so arranging things that all men always as a matter of fact freely choose to do the right'; the idea of God arraigning and punishing anyone who freely chose the wrong, if he so arranges things that his victim does so act, 'outrages . . . the most ordinary justice and humanity'.[28]

(*b*) If the objector prefers to go on maintaining—and we should only very hesitantly suggest he was wrong—that this idea that we are all of us always as it were acting out the divine post-hypnotic suggestions is incompatible with saying that all of us sometimes act of our own free will, then two possibilities are open to him: both of which equally involve the annihilation of the Free-will Defence. He can say that God exists and as his creatures we simply cannot be free: for what the doctrine of creation[29] means is that all power is from God, that all things and creatures are always and utterly dependent on God, for their beginning and preservation, in and for their powers, their activities, and their limitations.[30] If he says this then clearly he cannot use the central

27 A dim realization of this may have been what enabled the Calvinists to think that 'God from all eternity did . . . freely and unchangeably ordain whatsoever comes to pass. Yet . . . thereby' is no 'violence offered to the will of the creatures'. What was wrong was to suggest that in such a case: 'neither is God the author of sin'; that *God* could fairly hold men accountable (quotes from the *Westminster Confession*).

28 Calvin scarcely pretended otherwise: the damned were damned 'by a just and irreprehensible, but incomprehensible judgment'. In thus seeing and accepting the implications of omnipotence he showed himself to have both a clearer head and a stronger—shall we say?—stomach than most believers.

29 See Ch. IX: we are concerned here with what I there call the theological sense of 'creation'; which neither entails nor is entailed by the also questionably significant proposition that the Universe was made by God in the beginning of time. (On this last phrase see M. Scriven in *Brit. J. Phil. Science*, 1954 and on the absence of the two-way entailment see St. Thomas's *de aeternitate mundi contra murmurantes*.)

30 C. S. Lewis puts it nicely, without I think realizing how disastrous this doctrine is for what he wants to say about human responsibility: [Men] 'wanted some corner in the universe of which they could say to God, "This is our business not yours." But there is no such corner. They wanted to be nouns, but they were, and eternally must be, mere adjectives' (*loc. cit.*, p. 68).

move of the Free-will Defence ' to justify the ways of God to man '. Furthermore if he continues to hold, as he must, with Kant and everybody else, that morality presupposes freedom then he has left no room for higher-order, or any order, moral goods attainable by man. The alternative option consists in reversing the argument[31] to produce a new proof of God's non-existence, an inverted Kantian postulate of practical reason. Thus he can say that since we clearly *are* free agents on some occasions we *cannot* be God's creatures; and hence there *cannot* be a creator God. In which case the question of defence, free-will or any other, does not arise.

(*c*) Besides saying that the idea that we all always as it were act out the suggestions of the Divine Hypnotist is or is not compatible with saying that all of us sometimes act of our own free-will there is a third possibility. We might argue that the whole notion of an omnipotent creator God is logically vicious. If this is so the problem of evil cannot arise, since the notions of God as either all-powerful, or all-good or as even existing at all will all be equally vicious. This is a position to which the present writer is very much inclined;[32] and the difficulties which arise in attempts to reconcile divine omnipotence with human freedom might be taken as an indication that the former notion ought to come under suspicion. We cannot here examine this position; and fortunately it is sufficient to make three points only. First, even if it is correct it by no means follows that there cannot be any right and wrong about such theological arguments as those we have been deploying: for our propositions may nevertheless be sound or unsound in much the same sort of way as those of proposed *reductiones ad absurdum* in geometry; which also and similarly make use of expressions which are, strictly, non-significant. Second, if it is correct the practical consequences here may seem very much the same as those presented by the second option of (4) (*b*) above. For the

---

31 On this move compare Smart in Ch. III above and Descartes: ' Some indeed might be found who would be disposed rather to deny the existence of a being so powerful than to believe that there is nothing certain' (*Meditation*, I).
32 See, for instance, my share of Ch. IX below, *ad fin.*

question whether it is that the Universe has as a matter of fact no creator or that this suggestion does not even make sense is clearly academic. Third our concentration at the end of (4) (*a*) above on the moral monstrosity of the doctrine of a Hell-filling creator must not be allowed to conceal from us that we were there dealing with only one and an evaluative aspect of the much more general fact that there is absurdity in the notion of any transactions at all between creatures and their Creator. It is not merely that his 'punishing' his creatures is morally repellent, but that it does not deserve to be called punishment at all.[33] Again it is not that only the notion of punishment is inapplicable but that a similar absurdity infects all concepts which apply originally only to transactions between autonomous and responsible human beings if we try to transfer them to describe possible transactions between Creator and creatures. Thus to speak of a creature 'praising', 'promising', 'being rewarded by', 'injuring', or 'defying' his Creator is equally to misuse language: it is far more inappropriate than to use these words unescorted by warning inverted commas of the 'activities' of a ventriloquist's dummy; because the ventriloquist at most *fashioned* but he did not *create* his dummy.[34] Though this is not to dispose of that whole range of questions: Are those propositions which seem to be about men's actual or hypothetical trans-actions with God, if transformed into psychological and other sorts of propositions about the universe, as a matter of fact true?[35]

(5) Finally a few words on the pictures associated with the Free-will Defence. These do much to ease the 'double-think'[36] which goes on here when people hold: *both* that

---

33 See my ' "The Justification of Punishment" ' in *Philosophy*, 1954, on what a standard case of punishment necessarily involves.

34 On the possibility that the doctrine of the incarnation circumvents this difficulty see Ch. X and Ch. XI.

35 See for the sort of 'desupernaturalization' we have in mind: Lucretius, quoted in Ch. VI (i) A, and John Wisdom, 'Gods' *ad fin.*, in *Logic and Language*, First Series (ed. Antony Flew: Blackwell, 1951).

36 See Ch. VI (i) D above for the definition of this term, quoted.

our faults, though curiously and arbitrarily[37] not our virtues, are to be laid not at God's but at our door because he made us free agents; *and* that all power is in God's hands all the time, that every move, every thought of his creatures depends on him for its initiation and conservation, and presumably therefore that he could change the heart of any man at any time if he wanted him to reverse his wants.

The picture of the Great Father and his (mainly prodigal) sons is attractive; but quite inappropriate here, where the Father is supposed to represent Omnipotence and the sons are human beings. It seems suitable, because it does take account of the manifest facts of human freedom and responsibility to one another. But it is radically inappropriate to the relation between Creator and creature. A human father has only limited knowledge and limited powers. Once he has begotten and reared his sons there is usually precious little he can do about it if he doesn't like the way they behave. So that, as he had no means of knowing before their conception how radically prodigal they would be, and so long as he did his best to bring them up in the way they should go, there are usually no grounds for ascribing responsibility to him. But the position with an omnipotent Creator must be different. There can be no question of ignorance or of inability to do anything about it or of creatures being even temporarily autonomous. On the contrary the doctrine of creation necessarily involves that God is as it were accessory before during and after the fact to every human action. Or rather, 'accessory' is a ludicrously weak word for the source and ground of all being and power.[38] Again, a human father may fairly and without absurdity reward or punish his sons and they can without absurdity or inverted commas be said to defy, promise or injure him. But these relations cannot subsist between a Creator and creatures.

[37] Perhaps the elusive doctrine of the negativity of evil seems to some people to remove the arbitrariness: but surely if you take creation seriously it cannot do this? For who is there but God who could have left the gaps?

[38] See C. S. Lewis again, as quoted above, on our being adjectives and never nouns.

The analogy offered by the picture breaks down in precisely the respects which are crucial.

The only picture which begins to do justice to this situation is the one we have already offered, that of the Great Hypnotist with all his creatures acting out, usually unknowingly, his commands. To fail to appreciate this is to fail to take the theological doctrine of creation seriously. And this, as both Mill [39] and Calvin [40] in their very different ways were at pains to point out, is what most believers most of the time do. Similarly to suggest that God might himself have limited his power is to fail in the same way: for if the limitation is real it must involve that the Universe is now to that extent out of control, and contains things independent of God; which is precisely what the doctrine of creation denies.[41] But this picture, though it represents perhaps as well as may be the relations of creatures and Creator, misrepresents the relations of creature to creature by suggesting that none of us could very properly hold another responsible or be held responsible by him. (All this section (5) is assuming the position of (4) (*a*) above).

(6) *Summary*. We first posed the dilemma and then (1) outlined the three elements of the Free-will Defence and (2) four counter-moves usually made against it. In (3) we argued that there was no contradiction in saying that God could have made men so that they all always freely chose the right, but indicated that this did not definitively dispose of the matter, since the apologist could regroup the two remaining elements in the Free-will Defence for a further, albeit rather

39 See *loc. cit.*, pp. 39–40 and 115–16.
40 See *Institutes*, Bk. II, Ch. 4 and Bk. III, Ch. 21.
41 Consider here C. S. Lewis' speculation that 'the "annihilation" of a soul' may not be 'intrinsically possible' (*loc. cit.*, p. 113). This idea no doubt seems more plausible dressed in the idiom of 'intrinsic impossibility': but Lewis has elsewhere (pp. 15ff.) rightly pointed out that only *logical* impossibility could without contradiction be said to apply to God (see (1) above): and it is therefore wholly irrelevant to try to support this present arbitrary piece of special pleading by an appeal to the fact that we have no experience of the *annihilation* as opposed to the *transformation* of *matter*. Which is in any case a curious appeal to come from one who certainly wishes to claim that it makes sense to speak of *creatio ex nihilo*: both in the 'popular' and in the 'theological' senses distinguished in Ch. IX below.

desperate, stand. In (4) we considered the suggestion that while determinism may be compatible with human responsibility predestinationism is not: concluding, tentatively, that this is not so, but only because and in so far as a creator could and must be taken as outwith the range of human transactions. This section was awkward and unsteady: but not in any way to comfort the orthodox. Finally in (5) we pointed out how a favourite picture used to illustrate the relation of Creator to his creatures misleads believers to overlook those radically disruptive implications of the creation doctrine to which the possible objection of (4) had led us.

University College of North Staffordshire
ENGLAND

IX
CREATION[1]

ANTONY FLEW *and* D. M. MacKINNON

A.F. 'In the beginning God created the heaven and the earth. And the earth was waste and void; and darkness was on the face of the waters. And God said Let there be light: and there was light. And God saw that it was good; and God divided the light from the darkness. And God called the light Day and the darkness he called Night. And there was evening and there was morning, one day'.

And so it goes on: through the seven days of creation: one of the most majestic visions in all literature. I think we might begin from this picture. The first thing I want to suggest is that neither you, who are a Christian, nor I, who am not, hold that this tremendous story is literally true.

D.M. No, I wouldn't want for one moment to treat the narrative as literal: it's not that sort of thing at all. Only, of course, the order of the work of God is interesting, once you learn to take the word 'day' with more than one grain of salt. In the Bible time-words like 'hour' and 'day' have varied and elastic uses. Even schoolboys see there is a difference between the day of the Lord and founder's day or parents' day or what day have you. Even someone reading St. John's Gospel for the first time realizes that when Christ speaks of his hour he means something more than the mere revolutions of the clock.

A.F. This isn't just a peculiarity of the Bible either, for —perhaps ultimately owing to the influence of the Bible—

[1] This dialogue of elucidation was first presented on the B.B.C. Third Programme, and afterwards printed in the *Church Quarterly Review* for January 1955.

we all talk of, say, the things that happened in grandfather's day: regardless of the fact that he had a great many days.

D.M. Yes, but to go on, you know as well as I do that a great deal of critical work has been done on the book of Genesis which has turned up all sorts of similarities between the creation myth of Genesis and, say, the Babylonian cycles. For instance, the tradition which sees Marduk subduing Ti-amat the Dragon of the Great Deep is said to be a kind of parallel to the breathing of God on the face of the water in Genesis. Even that it is the same thing said in other words. To argue out these issues would take a long time, but what I want to suggest is that if you take the Genesis narrative, together with the whole tradition of Israel of which the Old Testament is the classical expression, you find that for all the impact of Babylon on the Jewish people finally they saw their creator God differently. They did not think metaphysically, but the absolute lordship of their God Jahweh over the world and, I would say, his authorship of *all* that was: these were axioms of their thought and judgment. And it is in the light of this that we should interpret the language of Genesis. As, in effect, asserting *creatio de nihilo*, creation from nothing.

A.F. Yes, indeed. But before moving on to that I think there are two points—on which I'm sure we agree—to be got out of the way. First: I'd like to emphasize how *different* the Genesis story is from any of those of its opposite numbers in other traditions which I myself have ever come across. Second: this notion of myth. Some tales which are not literally true are what I want to call myths—but not all. (There are also, for instance, legends and works of fiction as well as myths). A myth, as I want to use the word, in a more restricted sense than those of the dictionaries, may have point, and contain a great deal of truth. This is the case with the stories of the Social Contract in all their various versions. Social Contract theorists have been saying things about the *present* obligations of States and citizens, or about their *present* interests: but saying them in the mythological form of a story about a *past* contract; a contract having such and such terms and sanctions and supposedly made long ago by the remote ancestors of our present citizens. Some of these theorists have been unsophisticated, believing in the historical truth of their stories—for instance, Locke.

D.M. Yes, though Locke had the excuse that some things like social contracts were actually being made in America in his century.

A.F. Quite: and we know he had his eyes on American developments. But there were others—Rousseau and Hobbes, for example—who were the very reverse of unsophisticated about their use of myth. These recognized their stories as useful fictions. But all said things which matter—which could be said (though less interestingly) in a literal way—in the form of this myth of the Social Contract.[2] A story may be a myth: but not every myth is a *mere* myth. Now can we locate a literal core in the creation story in Genesis: what are the literal propositions which anyone who was to accept it, but as myth, would have to commit himself to?

D.M. I must admit that I am very conscious of the critical problems Genesis raises. But I say quite confidently that if you take the Genesis narratives in relation to the Old Testament as a whole, what the Creation doctrine suggests is something like this: God is the author of the world: of all things. The Nicene creed speaks of things visible and invisible; what we see and what we don't see: whether by that we mean the laws of nature that we frame, or the vastness of universes unperceived and unsuspected. 'All' is a little word, but here we try to measure up to what it speaks. 'Nothing but by God.' Nothing: this has to be taken seriously: there is no suggestion of a stuff existent alongside God out of which he fashioned the world as a modeller may mould his clay to bear the impress which he wants. All, absolutely, comes into being by God's will.

A.F. Just so: and this is one of the peculiar, perhaps unique features of the Genesis account, as against its opposite numbers.

2 See J. D. Mabbott, *The State and the Citizen* (Hutchinson, 1948), pp. 12–18 and 27.

D.M. Then when any sort of dualism has thus been ruled out, this 'Nothing but by God' is further picked out by insisting on an absolute dependence. That's a difficult enough phrase. Archbishop Temple tried to interpret it by saying: God minus the world equals God; whereas the world minus God equals nothing at all. You might put it in another way by saying that the universe exists not of itself but only in relation to another whose existence is in himself.

A.F. Besides this insistence on absolute dependence and this rejection of any sort of dualistic account of the universe, there must surely be moral suggestions too. I think of Emil Brunner's statement that in recognizing God as 'My creator and the creator of all things I become aware that I am . . . his servant, his property, because all that I am and have I have from him, because not only I but all that is has been created by him'. This insistence that this is God's world surely suggests that we should behave, as it were, as guests and borrowers: not as owners who have a right to do what they like with their own.

D.M. Yes. Aquinas says that to hold creatures cheap is to slight divine power. Others today, like Michael Roberts, warn us of the possible consequences of wanton and uncontrolled squandering of natural resources: finding in such improvidence a kind of irreverent disrespect of the order of creation.

A.F. We have now three elements which are essential to any interpretation of Genesis, which is to be an interpretation and not a travesty. First: the insistence on absolute dependence; second: the rejection of any really fundamental dualism; and third: the suggestion of certain conduct and attitudes as appropriate. Surely there is a fourth (which many would treat as the prime point)—the assertion that the world had a beginning?

D.M. This is crucial, both theologically and metaphysically. I must go very carefully here. Aquinas thought that only by revelation did man learn that the world had a beginning in time. That the world was contingent was evident to natural reason. But the fullness of the doctrine of creation belonged to the data of the theologian. Now I think that in popular thought what St. Thomas so carefully and indeed painfully distinguished has often been telescoped. For the moment I want to fasten on this word 'beginning'. What do we mean by the beginning and indeed by the end of the world? Or, to raise something even more difficult (of which St. Augustine spoke) of the beginning of time? I want to venture an opinion here. Even if, as St. Thomas did, we invoke revelation to justify our speaking of the beginning of the world, we must find it very difficult to understand what we are saying. It is tempting to seek a way out of this by turning to the specula-tion of empirical cosmologists: who claim to date the world's beginning as a geologist might claim to date a rock. Simi-larly, those who are too sophisticated to accept the predictions of soapbox preachers as to the date of the end, are happy to use the second law of thermo-dynamics to establish the hour when the trump of doom shall sound.

A.F. Perhaps it would help to define two senses of the word 'creation'. In the first, the popular, sense questions about whether the world was or was not created are questions to which the latest news from the science front is relevant. Because if the world was eternal and had no beginning; then there would be no room for creation, in this sense. In the second, the theological, sense, questions about creation are questions about an absolute ontological dependence to which particular scientific discoveries are simply irrelevant. This distinction is important: but difficult, because almost everyone—including St. Thomas—who has believed in creation in the second sense has also believed that the world had a beginning, and that it was in the first sense, also, created.

D.M. Yes, I think that one is always conscious in reading Aquinas here that he lived in an age before the distinction between the domain of the scientist and that of the meta-physician had been drawn. We live in a more sophisticated age. However, I think that a Thomist would say that there was a kind of fundamental understanding of one's creaturely lot that was independent of the movement of empirical discovery.

A.F. Creaturely?

D.M. It is a matter of having a sense of being a created being. What I want to do is to get to grips with the meaning of this kind of language. Language whereby we, so to speak, take up the posture proper to us, indicate the sort of things we are. *Either* we must use in these contexts words borrowed from the familiar transactions of experience, *or* we must say nothing at all. There is no escaping here the problem of giving some sense to talk of the creation of the temporal world by the eternal God. This is going to involve us in what I can only call a labyrinthine process of intellectual twisting and turning.

A.F. Am I right that it was from the moment that you used the word 'creaturely' that we began to discuss creation in what I called the theological sense of the word?

D.M. Even before that. I only mentioned St. Thomas's distinction between temporal creation and the contingency of creatures because I didn't want to have the discussion go off into our old friend the cosmological argument. After all, the Epistle to the Hebrews says that it is by *faith* we know that the heavens were formed by the word of God. Certainly in the New Testament there is very much on creation that averts altogether from metaphysics.

A.F. And from science too.

D.M. Yes. It belongs rather to an imaginative vision of the world. It sees its every process as well as its history converging on a single centre, which is at the same time their ground and origin. I say *imaginative* deliberately: for writing in the New Testament is poetry rather than prose. Yet for all that —to take up a much earlier point—the vision is offered to exclude, shall I say, nightmares. Fears, for instance, that human life was at the mercy of malignant forces which were not themselves subject to any control. The gospel of creation as St. Paul, for example, in his later Epistles presents it, is a vision: but a vision that effectively took from men their fear of malignant powers.

A.F. Well: let me see if I have understood you. Is the idea that what we have is not theory about cosmology—not a sort of Hebrew Fred Hoyle—but a picture?

D.M. Certainly not a Hebrew Hoyle; no.

A.F. Yet a picture the use of which excludes certain nightmares about the nature of the Universe. That the heavens were created by the word of God is not a piece of literal theory. Nevertheless the acceptance of this picture, on the one hand, excludes certain sorts of theory about what literally does go on; and, on the other hand, clears the way for other different sorts of theory also about what literally does go on.

D.M. Yes! that is right. Of course, the issues with which Paul was concerned were religious issues, or put in religious terms: issues, that is, about Man and God, the conduct of life, and of course about human destiny. And some people today would argue that the outcome of this religious struggle was not without importance for the development of modern science. I don't mean that there were any scientific issues involved: but by clearing away all sorts of false and frightening views of the way the universe worked, Paul helped later generations to explore its secrets without fear of malign forces. And with confidence of success too: for its processes were no longer regarded as governed by their caprice.

A.F. Yes. Now I am sure that people like Michael Foster in his articles[3] and the late Professor Collingwood[4] in his books, who have said at length the sort of thing which you are suggesting, have been on to something of the very greatest importance: (Though I, for one, have found their way of presenting assertions about the theological and other pre-suppositions of science both apparently arbitrary and mysterious). Yet I myself feel also fairly sure that it is wrong to speak of the Principle of the Uniformity of Nature and of the Law of Causality—principles and laws which curiously find no place in science text-books—as the fundamental *presuppositions* or *assumptions* of science: as if all the work already done and fully confirmed in one field would collapse

[3] See, for instance, 'The Christian Doctrine of Creation and the Rise of Modern Natural Science' in *Mind*, 1934.

[4] E.g. *Metaphysics* (O.U.P., 1940): his ' absolute presuppositions' are supposed, of course, not to be assumptions.

on to its undermined foundations if we found that in another field disorder reigned, and our present concept of, say, *cause* could not there be applied.[5]

D.M. I confess I'm always on edge when the Law of Causality (in capital letters) is mentioned. Moreover this expression 'Principle of Causality' slurs over a great many distinctions that should be drawn.

A.F. Yes this expression 'Principle of Causality' seems too often—like certain others in philosophy—to be taken as the name of a solution when it is only the label of a problem. And the fact that these principles are so excessively difficult to formulate in words suggests that the word 'presupposition' (which in spite of Collingwood suggests a *proposition* assumed) is in any case the wrong label. I think you gave us a clue when earlier you spoke of a *vision*. It seems to me that what is involved is something more like a *model*, an *image* or a *picture*. When Paul writes, 'In him were all things created in the heavens and upon the earth, things visible and invisible, all things have been created through him and unto him': Paul was not, as we both agreed, to be taken as making a literal statement *à la* Hoyle; nor is he doing—rather lamely —scholastic metaphysics. He is offering us a *picture* in terms of which to think of the universe around us. And this picture encourages and justifies one sort of religious practice. And was, as you hinted, later to encourage the beginnings of scientific inquiry as we know it today.

D.M. Of course, these struggles of Paul were about particular concrete superstitions; but the vision he evoked to deal with them proved remarkably fertile. You see, the gods and the devils had to be banished from the world if men were to begin to see its processes as capable of precise determination and description. If you thought that, for instance, the world had the sort of relation to God that a child may have to its parents: which is a view which Michael Foster finds deeply embedded in Plato's *Timaeus*—if you had this view (and if you had even a vague belief in God's existence) you

---

5 *Vide* G. J. Warnock in *Logic and Language* (Second Series: ed. A. Flew) and S. E. Toulmin in *The Philosophy of Science* (Hutchinson, 1953).

177

might be reluctant to pry and probe into it. It's a paradox: but if there is anything in our argument here you could say that Christianity by encouraging men to think scientifically was digging its own grave. It thereby stimulated the rationalism which threatens to undermine its foundations.

A.F. This would make a parallel to Spengler's remark—which was directed only at the egalitarian ethical aspect of Christianity—that 'Christian theology is the grandmother of Bolshevism'.

D.M. Quite: though I was not thinking of Stalin and Malenkov but of the whole family of views loosely called scientific humanism. There is something in the attitude of Prometheus which the doctrine of Creation endorses and upholds. There are secrets which men are right to wrest from the multiplicity of phenomena, although, as we suggested earlier, there may be limits to the extent human interference can go without destructive consequences. After all, although in a profound sense men and women do not belong to, are not part of nature, yet they are themselves creatures whose lives are not in their own hands or of their own fashioning.

A.F. I can see how these are consequences of the acceptance of a certain picture of the world; and how people who do not accept that picture might not accept these. But where is our discussion going?

D.M. Well, I plead that working out the consequences, even the historical consequences, of its acceptance may help us to see what the view is. A man might shy at the idea of broaching the Doctrine of Creation out of nothing, directly. Nevertheless he might be inclined to take seriously the intellectual differences between men who accepted it and men who accepted some other view.

A.F. Yes, I can see that. In the field of political thought, too, it seems to me that *one way* to see the implications of what Rousseau is saying is to study the political behaviour of his intellectual children and grandchildren. This may help to bring out that his ideas *do not* chime in with the toleration and civil liberty of liberal democracy, but rather with the nationalist statism of Mussolini's Italy and Kemal's Turkey.

D.M. And among those intellectual children of the believers in Creation I included some prodigal sons whose capital, inherited from their parents, is not yet exhausted.

A.F. A palpable hit, a very palpable hit.

D.M. But let's go back, shall we, to the doctrine itself? What have we unearthed about it? How is it to be understood? One thing has, I think, come out quite clearly. You can't talk about Creation as the Deists did: that is, as the winding up of a cosmic watch by a cosmic watchmaker; who then sits back with his work done. To believe in Creation is to see the world in a certain way: to have one's responses to its manifold being coloured in a certain style. That is part of the *content* of the doctrine, as Brunner well brings out.

A.F. Yes, the watchmaker-watch picture clashed, at more than one point actually, with their claims to believe in *creation*. But though seeing the world in a certain way may be *part* of the content of the doctrine, surely it can't be the *whole* of it. For surely any doctrine of creation worthy of the name must say *not merely* that for some reason this is the right picture to have of the world, *but also* that it is right mainly, if not entirely, because as a matter of fact there is a God, and his relations to the world can be best represented in this way.

D.M. Again, you are quite right. That brings us back to the question of the existence of God and the manner of his relation to the world. Actually, the recognition of God may be one with the acknowledgment of a Creator. That is, of one who stands to the world in that relationship. And what of that recognition? Or what of the language in which we make our confession of God's existence? What meaning can we attach to it?

A.F. Yes, I think that is crucial. For in any sophisticated theism God has to be conceived as a being beyond all finite human powers of understanding. (By the way, I do want to stress the word 'sophisticated', which I do not here intend to have any emotional overtones favourable or otherwise. I want to stress it because it seems to me that many sophisticated people—especially among our professional philosopher colleagues—simply overlook the possibility of unsophisticated belief in something called God or in gods). To return to the point, though: it does seem to me that if you are going to stress the enormous transcendence of God you are—to put it gently—in danger of undermining the possibility of saying anything intelligible about him. The theologian will find himself forever saying things about God by applying some analogy drawn from human experience. (For where else is a human being to get his vocabulary if not from this world we live in?) And then admitting that, of course, as God is transcendent, infinite, the ground of all being, and so on; this analogy breaks down in this and this respect. Again and again he is going—and I think necessarily so from the very nature of his project—to erode his promising analogy by qualifying it till there is nothing left. Till it has tacitly, or even explicitly, been admitted to break down not only in some but in all respects. His analogies are all going to suffer—if I may borrow a phrase I used in an earlier broadcast discussion—the death by a thousand qualifications.[6]

D.M. Yes, writers on the 'sovereign principle of analogy' insist that the thousand qualifications—the so-called 'negative way'—precedes and preconditions the use of the so-called 'way of eminence'. I suppose you could call the Negative Way a sort of putting to death. Penido, one of the modern masters of this doctrine calls it *épuration* (purging). Now, those who make play with the notion of analogy have much to teach us. They throw a lot of light on what I earlier called the labyrinthine windings of this sort of thinking. But the crux is their starting-point. For their master, Aristotle, it was his scheme of categories of being—with Substance, Quality and Relation forming a kind of declining series pivoted on Substance, *things*, for him, having being, *par excellence*. The schoolmen learnt vital lessons from him, but I don't think I misrepresent them entirely in saying that consciously or unconsciously they went for analogical

6 See Ch. VI (i) A above: these papers in *University* formed the basis of a Third Programme discussion.

thinking in a big way because they were theists; and analogical schemes helped them to work theism out. A theist isn't a dualist, as came out earlier, but he can't be a monist, either, for the sovereign lordship of God which Brunner so emphasizes is somehow necessary to him.

A.F. I'm sorry. But though I can see the enormous importance of thinking of the universe as somehow a unity and not, as you would put it, as just-a-lot-of-things, I don't see *either* how thinking in this way gives independent authority to analogical thinking about God, *or* how this is going to provide a basis for meeting my difficulty about using analogies from the finite world to describe, what is (by definition) infinite: namely, God. The difficulty that what you say, as it were, out of one corner of your mouth, you necessarily deny out of the other.

D.M. You put it nicely. I suppose you see yourself really as a speech therapist trying to cure me of these oral contortions. But actually what I was saying just before, was that it may be that analogical language is the language the theist must speak, and its sole justification is that it is the only language he can use. Now, I agree it is an awfully difficult language to talk. Your jaws ache and your hearers accuse you of trying to have it both ways. Of using the familiar word but of referring to the ultimately unfamiliar thing. I think you've got me there. What am I to say? I might say one or two things. That I am forced to enlarge the compass of my language to take in or to indicate what lies perhaps at the foundation of my experience. Or even—and this perhaps Paul and the New Testament writers did—because particular events in which they had been personally involved have commanded such an enlargement of their ordinary speech. I'd like to put a question to you: How are the horizons, the boundaries fixed? That's what our discussion makes me ask you. (That's larger, I know, than the issue of creation).

A.F. Yes, that seems to me a question as fair as it is fundamental. But we are at the parting of the ways: *either* we try to tackle this question *or* we get back to analogical thinking.

D.M. As you know, there was a lot of controversy among the schoolmen about analogy—the analogy of proper proportionality and the analogy of attribution. These are terrible terms, I know. I will give examples though of each. Geometry, I think, will do as an example of the latter, of the analogy of attribution. We all learnt Euclid's geometry at school, and in the history of the subject it came first. But now Riemann and Lobachevsky have devised new non-Euclidean Geometries. Why call them geometries? Well, they stand in relation to Euclid, taken as the proper standard of what geometry is. They borrow their name from this archetype. Now, when scholastics speak of God and beings they think of God as Being *par excellence*, and creatures as being by his leave. God is the standard being. He sets the standards for existence. We don't come up to that standard, but in our little way we, too, *are*. With the analogy of perfect proportion it's different. There the line is: as *A* to *B*, so *C* to *D*. For instance, to get back to our subject, as God to world, so artist to his work. Now I must be dogmatic here, and I may be attracting scholastic thunderbolts to my brow. But it seems to me attribution is fundamental. For that gives you what you must take over into the latter—that is, the break in the line. What the schoolman calls *summum analogatum*. Which sets the analogical ball rolling, spinning down the scale of being. God isn't on a level with any of the others, for the infinite God isn't an artist: that is anthropomorphism, If I think of him on that image it is only after I have got hold of the break between his work and that of any other craftsman.

A.F. I begin to see now how the analogical statements can be made once one can get started. But my difficulty is to know how you can get started, how you know that there is the basic *X*, God, to which all the analogies are to be applied. How is it possible to say the sort of things you want to say, and particularly to say that God is, as it were, the standard of being? Which was, as I understood you, the crucial move on which the development of the analogical thinking about God depends. And I must suppose that brings you back to the question you wanted to put to me : how are the boundaries of language to be found or fixed ?

D.M. We were discussing creation and we have gone on—as we must—to discussing the possibilities of metaphysical and religious language. How does one know one has any right to speak of creation? To frame the complex scheme of ideas it suggests. To articulate a language, the language which hails God the creator. How can one justify a chapter or a section of a chapter of language, the language of religion? I suppose I can only answer, by what it makes possible, a view of the world that is fertile and illuminating, a posture for men under the sun that vindicates itself. Yes, and more. Shall I say the opening of doors on to the unseen? That is the difficulty, there in those last words, deliberately metaphysical as they are. Can forms of words help men to launch out, if I may quote Boethius, to launch out into the sea of being? And what is such a launching? I know I have failed in this particular matter of creation to do more than indicate some of the ways in which the language of religion works. I know I haven't given anyone who thinks its idiom improper grounds for changing his decision. But then what made the writers of the Epistle and the Gospels adventure into language as they did, and speak the mysteries of creation, was more perhaps the riddle of a life lived and a death died than any sort of arguments.

A.F. That seems to me climactic. Philosophers who study the jobs which different parts of (chapters of, if you like) language do are usually concerned with, and often prefer to concentrate on the chapters—and these are the majority—which they feel do not require serious justification. (To concentrate on these ensures a placid life.) Talk about tables and chairs—the usual equipment of our sparsely furnished philosophic studies—doesn't need justifying: because absolutely everyone uses and has to use this part of language; to say simple, harmless, necessary, everyday things. Talk of a more theoretical and remote kind—the scientist's language of electrons, light rays, *gestalten*—isn't nowadays felt to require much defence : even though many of us are not scientists of any sort, and hence have little occasion to use it ourselves. Philosophers consider they have only to give an account of it, and to try to clear up the misconceptions which proliferate around it. Ethical language, perhaps, is rather more controversial. But still, on the whole, philosophers feel that if they can give an account of the jobs done by the moral words these will pretty well justify themselves as obviously necessary and proper jobs, essential to humans living together. And so on with most other elements in language. But religious talk, the religious chapter, is in a less secure position: it's a sort of appendix, an apocrypha in the book of language.

D.M. Now just why; surely not because it is merely different because *you* can't fit it into any of *your* permitted pigeon-holes?

A.F. No, indeed. Not merely because it won't fit neatly into any of the other available categories. No, indeed; philosophy has seen too much of this 'if-X-isn't-Y-or-Z-it-can't-be-allowed-to-be-X-but-must-be-junked-move'. I think I can suggest two reasons—apart from my earlier argument about theological description being an attempt to say something with the vocabulary of the finite about something by definition infinite.

D.M. Sorry; I ought, you know, to have said something about the word 'infinite' and now it's almost too late. But can I just say this? There's the mathematical 'infinite' which Cantor and Co. discussed. There's the 'infinite' of Newton: a sort of physical boundlessness. And there's the 'infinity' of God. That means, I think, that he is not bounded or limited by anything outside himself, so the models we make of him need to be continually discarded: a sort of intellectual fulfilment of the commandment to have none other Gods before him. But in this riddle of Christ's life lived and Christ's death died we see through a glass darkly the infinite boundless love, love without condition, translated into terms of the finite and the bounded.

A.F. I agree entirely that this is the heart of the matter, and I will try to return here. But first I must give my two reasons for thinking that religious language has an insecure status. The *first* reason is that only some people find it necessary to use it. While others do not; perhaps positively rejecting it. The *second* reason is that religious talk seems so often not merely deceptively like, say, ethical or scientific talk: but as if it really was in some way failed science or fraudulent ethics. *Either* perhaps the result of a misguided attempt to do super-science; God as super-science about the Cause of Everything. *Or* as a mere failure to do proper science; God as exploded science about the cause of, say, the weather. Then there is the 'pretentious ethics' aspect. Talk of God adding force and appeal to the commands of duty.

D.M. I have absolutely no sympathy with the suggestion that God can be invoked to underwrite our righteous causes. He is not a kind of stimulant for flagging hearts.

A.F. I'm sure that *you* yourself haven't. The two peculiar troubles about religious discourse are *first*, that religious language *as a whole* is controversial in a way in which scientific language is not: and *second*, *as a whole* it may appear either as a fraudulent way of doing ethics or as a discredited way of doing science. But it does seem to me that you said something crucial about this at the point earlier which I then agreed to be climactic. The heart of the matter is that the only satisfactory and the perhaps sufficient justification for the whole enterprise of trying to say things which it seems necessarily cannot be said lies just there; in Christ. 'In the riddle of a life lived and a death died.'

D.M. Good, I'm glad there is agreement there. We began by talking about creation, the status of the language of Genesis: how much is literal and how much is myth. Then inevitably to the claims of myth sometimes to be taken seriously, and so on to the drawing of distinctions; between the popular idea of creation on the one hand (involving a beginning of the world) and the creation of the theologians on the other (a recognition of man's absolute dependence on God). Next we discussed the very interesting arguments of Michael Foster and Professor Collingwood about the influence of creation ideas upon the history of science. We agreed that it was wrong to think of these ideas as presuppositions, *assumptions* upon which the fabric of science rests. They are rather *pictures* excluding other pictures and encouraging—or discouraging—scientific confidence. But of course the metaphysical issue could not be burked. After some discussion of the traditional doctrine of analogy and the difficulties which it was designed to meet, we went on to consider the impulses behind religious language, and the peculiarities which make its justification at once so necessary and so hard. Finally, we agreed that among the most important of these impulses are questions raised by the person of Christ.

<table>
<tr><td>*University College of*</td><td>*King's College*</td></tr>
<tr><td>*North Staffordshire*</td><td>*Aberdeen*</td></tr>
<tr><td>ENGLAND</td><td>SCOTLAND</td></tr>
</table>

X

TERTULLIAN'S PARADOX[1]

BERNARD WILLIAMS

*Non pudet, quia pudendum est . . . prorsus credibile est, quia
ineptum est . . . certum est, quia impossibile.*—Tertullian, *de carne
Christi,* v.

(1) This paper does not deal directly either with Tertullian
or with his paradox. In considering the most famous and
most widely misquoted of Tertullian's paradoxes, I do not try
to explain it, still less to explain it away; but take it as the
starting-point and end of a discussion of religious language
and of its relations to theology and to the kind of philosophical
inquiry with which this book is principally concerned. In
particular, I try to bring out a certain tension, a pull
between the possible and the impossible, a sort of inherent
and necessary incomprehensibility, which seems to be a
feature of Christian belief, and to locate this point of tension
more exactly within the structure of the belief. This tension
Tertullian seems to have felt very strongly, and characteristically proclaimed it with vigour; but it is only by this
rather thin string that my remarks are tied to what Tertullian said, the strict interpretation of which would require
something quite different.

As the path of this paper is rather circuitous, a rough map
may help. After stating the paradox (2), I go on to a short
discussion of paradoxes in general, their uses and demands
(3). I then leave Tertullian for a while, and attempt to show

---

[1] This paper, substantially in its present form, was read in May 1954 to the
Oxford University Socratic Club; I should like to express my gratitude to
the Chairman of that Club and the editor of its publication, the *Socratic
Digest,* for allowing the paper to be printed here.

some features which distinguish religious, or at least Christian, language from other kinds of language (4); this is done by presupposing the existence of God, which may seem a rather peculiar procedure for a sceptic, but which will, I hope, serve for a discussion which tries to show something about religious language as used by believers. The thesis is then proposed that Christian belief must involve at least one statement which is about both God and the world, and that this statement must be partly incomprehensible—which I hold to be suggested by Tertullian's paradox, if given its head (5). Some remarks are then made on theology, and its relations to religious language and to the philosophy of religious language; these raise considerations that stop an incipient discussion of the incarnation, and suggest some rather disheartening conclusions about both the philosophy of religious language and theology (6). I end (7) with some observations about faith and about what one may or may not be said to believe on faith.

Tertullian's paradox I represent as a paradox both about Christian belief and about theology, but it is the former that is the more important point. In both cases I consider it as a paradox about meaning rather than about truth; that is, it is with questions of what is being said in religious language that I am concerned, rather than with questions of whether what is said is true, although the two sorts of question are not (and cannot be) kept clinically apart.

(2) Tertullian, the first Latin father of the Church, started his career as a lawyer and ended it as a heretic. After his conversion from heathenism in 196 he remained for only five or ten years a member of the orthodox Church; both then and after his lapse into the Montanist heresy, he produced a series of theological works remarkable for vigorous reasoning, an unabashed use of legalistic rhetoric against his opponents, and an intransigent acceptance of paradoxical conclusions. The paradox I want to discuss comes from a work entitled *de carne Christi* which he wrote in the year 208, '*libris*', as the *Patrologia* (*Vit. Tert.*) elegantly puts it, '*iam Montanismam redolentibus*'—'at a time when his writings were

already stinking of Montanism'—but the work is not itself, I believe, heretical. He is attacking Marcion, who believed that Christ was not actually born of the flesh, but was a 'phantasma' of human form. Marcion's refusal to believe in a genuine incarnation, Tertullian argues, could come only from a belief either that it would be impossible, or that it would be unworthy, a shameful degradation of the divine nature. Against the view that it would be impossible he produces the sweeping and general principle '*nihil impossibile Deo nisi quod non vult*'—'nothing is impossible for God except what he does not wish to do'. In particular Marcion had argued that the idea of the incarnation of God involved a contradiction, because being born as a human being would involve a change in the divine nature[2]; but a change involves ceasing to have some attributes and acquiring others; but the attributes of God are eternal; therefore he cannot change; therefore he could not have been born as a human being. Against this Tertullian says that this is to argue falsely from the nature of temporal objects to the nature of the eternal and infinite. It is certainly true of temporal objects that if they change they lose some attributes and acquire others; but to suppose that the same is true of God is just to neglect the necessary differences between God and temporal objects (*de c. C.* iii). (I shall in section (6) of this paper say something about this, perhaps not immediately convincing, argument). Finally, against the view that, even if it were possible, God could not wish to be incarnated, because it would be unworthy of him, Tertullian, summing up his objections to Marcion in a passage of great intensity, accuses him of overthrowing the entire basis of the Christian faith: his argument would destroy the crucifixion and the resurrection as well. 'Take these away, too, Marcion,' he says (*ibid.*, v), 'or rather these: for which is more unworthy of God, more shameful, to be born or to die? . . . Answer me this, you butcher of the truth. Was not God really crucified? And as he was really crucified, did he not really die? And as he really died, did he not really rise from the dead? . . . Is

[2] For a similar argument see Ch. XI below—Editors.

our whole faith false? . . . Spare what is the one hope of the whole world. Why do you destroy an indignity that is necessary to our faith? What is unworthy of God will do for me . . . the Son of God was born; because it is shameful, I am not ashamed: and the Son of God died; just because it is absurd, it is to be believed; and he was buried and rose again; it is certain, because it is impossible.' '*Non pudet, quia pudendum est . . . prorsus credibile est, quia ineptum est . . . certum est, quia impossibile*': that is Tertullian's paradox.

(3) People who express themselves in paradoxes are in a strong position; and the more outrageous the paradox, in general the stronger the position. For an objector who insists on pointing out the absurdity of what has been said is uneasily conscious that he is making a fool of himself, for all he is doing is pointing out that the paradox is paradoxical, and this was perfectly obvious already: he is like a man who has missed the point of a joke or an ironical remark or an imaginative comparison, and insists on taking it literally. But ironical remarks and imaginative comparisons can have their point, and so can paradoxes; so it will not do, either, for the objector to dismiss the paradox in the hope that its evident absurdity makes it unworthy of discussion; for this is again to suggest that the person who uttered the paradox had overlooked its absurdity, but on the contrary he knew that it was absurd, and that was one reason why he uttered it. Because people do not in general utter absurdities unless they make a point by doing so, it is felt that the paradoxographer must have been saying something important. He not only prevents the critics answering, but makes them feel that in some mysterious way he is in a better position than they are; he is rather like a normally well-dressed man who appears at a function in a black tie and tails: the others present can't mention it to him, they can't overlook him, and they feel uneasy about their own turn-out. Or, again, he is something like a man who firmly closes a door in one's face: not only preventing one from going on, but making one feel one has no right to.

So far the paradoxographer has everything on his side, but

it is not entirely so. For, as the man in the black tie, to make his effect, has usually to be well-dressed, and the man who closes the door has to be someone one respects, so the paradoxographer has to have some other claim on the attention of his audience: for in general a paradox, however suggestive in itself, does not represent solid earnings—it draws a little on yesterday's credit or mortgages a little of tomorrow's. This claim on one's attention can be possessed in various ways: positively, by the utterer being a good and impressive and genuine person whose life commands love and respect, or by other utterances of his being original and profound; and negatively, by other conflicting, or apparently conflicting, claims on our attention being confused and unhelpful, or made by persons whose way of life seems trivial, evil or disastrous. If this is so, we might expect to find the beliefs of a religion, for instance, being put forward with a particularly defiant paradoxicality in two sorts of situation: first, when its believers are intensely bound together by a new and compelling faith, and fighting for survival in a hostile but decaying society whose beliefs they utterly reject; and second when, whatever the divisions and discredit that have fallen on the belief itself, those who reject it, their own hopes perishing, seem to have little to offer in its place except *angst*, tyranny or imminent thermonuclear annihilation.

This, however, so far as it goes, suggests only why people, and in particular religious believers, should tend at one time rather than at another to express themselves in paradoxes; it says little about why anyone should ever at all choose to speak in paradoxes, or suggests at most that they do this as a striking way of getting people to listen to or consider something else. Often it is not much more: to say, for instance, that the Holy Roman Empire was not Holy, nor Roman, nor an Empire, is, or should be, a brisk way of preparing for a new historical analysis. But there are other paradoxes which seem more important and significant; where to grasp the paradox seems an essential part of understanding what is being said. Here we have the feeling that a paradox, granted that it has to be understood against a background of other beliefs or a way of life, itself tells us something: that it is in a certain way the essence of what is to be believed. This is particularly so in the case of religious beliefs, where the feeling has itself been expressed in many ways: perhaps by saying, that there is an infinity of things that are beyond our comprehension; or that our reason cannot embrace the deepest truths; or that what we say can only be an unsatisfactory (or, perhaps, analogical) account of what we believe on faith. I shall try to show how such a point of tension, of failure of language, must occur in religious belief, and I think, therefore, that we should take Tertullian's paradox seriously; not as just a rhetorical expression of his objections to a particular doctrine, but as a striking formulation of something which I shall suggest is essential to Christian belief.

(4) There has been much discussion in recent years of religious language and its relations to other types of language; a good deal of this discussion has been concentrated on religious *statements*, and a good deal of this on the one statement 'God exists'. I think it is now time to consider whether such concentration has not been too narrow: for in each respect it has had undesirable results. First, there is an unclarity in the idea of a language—meaning by this, of course, not a national or dictionary language, such as French or Esperanto, but a logically distinguishable language or type of discourse. Second, the concentration on religious statements, as distinct from other types of religious utterance, has produced a string of disruptive effects: it has overemphasized the difference between the apparently unfalsifiable religious statement and the falsifiable statement of the sciences, which is indeed important and will appear later in what I have to say, but which taken by itself leads to an *impasse* which looks a little like a reduplication in linguistic terms of the barren nineteenth-century dispute between science and religion; and efforts to get out of this *impasse* have involved, in some cases, attempts to reduce statements of religion to statements of something else, for instance, of mystical experience, and in others attempts to reduce

statements of religion to other things that are not statements at all, such as commands or exhortations to a religious way of life—all of which either involve an evident circularity or omit the peculiarly religious character of the statements altogether. Third, there has been the concentration on the logic of the particular statement 'God exists'; this shows a kind of hopeless courage. It shows courage because this statement seems to be the lynch-pin of the whole system: to uncover what is involved in believing this should be to uncover the whole nature of religious language and the essence of religious belief. But it is just the peculiar importance of this statement that makes hopeless an inquiry that starts with it. Its peculiarity is such that it is extremely untypical of religious statements; a peculiarity emphasized by Collingwood, for instance, when he said that it was not a religious statement at all, but rather the presupposition of any religious statement. We might say that the statement of God's existence has indeed great logical power, but that it is the power not so much of a lynch-pin as of a lever: if we knew, from outside the religious system, how to work with it, we might move heaven and earth; but from outside we do not, because we know neither where we may fix a fulcrum nor where we can insert the other end of the lever. So rather than attempt such a direct approach, we must obey the Boyg, and go round.

I cannot hope to go far round, but perhaps something can be said. First, then, I think we must always bear in mind the fact that religious language is not used just for making statements, but that there are many other kinds of religious utterance: commands, for instance ('Thou shalt not take the name of the Lord thy God in vain'), and, very importantly, prayers, and expressions of trust ('Though he destroy me, yet will I wait for him'), and promises, and reprimands, and many others. Furthermore, none of these utterances, including the statements, is made *in vacuo*: sometimes they are used as part of a religious ceremony or observance, sometimes as part of a religious person's deciding what to do in a practical situation; and generally as part of the activities of life. This as a general point is one constantly emphasized by Wittgenstein; and in considering religious language it is, I think, particularly disastrous to ignore it.

But what is religious language? Is there one thing which is religious language? With what is it being contrasted? One thing, certainly, with which we must be wary of contrasting or comparing it is that nebulous and pervasive substance, 'ordinary language'. For one thing ordinary language should be is the language used by most of us in going about our ordinary occasions, and the question of how religious that is, is the question of how religious or professedly religious most of us are; and if some of us all of the time, and most of us most of the time, do not bring talk about God into our affairs, that seems to be at least as much something about us as something about talk about God. This raises the question of dispensing with talk about God, of what is involved in doing without it; and about that I shall later say a little.

So one might ask, 'What are in general the distinguishing marks of a language, of a type of discourse?'; and in attempting an outline of an answer, one can think at once of at least five possible distinguishing marks. For one language might be distinguished from another by the types of logical relation holding within it; by its subject-matter; by its use of technical terms; by its purposes; or, more generally, by the activities with which its use is associated. But it would, of course, be an illusion to suppose that these five, even if they were satisfactorily distinguished one from another, would be competitors for the position of the one and only distinguishing mark of one language from another; it is rather that from the inter-relation of features like these that we can, in particular cases, justifiably claim to distinguish one type of discourse from another. Which of these features one would particularly consider is a question partly of at what level the distinctions are being drawn. If we concentrate on distinctions between the sciences, at a low level of generality, we tend to fasten on distinctions of subject-matter, for we all learn at school that mycology is the study of fungi, and geology the study of rocks, and so on. But it is clear that in doing this we presuppose already a distinction between scientific and other discourse, and between one type of science and another: for not all talk about plants, for instance, and not even all scientific talk about them is botanical talk. Nor will the distinction of subject-matter apply at all to any but the most naïve distinctions between subsidiary sciences, the distinction elsewhere—for instance, between physics and physical chemistry—lying rather in the scope and terminology of the laws formulated and employed.

But it is not to the present purpose, even if it were possible, to attempt the high Aristotelian task of characterizing the differences between organized bodies of knowledge. For while it may be possible to characterize the language used by some type of scientist in his professional work, or to characterize a professional scientific activity to distinguish it from some other professional activity, such as that of the historian, this is beside our purpose, which is to characterize some *unprofessional* uses of language as distinct from others. It does seem clear, however, that when we, as laymen, speculate on the distance of a star, for instance, we are using language differently from when we remark on how beautifully it now shines; and that if we say that the first is a scientific use, part of what we mean is that we are asking a question to which the professional scientist is in the best position to give an answer—it is the sort of question he is asking. So we can at this point reintroduce the idea of a professional use of language, and say at least this much: that some of our utterances ask or involve questions that are properly to be answered by techniques and methods of inquiry professionally employed by some types of specialist, and others do not do this.

This distinction does not apply in any simple way to our investigation of religious language. In the case of religious belief, there is indeed the notion of a person who is a religious authority, but this is something quite different from a scientific authority. For first, the religious authority, if there is one, is at least not just someone who has a good training in the methods of answering certain sorts of question, but someone who *has* the authority to *lay down* what is to be believed or done. Second, the question of whether there is a religious authority even in this sense and, if so, who it is, has been the occasion of violent dispute, and many people have been killed in the attempts to settle it. But the dispute was about the settling of admittedly religious questions, so a reference to the authority cannot come into the characterization of a religious question. Third, even if we were to say that a specialist or professional use of religious language was to be found in its theological use (and about theology I shall have something to say later), it is clear that the relation of religious language to the theologian is different from the relation of scientific language to the scientist; one who speaks scientifically is at least an amateur scientist, but one who speaks religiously is not necessarily a theologian, even an amateur one.

How, then, can we attempt a characterization of religious, or at least of Christian utterances, made in their ordinary occasions by persons other than professional theologians? Could we say, for instance, to take up one of the suggested criteria, that certain language was to be characterized as religious, or more specifically as Christian, by reference to certain practices or observances in the course of which it was used? It is clear that such a reference could not give us enough. For, first, the ceremonies would themselves have to be characterized as religious ceremonies, and if we could do this, we should already have a clearer idea of what religious language was. Second, many religious utterances are made outside such ceremonies; unless everyone speaks religiously only on Sundays. The ceremonies might in the end have to be mentioned in a full characterization of a religious life; but what we are looking for must first be found elsewhere. We have seen that in attempting the characterization of other kinds of language, the distinction of subject-matter, of what the language is used about, did not take us very far; but in the case of religious language perhaps we should after all return to it. For religious language, we might say, is, peculiarly, language about God; and by 'peculiarly' I mean not only that all religious language is language about God, but—

and this seems to me an important point—that all language about God is religious language.

But to say that religious language is language about God immediately raises three related difficulties. For first, the word 'about' is misleading. In the most normal linguistic sense of 'about', it is statements that are about things or persons; but, as we have already seen, not all religious utterances are statements—a prayer, for instance, is not about God, but is addressed to him. If we are to say, then, that religious language is language about God, we have to take 'about' in an extremely wide sense. I take it that it would not be disputed by Christians that every religious utterance in some sense comes back to God, perhaps in the sense that if the purpose of the utterance is to be explained, God has in the end to be mentioned. In something like this sense, the word 'about' must be understood. I think we have to say, further, that the mere occurrence of the *word* 'God' in an utterance does not mean that it is actually about God, and so religious: for the most devout may use the word 'God' in idle phrases and not mean really to speak about God. An utterance which includes the word 'God' must be seriously meant to be about him for it to be actually about him.

Conversely—and this is the second difficulty—it is not the case that the word 'God' *has* to occur in an utterance for it to be religious. We could put this by saying that the distinction of subject-matter cannot be reduced to another distinction I mentioned, that of technical terminology. For there are many utterances that are religious even in the sense of 'Christian' but do not involve the *word* 'God'; and, more widely, there is religious language that is not the language of Christianity. To say that this other religious language is language about God, where 'God' is understood in a Christian sense, is at least to prejudge a particular theological issue, concerning the reference and truth of religious beliefs other than Christianity; but the fact that there is an issue here shows that there must be some characterization of a religion, and so of religious language, which is independent of the beliefs of Christianity. Thus we have to say that our characterization is one not of religious language in general, but of that of Christianity; and this will do for the purposes of this discussion.

But is it even this? For—and this is our third difficulty—saying that Christian language is language about God evidently presupposes the truth of Christianity in a far more radical sense, for it presupposes the existence of God. Therefore it looks as if we have to say that, if God exists, the language of Christianity is language about God, and this seems useless as a characterization of such language. For if we start from the statement of God's existence, the characterization is vacuous unless we already know that statement to be true; but if we know that statement to be true, the characterization appears superfluous. If, however, we start from the evident existence of Christian language, in the sense of language used by Christians, we might be tempted to arrive at the statement of God's existence, and so involve ourselves in a kind of ontological proof which might well be considered suspect. This all illustrates the peculiar relation to religious language of the statement of God's existence, which I have already mentioned. If we were seeking an independent characterization of Christian language these difficulties would be damning; but my present aim is not to do this, but to leave on one side the question of God's existence, and to try to show something about Christian language as used by Christians. So perhaps this rather paradoxical approach will not prove entirely useless. I shall therefore continue to speak of Christian language in a way that involves a suspension of disbelief, the suspension being achieved, evidently, by our own bootstraps. I have suggested, then, that all Christian language is language about God. I suggested before that all language about God is religious language, and this must stand, if it stands at all, in its original form: for to say that all language about God is *Christian* language is to prejudge to the opposite effect the theological issue, which I mentioned before, about the status of other religions.

But here perhaps we have an important point about religious language: for we saw before that, while the language of botany is language about plants, not all language about plants is botanical: for poets, painters, ramblers and so on may also speak of plants, but not botanically. But I want to suggest that all language about God is religious language— one cannot speak non-religiously about God. It does not follow from this that atheists are necessarily speaking religiously: for they are denying the statement 'God exists', and to do this goes behind the presuppositions of the present discussion. It does, however, follow from the present thesis that blasphemy is a kind of religious language, and such it must be—for how else could it give so much offence? Blasphemy is the misuse of religious language: it is to say things about God, or to ask things of him, but the wrong things. Yet there seems to be a sort of paradox here: for the blasphemer says, for instance, that God is wicked, and gives offence by so speaking of the Christian God. But the Christian God is good; so must not the blasphemer be speaking of some other God? But if he does this, he either gives no offence, because it was not of the Christian God that he was speaking offensively, or gives offence only by suggesting that there is another God—a line of argument that might lead to the intriguing conclusion that the only form of heresy is polytheism. Perhaps here we must say something like what we say about disagreements concerning characters in the historical past, that there must be some beliefs, and in the case of religion some practices, in common, between the blasphemer and the orthodox to support the idea that they are both talking about the same God: when Housman referred to 'Whatever fool or blackguard made the world', the description 'He who made the world' provided the place from which the offence was to be taken.

If we say, then, that all language about God is religious language, we have said something about religious language and its subject-matter which distinguishes these from, say, botanical language and its subject-matter. We must next consider one type of utterance which, very importantly, occurs within the body of religious language. I have stressed the fact that religious utterances can be of very various types: statements, commands, prayers, etc.; but it is important also that when we consider only those religious utterances that are statements we find that they as well can be of very various types. Some may be statements directly about the nature of God: 'God is three Persons'; some about historical events: 'God sent the Jews into exile'; some about human nature: 'God has given men free-will'; and so on. That is to say, there are many religious statements that are not just religious—although they are about God, they are about something else as well, something involving the affairs of men.

(5) We must now look more closely at the way in which some religious statements, to confine ourselves to statements, are not purely about God, but about human affairs as well; for by doing this we may become clearer about the range of religious language, its relation to other language and to theology: and we shall return, at long last, to Tertullian's paradox. Because religious statements are so various, many different ones should be discussed, but here I shall mention only one. It raises in itself some well-flogged issues, but these I do not want to discuss: I take this example only to illustrate a more general point.

If a people suffer from occasional failure of their crops and subsequent starvation, a person of rather Old Testament faith might say: 'God makes the crops fail to punish the people for their wickedness.' Such a statement is certainly a religious statement of a sort, but it is also a statement about certain events in human life, and seems in fact to provide an explanation of them; and it seems most clearly to do this, and looks logically like a non-religious explanation of the same events, because it connects with each other two sets of human events—the wickedness of the people and the failure of their crops—with God, as it were, as a middle term. As such, the statement seems also to be in a crude sense falsifiable. For when the agriculturists arrive, the irrigation is improved, the crops never fail, and the people riot in wickedness in the midst of plenty, the man who said that the crops failed because of the people's wickedness notoriously falls into discredit. People will cease to talk of God in explaining the success or failure of the crops: one sort of religious statement will cease to be made. This is the familiar phenomenon of the elimination of religious language from a context; and it has been eliminated here not just because people have come no longer to speak in a certain way—as a people might cease to write some sort of poetry—but because the religious statement, in this particular crude example, was a kind of explanation, and was run over by a rival and better explanation. We mentioned before a distinction of languages in terms of specialists and their techniques, and where a language in the specialist sense can clash with religious language, religious language tends to be driven out; because the specialist techniques give explanations which are recommendations for effective action, and where religious language claimed to do that, it failed: for either it gave an 'explanation' which wasn't an explanation in this sense at all, and provided no recommendation, or it gave an explanation, as in the case of the crops, but a very bad one—for if anyone believes that the best way to prevent natural disasters is to live a better life, he appears to be in error.

It would, of course, be a crude mistake to suppose that these antique considerations could, in some sense, 'disprove religion'. What they do show is that if religious language is used to give certain sorts of explanation, it clashes with a more effective explanation and tends to be eliminated. Such elimination has its effect, too, on the theology of the user of the language. For the religious explanation, as we have seen, was a statement both about certain events and about God; and if these statements are seen to be inapplicable to events, they are seen to be inapplicable also to God. Hence it will come to be seen, perhaps, that certain things cannot be said of God: for instance, that he produces particular disasters as a punishment to men. This in turn leads to new speculation about the nature of God and his relation to the world; so that a change in the possible uses of religious language is connected with a change in the views about the nature of God. This works also the other way; for it would be false to represent the situation as one of the constant retreat of religious language, with consequent trimming of theological doctrine. Undoubtedly this has happened; but there may also be new thoughts about God and new moral views and following from these, changes in what can be said in religious language; as with the coming of Christianity less was said about the anger of God and more about his mercy, and as there comes with a change in religious belief a change in what it is considered proper to ask of him in prayer. An attempt may be made at each stage to co-ordinate the implications of what men think they can and ought to say in religious language, and such co-ordination takes the form of a series of statements about the nature of God: and this is systematic theology.

But although the changes in the range of religious language are not to be described entirely as a retreat, the retreat, as we all know, has its dangers for the religion. The supposed religious explanation that we mentioned was in its rough way one statement about both God and the world; and if all statements that are about both God and the world were to be abandoned, what would be left? Such statements would not need to be, as that one was, explanatory of what goes on in the world, and indeed could not be; but there are connections other than explanations, and some such there must surely be. Wittgenstein said (*Tractatus*, 6.432): '*How* the world is, is completely indifferent for what is higher. God does not reveal himself *in* the world.' But if all talk about God were talk only about God, and all talk about the world talk only about the world, how could it be that God was the God *of* the Christian believer, who is a toiler in the world of men? Would not the views about the nature of God retire more and more away from the world of men: his existence would become like that of the gods of Epicurus, 'far remote and cut off from our affairs' (Lucretius, *de Rerum Natura*, II, 648). And if that happened, it could not be of much concern whether he were there or not.

(6) This is where we return to Tertullian. Tertullian's paradox is relevant to this question both because it is a paradox and because it is about the incarnation. For the incarnation seems to be the point for the Christian faith, where there must essentially be an intersection of religious and non-religious language; it has to be said not only that a certain person was crucified, but that that person was the Son of God. This has to be said, as Tertullian clearly saw, if there is to be a Christian faith; and as he equally clearly saw, it is a paradox. The paradox comes about because, although we must have some statement which says something about both God and the world, when we have it we find that we have something that we cannot properly say. For when God is spoken of in purely religious language, he is said to be a Person eternal and perfect, that is, we do not speak of him in terms appropriate to the temporal and imperfect objects and persons of this life; or if we do, it is notoriously by the analogy of which theologians speak, and therefore imperfectly. For there is no language for God's eternity and perfection beyond the statement of it: it can be said *that* God is eternal and perfect, not *how* he is, for God's eternity and perfection must be beyond the reach of our understanding. So when we come to a statement that is about both God and temporal events, it must be unsatisfactory; for if it were not, we should have adequately described the relation of the temporal events to God in terms appropriate only to the temporal events: and this would mean either that we had described only the temporal events, and left God out, or had described God as a temporal being, which he is not.

The difficulty seems to follow not from the eternality of God by itself, but from the conjunction of this with his perfection as a personal being. For some have held, for instance, that the numbers are eternal objects, although mathematical statements about things in the world can satisfactorily be made. One difference of this case from that of God could be marked by saying that, leaving aside the question of application, the nature of the numbers in themselves can be adequately expressed in the language appropriate to this, the language of pure mathematics, but the nature of God cannot be adequately expressed in any human language. But if we say this, it looks as though we were defending now a different thesis about religious language. For this seems to say that any statement about God, whether we say that there is a relation between God and the world or not, will be unsatisfactory, just because it is made in the words of human language; but the thesis was that it is the fact that there must be a relation between God and the world that made religious language unsatisfactory. But it is not really a different thesis; for it is just the fact that there is at some point such a relation, and a statement or set of statements that tries to express it, that makes religious language elsewhere also unsatisfactory. The question of the applicability of mathematics to the world does not affect the question of the expression of the nature of the numbers by pure mathematics; but the question of the relation of God to the world does affect the question of the expression of the nature of God in religious language. The actual effect is that God is said to be a perfect personal being; because, for instance, prayers are addressed to him, and because he has a Son who was born into the world. The statement of these relations will be itself unsatisfactory, and will involve others that are so: because the concepts required—of fatherhood, for instance, and of love, and of power—are acquired in a human context; the language of these things is a language that grows and is used for the relations of humans to humans. To say that, while this is so, religious language requires merely an extrapolation from the human context,[3] is not to solve the problem but to pose it again. For the extrapolation required is an extrapolation to infinity, and in even trying to give a sense to this we encounter the incomprehensibility. This incomprehensibility Tertullian has brought out in his paradox.

In fact, it is a double paradox: 'because it is shameful', Tertullian says, 'I am not ashamed . . . it is certain, because it is impossible'; that is, there is something that is morally

[3] The connection of this with the idea of an immortal soul will be obvious, and is basically important; but it cannot be pursued here.

outrageous about it, and there is something intellectually outrageous. The two paradoxes can perhaps be seen by considering the incarnation from two different directions. That God, a perfect being, should be willing to be born and to be crucified, is morally astonishing; that this man on a cross should actually be God is intellectually astonishing. Of these, the moral paradox is perhaps the more readily comprehensible to the unbeliever; for this at least he has a model, in the ideas of humility and sacrifice and the finding of the greatest value not where the worldly are looking for it. So the unbeliever, perhaps impertinently, may feel that he sees a point to the moral paradox—that it has turned upside down the standards of what is to be admired and loved. The feeling is easier, perhaps dangerously so, because we have a Christian tradition: to the educated Roman, for instance, it must have been deeply shocking. In this case, too, we can understand to some extent what is in fact the centre of the paradox, Tertullian's saying not just that it was absurd and he believed it, but that he believed it *because* it was absurd. It was just the outrageousness of the crucifixion that pointed the new way one had to try to follow in one's life,[4] and how can any of this be applied to the second part of the paradox, to the fact of the incarnation? How can it be certain, because it is impossible? How can we come to understand, how can we give any sense to, the statement that this man who was crucified was God?

Here I encounter fully a difficulty that has been gradually making itself felt throughout. For the examination of the meaning of statements about the incarnation is, or certainly has been, a task for the theologian; and not being a theologian I cannot feel competent to undertake it. And yet, by starting out to look at religious language I seem to have reached a point at which it is necessary to turn into a theologian. I think we can see the reason for this if we consider what has already been said about religious language and theology. I suggested before that there was a relation between

---

[4] But clearly we cannot properly understand the first part of the paradox unless we understand the second.

what can and cannot be said in religious language and systematic theology; that a contraction or extension in the use of religious language leads to changes in the theology; and that the systematization and explanation of the implications of what can be said about God is a task of theology. But this seems to have two consequences. For the theology examines and changes by reference to the logical consequences of speaking in this or that way about God: if we cannot say 'God sent the drought to punish the people', we must say that God does not intervene in the operations of natural law; if we say this, are we to say that God's power is limited or that he himself is willing not to intervene?—and so on: all traditional problems of theology. And if we say that God was incarnated, are we to say that he changed?—Marcion's problem. But if the raising of these questions is a task of theology, then theology seems to include the logical analysis of religious language; for surely the logical analysis of religious language is just this, asking how, and with what implications, utterances are made in religious contexts. So the philosopher who regards his task as the logical analysis of language and who sets out to examine religious language will find himself, I suspect, as I have done, doing theology. This, which is the first consequence, seems to me not too happy a one for the supposedly independent analyst of religious language. For I have a suspicion that as a theologian he will turn out rather poorly; as some indeed have, supposing themselves to be raising for the first time logical difficulties in Christian language which have in fact in one guise or another been the concern of theologians for centuries. If he is not a believer at all, his case will be worse still, for the utterances are not just *there*, to be pulled to pieces without understanding of the context in which they are used; but can he understand what is the context and importance of a prayer, for instance, unless he understands what it is to pray? Any more than a man can write on the language of aesthetics who cannot see beyond a coloured photograph of 'The Laughing Cavalier'.

The first consequence I suggest, then, of the status of

theology is that there is not much hope for an independent logical analysis of religious language; and the second is its converse: that if one task of theology is such an analysis, theology is committed to making itself coherent, and coherent not only with itself, but outside as well. We have already seen how religious language might retreat from human affairs into an Epicurean remoteness, and that this must not be, if it is to be of any use. So it is that theology must show how religious language can gear into other language, and must lay bare the points of intersection. Yet in the end, it seems, it cannot be successful in this; for the points of intersection, as I have tried to say, must contain something incomprehensible. In saying this, I am only saying what theologians and other religious people have nearly always said; and this shows, what in any case follows from the nature of the thing, that while one should be a believer to be a theologian, being a believer does not eliminate the incomprehensibility. For if the belief is true, it is a belief in an eternal but personal God with a concern for the world, and it is from this that the incomprehensibility follows.

Having just disqualified myself from becoming a theologian, I shall not pursue the question of the logic of statements of the incarnation. I shall say, however, that I think it is clear that one cannot deal with the difficulties in the summary way which, in the work under discussion, Tertullian takes. It will be recalled that Marcion had said that if God had been incarnated, he would have changed; but change involves losing some attributes and gaining others; and God cannot do this. Tertullian briskly replied that what Marcion had said was true of temporal objects, but God is not a temporal object, and that therefore what Marcion said did not apply. But this is to counter one's opponent's move by smashing up the chessboard. For Marcion's objection, we might say, is a point about the logic of the word 'change'; we only understand the word 'change' in terms of the losing or gaining of temporal properties: so how can we use it of God? So something else must be said; but then, again, if the beliefs are true, nothing can be said that will really do.

Tertullian's paradox is also a paradox of theology: it seems committed to what on its own premisses must be an impossible task.

(7) If it is impossible, what is to be done? Here it may be said that we must have faith; and further that the incomprehensibility I have been discussing is not only a necessary feature *of* Christian belief but is necessary *to* it, for it is this that provides a place for faith. Tertullian himself I take, on my freewheeling interpretation, to suggest this in the core of his paradox: it is certain, he says, *because* it is impossible.

We must distinguish here several things that may be meant by having faith. For we may have faith in a person, in the sense that we continue to trust their honesty, good intentions, wisdom, etc., despite perhaps an apparent perversity in their actions. Or we may believe on faith a statement that such-and-such is the case, despite all the evidence being to the contrary. Or we may have faith that such-and-such is what ought to be done, despite the fact that actions and the results of actions involved in carrying out this policy are such as otherwise we should consider wrong. These kinds of faith are, of course, found together: when, for instance, Lenin asked the Bolsheviks before the Revolution to have faith in him, although many of his actions would appear to them inexplicable, he was asking them to believe, among other things, that the aims of the Party would be effected by his policies, although often they seemed to be moving in the opposite direction; and a humanitarian member of the Party had to continue to believe that the Bolshevik state was the right thing to aim at, although murder and misery was involved in doing so. These kinds of faith can be paralleled in the case of religious beliefs; but in the former cases, one thing at least seems to be clear, *what* it is that is being believed; for if a man had faith in Lenin as leader of the Party, or in the belief that his policies would forward the Revolution, he knew what it was he was believing, although he might be able to give very little in the way of rational grounds for believing it. But it is a stranger request to ask someone by faith to believe something that he does not properly understand; for what is it that he is being asked to believe? Faith might be a way of believing something, as opposed to believing it on evidences; but how could it be a way of stepping from what is understood to what is not understood?

Well, it might be said, faith can be a way of coming to understand something; and here it might be suggested that there is an analogy in the arts. 'You think this stuff is all nonsense,' someone might say about a poem; 'but just believe that the poet is not trying to fool you, take it seriously, and you will come to see what it is about.' The eighteenth-century hymnologist, in slightly more utilitarian terms, made something like this point when he wrote: 'O make but trial of his love; Experience will decide How blest are they, and only they, Who in his strength confide.' But the analogy is not good enough. For here again the initial faith is in a belief that is itself comprehensible: the belief that the poem has a meaning, if one can only find it. But in the case of religious belief it is just the belief itself, and not a prior belief about its comprehensibility, that one has, on the position being discussed, to take on faith, in the hope that afterwards it will become clear what it means. Here again I encounter the same difficulty: for if you do not know what it is you are believing on faith, how can you be sure that you are believing anything? And *a fortiori* how can such belief be the means to something else, viz. coming to understand?

In any case, this is beside the point; for the original argument was that certain religious beliefs must be inherently mysterious and remain so, and that it is the part of faith to accept them. My difficulty is that, if the belief is incomprehensible and necessarily so, one cannot see what is being accepted, on faith or otherwise.

St. Paul (I Cor. 1.20 f.) writes: 'Where is the wise? Where is the scribe? Where is the disputer of this world? hath not God made foolish the wisdom of this world? For after that in the wisdom of God the world by wisdom knew not God, it pleased God by the foolishness of preaching to save them that believe ... the foolishness of God is wiser than men';

and in explanation a French commentator, F. Godet, has said: '*l'évangile n'est pas une sagesse, c'est un salut*'—'the Gospel is not an intellectual system, but a salvation'. It might be objected that my argument has been treating Christian beliefs too much as a '*sagesse*', and that a system of coherent and comprehensible beliefs is not to the point. This might be put differently by saying that in the later part of this paper I have neglected what I emphasized in the earlier, that religious language is not used only to make statements but for many other purposes as well; that the statements of religious belief are to be understood only as part of a way of life, which includes prayer and religious observance and so on; and it might be said in connection with the previous discussion that want one chooses, when one chooses to believe, is to live in a certain way, in which the statements play a part. This is true; but the statements do play a part, and the beliefs must be there, and that is the point. We may consider again the possible contraction of religious language, the lessening of its scope, which I discussed before, God may cease to be mentioned in explanations of particular physical events, for instance, or in moral discourse, and they will continue as forms of discourse on their own. What would not make sense would be for God to cease to be mentioned in the forms of religious observance or in prayer, for then they would no longer exist at all. But religious observance and prayer stand for nothing, so far as I can see, unless there are also behind them some beliefs about God, some statements about him: for this would indeed be the end needle point of faith, to pray just to the unknown God, in complete ignorance of whether such an activity had any sense in relation to him or not—or rather, in such ignorance, one would have to say 'it' rather than 'him'; and could one even say that? Something must be believed, if religious activities are not just to be whistling in the dark without even the knowledge that what one is whistling is a tune; and something that connects God with the world of men. But such a connection must involve saying something about God that is interpreted not just in terms of other statements about

God, but in terms of the life of men. If this is said, it seems that it must either be so like some non-religious statement, as in our crude pseudo-scientific example of the failure of the crops, that it can conflict with such a statement, which would make the central religious belief falsifiable and in no way what was required; or it must be sufficiently a statement about God, as it were, for it to be mysterious, as involving an attempt to express the appearance in, or other connection with, a human situation of the infinite perfection of God. If it is inherently mysterious, then it cannot be explained by reason; but to say that it is to be believed on faith, and not by reason, does not face the difficulty: for the question was not how it should be believed, but what was to be believed. If, then, the Christian faith is true, it must be partly incomprehensible; but if it is partly incomprehensible, it is difficult to see what it is for it to be true.

(8) This is only Tertullian's paradox with a converse: *credibile est quia ineptum*; *et quia ineptum, non credibile*. It follows further, if this is the case, that it is difficult to characterize the difference between belief and unbelief. We can indeed point out that the believer *says* certain things which the unbeliever does not say; but we want not just this, but to know *what* it is that the believer believes and the unbeliever does not believe; but this we cannot properly do. But if we cannot adequately characterize the difference between belief and unbelief, we may not be able to characterize the difference between orthodoxy and heresy: for the difference between persons believing different ineptitudes is as obscure as that between those believing one ineptitude and those not believing it. Tertullian, as I mentioned at the beginning, became a heretic.

New College
OXFORD

XI

THE PERFECT GOOD

C. B. MARTIN

In Part I of this chapter I attempt to bring out into the open basic analogies that are implicit in much talk about God. Very often, in such talk, analogies are suggested and, if pressed, withdrawn. It is suggested that the authority of God is *in a way* like the authority of a father, and the goodness of God is *in a way* like the goodness of a man. Such analogies are desired by those who do not wish the nature of God to pass '*all* understanding'. My method is to make the analogies explicit and by degrees to show how they cannot hold.

In Part II I try to show that there is an inherent contradiction in the notion of God's perfect nature. The attempt to avoid such contradiction and the subtle ways in which difficulties are obscured are brought out by examining carefully relevant analogical cases. The classical distinction between the human and divine natures of Christ is shown to be of no help. The following quotation may serve to introduce the discussion.

'The problems raised by Ethics find their solution in Religion, and it is here that the inner connection of the two comes to light. For the religious consciousness states explicitly the implications of the moral consciousness: it affirms the reality of an Ultimate Good in the form of a supreme and personal Will, who is the Ground and End of the natural and the spiritual order of things. The God who is ethical Ground of the world guarantees the validity and persistence of the ethical values; and it is in and through man's relation to God, the perfect Good, that the ethical ideal can be transcended and completed.' (*The Philosophy of Religion*, Galloway, pp. 202–3.)

I

Let us imagine conversations of the following sorts:

A. MARY. 'What *ought* we to do about Mother? We've
     thought and thought about it and there just doesn't
     seem any way to decide.'
   JANE. 'I swear I don't know what is the right thing to
     do.'
   MARY. 'How I wish Father were still alive. He would
     know.'
   JANE. 'Somehow he always seemed to know what was
     right.'
   MARY. 'Yes, he did, except towards the end when he
     began to fail so fast.'

B. MARY. 'Even though Father is gone, I feel that I have
     to do what is right just because that is what he wants.'
   JANE. 'I know what you mean. That feeling is even
     stronger than when he was alive.'
   MARY. 'Yes, and if I didn't know that he was somehow
     there I don't think that anything would matter.'

C. BETTY. 'But I don't see why I ought to do this and not
     that.'
   MOTHER. 'Because Father says so—that's why.'

The use of 'Will of God' is like and unlike the use of
'Father' in the above three cases. I shall talk about these
cases in themselves and then to relate them to theological
cases.

Case A

Mary and Jane have tried to reach a moral decision, and
because the choice is a very complex one and there is no
obvious way in which to decide, they feel at a loss. They
remember Father's superior moral vision and wish that he
were there to help them make the decision, because 'he
always seemed to know what was right'.

Time after time they found that his decisions were wiser
than theirs. They had good reason, were justified, in trusting
him. Of course, Father could be wrong and towards the

15   213

end of his life, when his faculties were failing, they found that he often was.

Case B

Mary and Jane remark that since Father's death they have come more and more to feel compelled to do what is right because that is what he wants them to do. It isn't just that they feel they ought to behave in certain ways now because if he were alive that is how he *would* want them to behave. It is more than that. It is that the strength of this compulsion comes from their belief that in some sense he still, even now, wants them to behave in this way. Their allegiance is to Father dead yet somehow alive. The unseen guiding hand and the unheard approval or disapproval are more powerful than the seen and heard. They also feel as if the difference between doing right and not doing right would not matter or concern them if they didn't believe that Father still wanted them to do right. 'What is right' has become (by induction) closely tied up with 'what Father wants us to do'. The tie-up has come about by induction because Father has so often been right, so that when asked why they say something is morally right, they might give as a reason 'Father says so' or 'Father wants us to do this'. This would be a good or bad reason just in so far as Father has shown himself wise in the past about moral issues. After his death, they still want to have this reason ('Father says so' or 'Father wants us to do this'), though, of course, they no longer can hear his judgment.

Case C

Betty is objecting that she sees no reason why she should act according to another ethical choice. Mother's answer ('Because Father says so—that's why') is supposed to provide that reason. If this answer is interpreted quite literally and Betty is intelligent, she will answer, 'But that isn't any reason at all. Father's saying so doesn't make it right.' Mother's answer, however, isn't meant literally. It may mean a number of things such as the following: 'You ought to obey

Father.' 'Do as you are told.' 'There isn't any particular reason why, except that Father wants you to do it.'

These three cases must now be related to theological cases. God is totally different from Father. The difference will come out as each case is examined.

Case A

Mary and Jane feel in need of justification for choosing one alternative instead of another in a difficult moral choice before them. Father could have provided that justification because his decisions had always proven wise, therefore his judgment would have amounted to justification.

The situation is different with theologians and God. Justification, by means of reference to God, is sought not only for difficult ethical judgments ('Pacifism is right') but also for obvious ethical judgments ('Lying is wrong'); indeed, *all* ethical statements equally require justification of this sort. The justification must be peculiarly general. It will be seen later what the nature of its generality is.

The nature of the justification in terms of 'Father says so' or 'Father wants us to do this' depends upon the success and failure of Father's judgment in the past. The nature of the justification in terms of 'It is the will of God' does not depend upon the success and failure of God's judgment in the past, because God is defined as perfect. God can't be wrong, so investigations as to whether he is right or wrong are irrelevant. If God is perfect then nothing *could* count as evidence against his rightness. If anything *could* count as evidence against his rightness then the justification of ethical statements in terms of God's will is not absolute.

Case B

In this case Father is as close to God as he can be. He is dead. Yet there is all of the difference. In a way, statements about Father dead are no closer in their logic (in their use) than are statements about Father alive. With Father dead, he seems more infallible than ever. Mary and Jane have the glowing memory of his wisdom and he is no longer around to be wrong. When (e.g. in dreams) Father now makes

215

known to them his judgment, they test whether it was really Father who 'spoke' to them by the wisdom and success of the judgment. If it proves unwise then it couldn't have been Father. If it proves wise then it was Father, and they have something of the reason (Father's wisdom of the past and his saying something is right or wrong) they had for a moral decision when he was alive. Father's 'speaking' in dreams is like God 'speaking' in prayer. In both cases neither can 'speak' evil counsel, for then it wouldn't really be Father in the dream or God in the prayer, it would just seem so. It almost seems that Father has been deified. But, no, the difference between him and God is as unbridgeable as ever. There is still a way of proving Father wrong—he is not perfect.

Imagine that Mary and Jane dreamt that Father spoke to them saying, 'You ought to tell Mother of your plans for marriage, for she must be encouraged to live her life according to new patterns. Protecting her as you have done only makes her lack courage.' They might, on the basis of this dream, think they ought to do this, because it is what Father says to do. They will be struck by the similarity of the moral wisdom of Father in the dream with the moral wisdom of Father when alive. Imagine, however, that they dreamt that Father spoke to them saying, 'Lying is never wrong; take advantage of others or they will take advantage of you.' They would not, on the basis of this dream, think they ought to do this because it is what Father says to do. They will be so struck by the dissimilarity of the evil counsel of Father in the dream with the moral wisdom of Father when alive, that they will not count this counsel as coming in any way from Father. Or say that they accept the counsel of Father in the first dream as coming in some way from Father and act in accordance with it. Circumstances which should have been anticipated then prove the counsel to have been foolish. They would then say that it couldn't have come from Father though it seemed at the time to do so. How well the wisdom and right judgment of Father dead are protected! How strong the faith of the daughters! But it is only when nothing *could* count against their confidence that it is of a logical sort.

Now, what if Father's diary were found by Mary and Jane some time after his death? In this diary, in Father's handwriting, are written accounts of the most evil exploits and also descriptions of how he has been exploiting the trust of his wife and daughters all through the years, and evil maxims are suggested as the rules by which all ought to live. Further still, it comes out that Father had committed bigamy. The daughters are shocked and disillusioned beyond description. Their faith and confidence in Father are completely destroyed, and never again will they give as reason for the rightness of an action that 'Father says so' or 'Father wants us to do it'. Losing this reason, which had seemed so admirable and sure in the past, may seem like losing *all* reason for judging between right and wrong. *This feeling of ethical defeatism would be inconsistent, however, because Mary and Jane are able to judge between right and wrong apart from what Father says and wants, because their final disillusionment comes as a result of judging what Father says and wants as wrong.* Yet something very precious and certain has been shown to be past and false. The loss may well be demoralizing.

Now, it is not in any way essential to our argument that the things we have imagined should actually happen. In order to understand the use of the statements made about Father by Mary and Jane it is enough to keep to the world of imagination. The diary doesn't have to be found. Instead, we can ask Mary and Jane how finding such a diary *would* affect the way in which they talked about Father. The answers they give make clear the way in which they *are* talking about Father. If they say that finding such a diary would dissuade them from their previous beliefs about Father, then this shows that even in the absence of the diary their beliefs about Father are such that they *can* be doubted —something like the diary *could* prove their present beliefs false though nothing of this sort, as a matter of fact, happens.

We have seen how Father, even as dead, is not secure

enough from discredit for the strict equivalence of '*X* is right' with 'Father says *X* is right' and 'Father wants us to do *X*'. But, of course, Father is not God. God is totally different. He is the *Ultimate* Ground and Justification of Value. It is time now to turn to the last case.

Case C

    BETTY. 'But I don't see why I ought to do this and not that.'

    MOTHER. 'Because Father says so—that's why.'

    BETTY. 'But that isn't any reason at all. Father's saying so doesn't make it right.'

Betty's literal interpretation of Mother's remark works as a kind of escape from the disciplinary force and meaning of the remark. If Mother had said instead, 'Father knows best', Betty could still have taken this literally by answering, 'Father can be wrong like the rest of us. He doesn't know everything.' Again she has avoided the disciplinary force and meaning by an obstinately literal interpretation. Mother's only recourse is to say what she has meant all along—'Do as you are told', 'You ought to obey Father.'

Father alive and dead is fallible. He 'can be wrong like the rest of us'. He isn't God. Just because he is fallible, 'can be wrong', 'doesn't know everything', he is totally different from God. Finally, we come to talk about God, but it couldn't have been done without the talk about Father, for we come to know what God is by coming to know what he isn't.

God is the 'Ultimate Good in the form of a supreme and personal Will'.[1] God is 'the perfect Good'.[2]

This may be put in more logical form in the following way:

A. It is one's ethical duty to love one's neighbour as oneself.

B. It (the moral judgment expressed by A) is in accordance with the will of God.

If B is asserted then A must also be asserted. The phrase

[1] Galloway, *The Philosophy of Religion*, p. 202.
[2] *Ibid.*

'in accordance with the will of God' works in this way like 'is valid'.

If B is denied then A must also be denied.

The Good is defined in terms of God's will. Yet this is not enough, for it must be added that God's will is Perfect. Being 'perfect' it cannot but be 'good'. This is how moral values are established in 'the ultimate constitution of things'.[3] But what have we come to? Absolute justification and absolute perfection; circularity and logical vacuity.

The good is defined in terms of God's will.

God's will (as perfect) is defined in terms of the good.

Nothing in the world of fact or the world of imagination can disturb this equivalence—it rests secure in the cold and barren world of logic. No wonder we found such difference between Father and God.

The circle must be broken. When it is asked, 'what is good?' the answer must be more than 'The will of God'. When it is asked, 'What is the will of God?' the answer must be more than 'The perfect good'. The concepts cry out for content and application. And, of course, this is supplied. 'The Word was made flesh.' The Father analogy with its implications of uncertainty and fallibility, as we have seen, does not apply to the perfect, infallible God. But, it does apply to Christ!

There are answers to the question 'What is the will of God?' other than the circular answer 'The perfect good'. The Bible is the revelation of the divine will and the life and person of Christ is the embodiment and fulfilment of that will. Answers might be, 'Read the Bible, pray, and learn of Christ.'

Christ lived and taught on earth. He was seen and heard by men. Some of these men came to think of him as never being wrong. His moral wisdom was proven in case after case. When we read of him we may be struck by the consistency of his ethical profundity. But can we imagine cases in which we would have reason to lose our confidence in him? Is there anything comparable to Father's diary?

[3] H. H. Farmer, *Towards Belief in God*, p. 200.

Though highly imaginary, it is conceivable that manuscripts should be discovered that proved beyond reasonable doubt that Christ was some sort of mad villain. This is not a self-contradiction. As long as these frightful imaginings did not become fact, Christ the good man would be safe from censure. But Christ is God—the Father, *the Son*, and the Holy Ghost! Imaginings that never happen do not upset the reputation of men, but it must be inconceivable that God should err. Christ is used to bridge not only the world of heaven and the world of earth, but the world of logic and the world of fact. This will be made clear in what follows.

It is sometimes said that doing evil is inconsistent with God's perfect nature. But men go against their nature occasionally; why is it inconceivable of God? The answer is that we have so defined the concept of 'God' and 'God's nature' that evil action should not be predicable of God. But let us move slowly. A detailed examination of this gives the opportunity for putting the point of the argument concerning God's infinity in a new way.

II

'Therefore, everything that does not imply a contradiction in terms, is numbered amongst those possible things, in respect of which God is called omnipotent; whereas whatever implies contradiction does not come within the scope of divine omnipotence, because it cannot have the aspect of possibility. Hence it is better to say such things cannot be done than to say that God does them. . . . To sin is to fall short of a perfect action; hence to be able to sin is to be able to fall short in action, which is repugnant to omnipotence. Therefore it is that God cannot sin, because of His omnipotence.' (St. Thomas Aquinas, *Summa Theologica*, Q. XXV, Art. 3.)

'You cannot be corrupted, You cannot lie, You cannot make that which is true to be false. You cannot make that which has been done not to have been done and so forth'. (St. Anselm, *The Proslogion*, Ch. VIII.)

Unfortunately, Protestant writers have nothing clear to

say on this subject. Typical of their failure to see the problem is the following passage:

> . . . omnipotence means only that he is wholly competent to achieve what he wills and intends; it does not mean that he can do anything that any clever person likes to 'think up'. To silly conundrums such as whether God, being omnipotent, can tie a knot that he cannot untie, the only right answer has always been—and it is not an evasion— 'we are not interested'.
>
> Perhaps the best way to realize that these great thoughts of God are not meaningless, though they baffle the understanding—one way too, to get away from the dullness and deadness of the merely abstract statement we have been making—is to come 'at them once again through the personal relationship in which we ourselves stand to God, and through which God reveals himself to us.' (H. H. Farmer, *God and Man*, p. 111.)

Imagine a conversation between Mary and James in which they are discussing human frailty and James cites an exception to the general rule and says of John, 'It is his nature to be kind.'

MARY answers, 'Yes, but we can imagine all too readily how even John could go against his nature.'

James may resist this in two ways, one of which is unnatural and analogous to theological talk of God's nature.

The natural resistance might take the following form:

JAMES. 'No, I don't think that I can imagine at all readily that John should go against his nature. It seems to me just inconceivable that John should ever do anything unkind.'

MARY. 'Oh, I suppose it really is terribly unlikely, but all the same we can imagine that he should have been brutal in the past or be brutal in the future.'

JAMES. 'Good heavens, if that is all you mean, then just because we can imagine this of John, it doesn't in the least reflect upon his character or throw any doubt on the fact that it is his nature to be kind. I thought at first that you meant by "imagine all too readily" that his being unkind was somehow likely, and this just isn't true. After all, we can deny that he is unkind, has been unkind, will be unkind, and still be able to imagine what it would be like for him to be unkind, to go against his nature.'

Now let us have James make the unnatural resistance to Mary's suggestion. The dialogue can begin in the same way.

JAMES. 'No, I don't think that I can imagine at all readily that John should go against his nature. It seems to me just inconceivable that John should ever do anything unkind.'

MARY. 'Oh, I suppose it really is terribly unlikely, but all the same we can imagine that he should have been brutal in the past or be brutal in the future.'

JAMES. 'It isn't a matter of likely-unlikely at all. I said it was inconceivable and that is what I meant. If he did something brutal he wouldn't *really* be John, and even imagining brutality of him is impossible, because what you imagine couldn't apply to the real John.'

Connected with this last speech of James is a further alternative. He might have said the following:

JAMES. 'It isn't a matter of likely-unlikely at all. I said it was inconceivable and that is what I meant. I don't say that John might not do something or be imagined to do something that had the *appearance* of brutality, but whatever he does or can be imagined to do would *really* be kind no matter how it *appeared*.'

This position of James might at first appear to be that of a man whose faith in a friend is abnormally strong. This, however, is not so, and cannot be so if the case is to be analogous to the theological one. Yet, it is impossible to mark off any boundary line between unshakable faith and logical certainty or vacuity.

The statement made by James is: 'John cannot in fact or in imagination be said to go against his nature and be unkind.'

He may keep this statement logically secure in two ways, even in the face of the strongest opposition.

MARY. 'Look, let us both agree that John is in fact kind by nature, but still it is consistent with this assertion to imagine him to have been otherwise than he in fact is, for this imagining doesn't affect what we say he is actually like. Though we assert that John is by nature kind we can imagine that he might have been unkind, that is, beaten his wife, starved his children and done all sorts of unkind things. This kind of supposing needn't worry you, James. It doesn't in the least denigrate the actual character of John, for this sort of thing can consistently be said of the most angelic, perfectly blameless creature conceivable.'

The above comment by Mary is the strongest opposition to the statement made by James. The two ways in which he keeps his statement logically secure are the following:

(1) Deny the subject. If an opposing statement made by Mary is 'John might have (though he didn't) beaten his wife, starved his children and so been unkind', then James may deny that this supposition could be made of John.

(2) Deny the predicate. James can deny that any acts predicted, even in supposition, of John could be called unkind. They would only *seem* so, *appear* so.

In the first alternative James uses the name 'John' not to apply to a creature, but to apply to a concept such that it is inconsistent with the concept 'unkind'. Confusion arises because as long as unkindness is not asserted of him, it appears that 'John' is not a concept but a person. It is only when the possibility of predicating unkindness in fact or in imagination of John is denied that we discover that for James the name 'John' applies to a concept, not a man.

In the second alternative James uses 'kindness' and 'unkindness' in such a way that when he applies 'kindness' to John it is not used to mark off instances of kindness from instances of unkindness. Again, this monstrous use is not discoverable when James uses 'kindness' of John when John is in fact kind. It is only when the possibility of predicating unkindness in fact or in imagination of John is denied by James that we discover that James fails to mark off 'kindness' from 'unkindness' as applied to John and therefore

223

leaves his statement vacuously, certainly true, and consequently it does not describe in any way the character of
John though it has the form of doing so.

But is the situation really as pure, unalloyed and clearcut
as this account makes it appear to be? No, it is not, but from
this it does not follow that the account is incorrect. The case
must be examined more closely.

We have granted that John is in fact kind by nature. It has
been shown how very differently James thinks of the 'kindness' of John and we have gone so far as to accuse James of
using this work vacuously when he applies it to John. This
accusation has not been in impulse, it has been carefully
worked out. Yet something seems not exactly right about it.
It smacks of lack of sympathy and of classificationism. The
statement has been fitted rather uncomfortably into a box
labelled 'Logically Vacuous'. James may well complain.
Let us hear him out.

He may say, 'You fail to emphasize our agreement. We
both agree that John is in fact kind by nature. If we were to
write testimonials as to his character, we should not write
differently. Yet you say that my statement does not really
describe his character at all. We both use our statements to
approve of John. Yet you say that my statement is logically
vacuous. After you get through describing my statement, I
no longer recognize it as my own. You don't seem to be
aware of the possibility of a man having unlimited faith in a
friend.'

This is an example of how sensitive statements are to
philosophical treatment. As we get more and more clear
about a statement it seems to change. This is inevitable. But
unfortunately there is more to it than this in our present case,
for James's statement has not been seen clearly enough.

It is not that James talks in a completely different way
from Mary about the kindness of John. The point is rather
that he does not talk in one sort of way, but in two ways at
once. Each way must be brought out by a different procedure. I want to suggest that there is a similarity here to
theological talk about Christ.

Remember, John really is kind by nature and we are allowing no doubt about this.

James speaks and acts like Mary in many ways concerning the matter of John's character. He approves heartily of him, writes testimonials, holds him up as a good example and desperately tries to imitate him and urges his children and others to imitate him. He has faith in John in the sense that when others may doubt his kindness he does not; he does not believe bad reports, slander, gossip. His faith is strong, but as seen from this perspective only it is not religious.

But James's 'unlimited faith' has another aspect which we have already treated in some detail. This aspect is revealed by the peculiar way in which James reacts to certain suppositions we make of John. We assert that though John is by nature kind, he might have been different, and could (though we assert he won't) be unkind in the future. This is not an attack upon John's actual character, but it *is* an attack upon James's concept of the nature or character of John. We have shown how this logical security has led to logical vacuity. The 'faith' of James is 'ultimate' indeed.

The uneasy and impossible combination of the two ways of talking is what makes James's 'faith' in John religious in kind. It embraces the identical paradox to that embraced by theologians in their account of the incarnate Christ. We must turn once again to God and his incarnation. The analogy must already be clear.

All seems to be well as long as the goodness of Christ is not really called in question. Theologians admit freely enough that if the goodness of Christ is in doubt then his divinity must be in doubt and, of course, if the goodness of Christ is denied then it must also be denied that he is God. However, they think that there is nothing contradictory remaining if the goodness of Christ is asserted without qualification and he is called God, the 'perfect good'. I have been at pains to point out that a contradiction of an irresoluble sort remains still. The contradiction is that Christ can be conceived to have been other than he was, that is, not good, yet as God it is inconceivable that he should have been not good.

But is the contradiction resolved by the theological device of the dual nature of Christ? Let the suggestion be that the human-finite nature of Christ is that which could have been otherwise and that the divine-infinite nature of Christ is that which could not have been otherwise. What is accomplished by this move?

We have assumed Christ's human nature to be good. This is supposed to allow for the consistent addition of the perfectly good divine nature. This divine nature cannot be asserted if the goodness of the human nature is called in question. But, now, just what does this divine nature add?

It is that about Christ, when we assert his human nature to be good, that could not have been otherwise. But *what* about him couldn't have been otherwise? We can conceive to have been different from what it in fact was, every thought, word, action, capacity and disposition. Let the divine nature express itself and by that expression contradict itself. Let the divine nature keep itself from all expression and by that sublime reticence say nothing to us. There is the choice between self-contradiction and vacuity. The charm of Christ has been thought to be his union of the human and the divine. We have considered the logical nature of the impossibility of such a union.

University of Adelaide
AUSTRALIA

XII

DEMYTHOLOGIZING AND THE PROBLEM OF VALIDITY

RONALD W. HEPBURN

It might seem as if the title I have chosen were either bombastic and empty, or claimed nothing less than the entire field of myth and the Bible as its theme. For does not every theologian aim at producing *valid* theology and is not 'the problem of validity' only another name for the theologian's problems as a whole? Yet it is all too easy in theology to muffle this question of validity, for all its importance, to veil and camouflage inadvertently the logical nature of what is being undertaken. Nothing is harder than to write so transparently that the reader is kept aware of exactly what claims are essential to the validity of the doctrine or theory concerned, and what are subsidiary, carefully distinguishing the logical from the psychological, the historical from the metaphysical—at every stage. This is far more than a peripheral matter of expositional technique: for to allow the logical structure of a theology to shine through its presentation is not only to prepare the way for assessing its validity; it is to have commenced assessment already. In this field clarification and verification constantly merge into one another. To see clearly what a theology demands is to begin seeing how plausible or implausible are those demands.

This is, of course, true not only of theology. If a piece of empirical science is dressed up to look like *a priori* mathematics, we shall be tempted to use quite inappropriate methods for testing its truth or falsity—looking for internal consistency in the use of symbols instead of conformity with a range of phenomena in the outside world. A mistaken account of ethics (say a crude subjectivism) can suggest irrelevant tests for moral rightness and wrongness (such as the occurrence of certain kinds of sentiments). But however widely spread this danger, the theologian is exposed to it in a unique way. Notoriously, his utterances about God put constant severe strain upon the vocabulary with which he is compelled to work: the lines of communication between the senses which he gives his words and ordinary use are ever on the point of being ruptured—a truth which he may learn from Kant as well as from Wittgenstein. It is, therefore, of paramount importance that he should show as far as he can what functions his language is performing—when literal, when symbolical, when descriptive, when evaluative.

In what follows, I want to ask how far the contributors to the recent debate on demythologizing have been alert to this problem of meaning and validity. How far, in particular, does Bultmann's *New Testament and Mythology* reveal an awareness of them? If my conclusions are unsympathetic, this must not be taken as evidence of a sceptical indifference to the subject itself. The relations between historical fact, mythological statement and existential concern are inescapably fundamental to the New Testament study of our day. It is rather my sense of their ultimacy which prompts this criticism of the procedures employed by one major protagonist in the debate.

The pith of my criticism is simply this: that Bultmann's methods and terminology tend to insulate his claims against the possibility of verification or falsification (using these words in their widest sense); that this happens not in conjunction with a reasoned assertion that theological disagreements are by nature unsettleable, but *by default* through ambiguities and confusions in crucial terms, which effectively prevent the question of validity being raised as it ought to be raised and even deny the language whereby this could be done.

My remarks may be grouped under five headings.

1. *The Definition of Myth*

Any instability in the concept of myth itself would be found to imperil the discussion at point after point. Yet Bultmann neither offers a satisfactory definition, nor abides by the definition he does offer. 'Mythology', he writes (p. 10)[1] 'is the use of imagery to express the other worldly in terms of this world and the divine in terms of human life, the other side in terms of this side.' By his own test this definition itself is partly couched in mythological language, which is cause enough for bewilderment. And it is sufficiently wide in its scope to include all pictorial, analogical and symbolical speech whatever. Now in another place Bultmann concedes that *all* utterance about God is analogical, and therefore (if the first definition is to stand) irreducibly mythological. Bultmann cannot mean this. For if it were true, it would make demythologizing a logically impossible task; and the contrast he constantly wishes to make between 'mere mythology' and authentic existentialist interpretation would be robbed of its basis. Perplexity does not end here: in a discussion on the expression 'act of God' (p. 196 f.) Bultmann decides against calling this 'mythological language', on the ground that 'mythological thought regards the divine activity . . . as an interference with the course of nature', and 'acts of God', to Bultmann, are not of this sort. Therefore to speak of such acts is not to speak mythologically, but *analogically*. This conclusion, however, violates his original definition of myth in two ways at once:

(1) Bultmann is saying: 'the expression "act of God" is not mythological language, but analogical', whereas on his definition this antithesis could not be made, since 'myth' is there plainly the 'genus' word, with 'analogy', 'pictorial image', etc., as species.

(2) The mythological has been redefined as that which depicts God as 'interfering in the course of nature'; while the first definition concerned itself only with myth as a form of language and said nothing at all about the *content* of any particular myths.

[1] References are to pages in *Kerygma and Myth*, edited Bartsch (S.P.C.K., 1953).

The contrast mentioned a moment ago between 'just mythology' and 'existentialist interpretation' (p. 110) reminds us that Bultmann frequently uses 'myth' and its cognates as pejoratives. For example: Bultmann may well be right when he claims that the New Testament myths are *in origin* Jewish and Gnostic. But he goes on to say that they are also Jewish and Gnostic 'in essence'—a very different claim (pp. 3, 15). 'Identical in essence with *X*' implies 'containing no more than *X*', 'of the same value as *X*'. Part of Bultmann's failure to justify his transition from 'in origin' to 'in essence' may be due to just this pejorative innuendo carried by 'myth' which militates against the scrutiny and evaluation of each individual myth (and modification of myth) on its own merits.

Here, then, in the definition of 'myth', is one point at which greater logical rigour is urgently required, if the discussion is to be set on a secure foundation.

2. *The Flight from the Evidential*

Bultmann's reluctance to face problems of validity manifests itself in a recurrent pattern of argumentation, which could be schematized in roughly the following way:

(a) A fact or argument appears, which *prima facie* is hostile to the validity of the Christian position;

(b) Bultmann turns aside from its negative evidential implication; and

(c) transforms the hostile fact in such a way as to make it yield positive support for a modified and freshly secured theological view.

The suspicion grows, as one reads, that no evidence at all would be admitted as finally detrimental to Bultmann's position. If he actually believes this (and it is not an *absurd* belief to hold), it ought to be clearly exhibited as the crucial tenet it undoubtedly would be, and argued for as such.

Two simple examples may bring out this pattern of thought.

(1) On page 11 of *Kerygma and Myth* Bultmann describes how antinomies are generated by conflicting imagery in the

New Testament. 'The virgin birth is inconsistent with the assertion of [Christ's] pre-existence', so is the creation doctrine with talk about the 'rulers of this world', and the law as God-given with the statement that it came from the angels. To Bultmann all this implies, 'Rise, therefore, *above* the mythological.'

(2) Christ failed to return in the way the disciples had at first expected. We ought, says Bultmann, to profit from their mistake; recognizing that the Last Things are mythological conceptions, not historical.

In both cases a difficulty is metamorphosed into a theologically acceptable 'truth'. But in each case too Bultmann has side-stepped an equally important sceptical option—without giving adequate reasons for so doing. In the first case we might say: 'Conflicting views? then so much the worse for the reliability of the documents!'; and in the second case: 'Jesus did not come, because the disciples were simply and tragically wrong about him.' Plausibility can be given to evasive moves like these in individual instances, but only so long as the by-passed sceptical options are never gathered together and faced *cumulatively* as a challenge, more or less formidable, to the Christian position.

One may go further: the whole category of the evidential is repeatedly pushed aside by Bultmann as of no importance, or, worse, as a snare. He speaks scornfully of the 'provable': 'It is precisely its immunity from proof which secures the Christian proclamation against the charge of being mythological' (p. 44). The language of myth is concrete and pictorial, concerned with stones rolling away and men rising into the sky, suggesting in many cases events that might be captured by the camera. Not so the truths of non-mythological Christian belief: for to Bultmann the removal of Christianity from the realm of myth up-grades it in value. So much so, that the reader is prepared to accept, if he is off-guard, that to remove it from the realm of the 'provable' must also be an act of up-grading, to be welcomed like a release from a long-standing bondage. But in this way Bultmann has again omitted to argue for a vital proposition, namely that absence of evidence does not disqualify a religion from being acceptable by reasonable men, or that 'unprovable' here is not equivalent to 'baseless' or 'unfounded', as it undeniably is in many contexts.

In speaking of faith Bultmann makes this turn of thought particularly plain: 'It is impossible to prove that faith is related to its object . . . it is just here that its strength lies' (p. 201). Once more the absence of evidence is taken as a commendation. For if the relation of faith to God *were* provable, then, says Bultmann, God would be reduced to the status of one item among others in the furniture of the universe: and only 'in that realm [are we] justified in demanding proof'. Unfortunately this latter sentence begs the question. It assumes that we know already—have had convincingly shown to us—that there are in fact two 'realms'—a belief which should surely appear as part of the end-product, not as the initial presupposition of a reasoned theology. Again, a sceptical option demands attention but does not receive it; that is, 'If God's being cannot be established, there *may* be no God'.

The furthest Bultmann goes in this extraordinary and fascinating flight from the evidential is to transform the failure to obtain proof into an aggressive refusal to accept any *possible* proof. Thus he rejects I Cor. 15.3–8 as evidence for the resurrection, not explicitly on critical grounds, but in his own words—'that line of argument is fatal *because* it tries to adduce a proof for the *Kerygma*' (p. 112; my italics).

This trend of thought, yoked with his critical standpoint, leads Bultmann to speak evasively and ambiguously of the Biblical narratives. As Schleiermacher could say of the ascension only that 'something happened', so Bultmann says of the resurrection with similar cloudiness, 'I have no intention whatever of denying the uniqueness of the first Easter Day' (p. 111), selecting a vocabulary which permits the retention of a reverent attitude but leaves altogether unclear the nature of the event towards which the attitude is adopted, and therefore leaves equally unclear what procedure could show whether the attitude was an *appropriate* one or not.

An avowed historical agnosticism about the events of
Jesus' life would be quite unexceptionable. What one finds in
Bultmann, however, is something more positive and dogmatic. At many crucial points he casts about in his mind
for an interpretation of an event which he thinks adequate
to the existential seriousness of Christianity and procedes to
read back his interpretation into the original documents
however these may resist the treatment, and however many
critical questions may be begged. It is one thing to say, 'I
have no idea what happened at the ascension, but it provides
an excellent symbol for Christ's oneness with the Father':
quite another thing to say, 'The ascension did not happen—
could not have happened: it is an excellent symbol, etc., etc.'
To speak of the 'unique and final revelation of God in
history' may be misleading as Bultmann claims, in its
tendency to lead to thinking of that revelation as a *revelatum*,
an event which happened once in the remote past, to which
we have access only by historical documents; in Bultmann's
words, 'something which took place in the past and is now
an object of detached observation' (p. 111). But anxiety on
this score has gone too far when it results in a fight against
history itself; and it cannot be invoked as justification for
abandoning the evidential as such.

It is hardly an exaggeration to say that Bultmann would
feel an *embarrassment* at the very possibility that certain
events might after all have taken place just as the documents
narrate them. Doubtless a Christian ought not to see a
miracle as a divine conjuring trick, but should interpret the
miraculous in personal and moral categories. But that does
not give Bultmann warrant to say, 'the God of revelation
is the God of judgment and forgiveness, *not* the Cause of
abnormal phenomena' (p. 121; my italics). It may also be
true that in the believer's passage from death into life
'outwardly everything remains as before, but inwardly his
relation to the world has been radically changed' (p. 20),
but Bultmann is over-eager to make this inner invisible
event the paradigm not only of conversion but of the New
Testament message in its entirety, for the most momentous

divine activity still leaves 'undisturbed' the 'closed weft of history' (p. 197). Can he also consistently say, 'It is indeed part of the *skandalon* that ... our salvation is One who is involved in all the relativity of history' (p. 111)? For he is as anxious to *escape* the level of the verifiable as the logical positivists were to remain within it, in making verifiability the touchstone of meaningfulness. Both are guilty through excess of zeal: the positivists in their belief that any simple verification procedure could prove adequate to every possible experience, Bultmann in refusing to make plain what states of affairs would be incompatible with Christian belief, or just how different the world would have to be before belief would have to be declared senseless.[2]

The historian's task would be impossible, were he forbidden to fill out imaginatively the reconstruction of events to which his sources bear witness. Yet at what point legitimate interpretation fades into fanciful and irresponsible refashioning of the past is often a hard question. We have no guarantee that any ingenious device we may introduce into a production of Shakespeare was actually present in the poet's mind when he wrote his play; how much more uncertain is the assurance of Bultmann that the demythologized, existentialist account of the New Testament proclamation does not in fact distort that proclamation, for all its philosophical attractiveness.

3. *Fact and Language*

A theology which aims at being logically transparent must carefully distinguish issues of fact from matters of linguistic convenience. Now, the very word 'demythologize' strongly suggests a venture in translation, the substitution of more literal language for pictorial and symbolic language. Yet this is thoroughly deceptive. If the ascension, say, is amenable to demythologizing, that is to say something not only about the language in which the 'event' is described, but to decide also about the actual status of the event itself, to deny

2 Compare the *University* discussion in 'Theology and Falsification', Ch. **VI** (i) above.

that Jesus did in fact rise into the air. And no linguistic investigation could lead by itself to such conclusions. Put it differently: to qualify for mythhood a statement must be (on Bultmann's definition) actually about 'the other world' or 'the other side'. The process of demythologizing must accordingly consist of at least two phases, of which the first is the recognition that the scriptural account concerned is mythological in nature; while the second phase re-interprets its substance non-mythologically. But the question whether any particular narration *is* mythical cannot be settled by Bultmann or anyone else while acting in the capacity of *translator*. An event such as a piece of prophetic symbolism may be historical (Jesus did enter Jerusalem in triumph, did curse the fig tree) and at the same time be mythological in Bultmann's sense. Or the alleged event may not have happened and the narrative still retain mythological value. What one must insist is that whether or not the imagery, etc., of the narrative yields itself to translation into existentialist terms, this does nothing to tell us which of those possibilities is more likely to be true. Yet Bultmann repeatedly suggests that '*X* is described in mythological terms' implies '*X* cannot have happened as narrated', and does not make it plain that the latter judgment requires a quite distinct investigation.[3]

Two brief examples of this may be hazarded. First, the expression 'the cross' is indispensable in devotional language; but the very reasons which make it valuable there make it a dangerous and slippery term in a theology like Bultmann's —namely its conflation of two distinguishable conceptions, the actual crucifixion of Jesus at Calvary and the 'meaning' that event can have for the Christian. This span of meaning permits a theologian to keep his reader in a state of sustained uncertainty about exactly what historical claim, if any, he is making when he speaks of 'the cross'.

[3] An analogy with Political Theory presents itself here. The idea of a Social Contract may be a valuable one in justifying political obedience under certain circumstances. To speak of it as a 'myth' is neither to assert nor to deny the historicity of such an original Contract. Compare D. M. MacKinnon and Antony Flew, in Ch. IX above.

Second, 'Take . . . the case of a child being sacrificed in order to ensure the success of an enterprise or to avert misfortune. Such a practice implies a "crude mythological conception of God"' (p. 108). Here the rejection of a primitive view of sacrifice (as in the stories of Iphigenia and Jeptha's daughter) appears to be part and parcel with Bultmann's general impatience with the mythological: its repudiation is represented as involved in the passage from myth to non-myth. But is this not misleading in the extreme? What is 'crude' about the sacrifice theory is not its mythological nature, but its *moral* inadequacy. Abandoning it is not a piece of linguistic spring-cleaning but a value-judgment, logically quite different.

There may be at least a hint of this fact-language conflation on page 7 of *Kerygma and Myth* where Bultmann says: 'The only criticism of the New Testament which is theologically relevant is that which arises *necessarily* out of the situation of modern man' (Bultmann's italics). One such 'necessity' is disbelief in the miraculous as interference in the order of nature. Now, as Austin Farrer remarks in the same volume, some modern men do not find such a belief impossible. But Bultmann whisks his reader past the possible objection, aided by this word 'necessarily' which is always ready to take on the logician's sense of 'analytically, logically necessary', therefore not falsifiable by any matter of fact. Again the controversial is made to seem less controversial, and objections on the score of validity are glided over by the hint that the truth of the statement is guaranteed by linguistic convention, that its denial involves contradiction.

4. *Myth and Oblique Language*

The project of demythologizing raises in an acute form the general problem of the religious use of language, the logical nature of statements about God. We may start with Bultmann's crucial statement, '. . . there are certain concepts which are fundamentally mythological, and with which we shall never be able to dispense—e.g. the idea of transcendence. In such cases, however, the original mythological meaning has been lost, and they have become mere metaphors or ciphers' (pp. 102 f.). '*Mere* metaphors', note; the phrase suggests that these concepts are 'as near literal as makes no difference'. But in fact it makes a great deal of difference. The gulf between literal (or direct) and oblique language cannot be bridged so lightheartedly. For if propositions about God are irreducibly oblique—that is, symbolical, analogical and so on, then to demythologize is not to remove all obliqueness, but only obliqueness of certain sorts: on the other hand, if it is possible to speak literally of God, then demythologizing is quite a different activity, not one of translation out of one code into another, but rather of *de-coding* altogether. The question which should be of greatest concern to the theologian is not whether this or that myth may be re-expressed in language less flagrantly pictorial, more abstract in appearance, but whether or not the circle of myth, metaphor and symbol is a closed one: and if closed then in what way propositions about God manage to *refer*. Bultmann's first definition of 'myth' gave the word a sense sufficiently extended to include every kind of oblique language; yet in practice he gives very little scrutiny indeed to this general issue, and even (as we have noticed) contrasts the mythological with the analogical—a procedure for which his definition gives no warrant. That is to say: the nature of demythologizing as an enterprise must remain logically obscured so long as we leave unsettled the question 'Is any direct talk of God possible, or can one talk only obliquely of him?' How inattention to this question can enfeeble the debate can be brought out as follows.

Bultmann's critics have often pointed out that his existentialist terminology is no less mythological than the New Testament ideas from which he wishes to deliver us. Bultmann is prepared to admit this: even 'transcendence' is a mythological concept, but one (he is assured) in which myth is merely vestigial, neutralized, reduced to the harmless status of 'mere metaphor or cipher'. But the more searching objection can still be made that this *appearance* of directness and abstract sterility can be (logically) a menace. If the demythologized talk of God is still oblique, then it should display its obliqueness overtly, for to carry it surreptitiously may be rather like treating measles by hiding the rash with face-powder. For all we know, the suppressed picture, the latent myth, may still be doing the work in the expression concerned; and the 'cashing' of it may be impossible without once more reverting to the concealed, but active, myth.

The importance of this may be made plainer by referring to a perceptive article[4] by Ian Crombie, where he considers the challenge to religious belief presented recently by certain linguistic philosophers. In particular, it had been argued that a proposition like 'God loves me' appears at first sight to be rich in meaning but is in fact qualified out of existence as soon as we attempt to describe in detail what precisely it claims. Although there are certain sorts of behaviour which give good grounds for denying that one human being loves another, the Christian is expected to go on saying 'God loves me' even when his child is born blind and he himself succumbs to an incurable disease. Even the proposition 'God exists' is eroded away to emptiness by successive qualifications: 'he exists—*but* is invisible, inaudible, intangible, not *in* the world nor a name for the world as a whole. . . .' Now, in his article, Crombie granted that any attempt to speak literally, directly of God was indeed bound to fail. Nevertheless, we can still speak of him—in 'parable' (using the word in an extended sense). We say 'God loves us'; what this is like as an experience in God's own being we have not the least idea (nor, without taking in the hereafter, can we exhaustively verify or falsify it): for to predicate 'loving' or 'acting' or 'suffering' of One who infinite and unconditioned is at once to snap the links with every intelligible use of these words. But if we think of 'God loves us' as a parable, an oblique utterance, the word 'loves' is being used not in a stretched sense but with its everyday familiar meaning. Without knowing what it is like for God to love, we do know now what thoughts of God and what sorts of behaviour are

[4] Ch. VI (ii) in this volume.

appropriate and what not. We accept one parable about God, rather than another, on the authority, primarily, of Jesus Christ. The parabolic is only one of the two 'parents' of religious belief: the other is what might be called 'undifferentiated theism', and springs from a sense of the contingency (or beauty, etc.) of the world, giving a 'direction' in which the revealed parable can be referred.[5]

Professor Tillich, in a conversation, once pointed out to me how closely this analysis followed the pattern of his own treatment of the same problem, however different his starting-point. Tillich maintains that all propositions about God are symbolic, except one: for without one direct proposition the oblique language, despite its internal coherence, would have no anchor in reality; the flotilla of symbols would be adrift, unpiloted. To Tillich this one direct proposition is 'God is Being—itself', and its resemblance to Crombie's 'undifferentiated theism' is obvious enough.

Neither Crombie nor Tillich was engaged on a project of demythologizing. None the less, my point is that demythologizing is only an artificially broken off segment of the problem with which they *were* grappling, and that both of them permit the logical structure of their enterprises to shine through with a clarity impossible to the close disciple of Bultmann. Thus Crombie's presentation, if acceptable, makes it at once plain what sort of procedure is relevant to establishing its truth: each 'parent' of belief requires a separate justification. With the theistic, for instance, we must ask how far it is exposed to the general difficulties of the classical arguments of natural theology despite its prelinguistic character[6]: with the parabolic we must investigate the grounds on which we accept Jesus' authority in uttering the parable.

5. *The Existentialist Interpretation*

So far I have been trying to lay bare some of the pitfalls which beset Bultmann's enterprise, ways in which the problem of validity tends to be side-stepped in demytholo-

[5] See, for instance, Professor J. J. C. Smart in Ch. III above, *ad fin.*
[6] Compare Smart again in Ch. III above, *passim.*

gizing and the logic of religious statements obscured rather than clarified. Something must be said in conclusion (however briefly), about the other half of the total programme—the revision of the *Kerygma* in existentialist terms. Do existentialist modes of thought, as Bultmann adopts them, help or hinder the fashioning of a theology whose logical structure reveals itself through its presentation and terminology?

In the first place, there is an undeniable advance from a sentimentalist analysis of belief (as in Schleiermacher) to an existentialist analysis. The advance is comparable to that recent progress from the positivist's dichotomy between 'descriptive and emotive' language to the recognition of the variety of actual linguistic functions as seen in the writing of philosophers like Wisdom and Austin. Existentialism provides the theologian (the poet and novelist too) with a rich vocabulary in which to express important elements of the human situation—decision, commitment, dereliction, anguish and many more. Indeed, its theological adaptability is not matter for surprise, since the roots of existentialism go back as far as Pascal and Augustine.

But the adoption of a twentieth-century existentialist terminology is not without its dangers. Certain of these were admirably discussed in Christopher Evans' broadcast review of *Kerygma and Myth*. It is as a tentative supplement to what he said there that I hazard these three additional criticisms.

The first is the most formidable, but space will permit only its bare statement. Overwhelmingly concerned with the phenomenology of faith and the life of faith, existentialist thought is in continual peril of failing to emerge from the subjectivist circle at all. A subjectivist account can provide an informative description of what it is like to think and act *as if* there were a God, of the 'inward' metamorphosis which accompanies belief. But it is unable to go further (and it is only here that the question of validity becomes relevant) unable to say whether the belief is justified or unjustified, whether or not there exists a Being before whom the believer has taken up the attitude of faith.

A second danger arises from the almost unlimited hospitality which existentialist thought gives to the paradoxical. Even granting that there are situations in which one is forced to say, 'This is a paradox—an enigma, a mystery', there are others in which the proper response is, 'This is paradoxical, contradictory and nonsensical'. The more cautious a theologian is of paradox, the less he revels in it for its own dramatic sake—the less likely he will be to revere the nonsensical and the invalid when he ought to be dismissing them. His ideal language is one which (by its reluctance to resort to paradox in all but unavoidable contexts) reduces the risk of such confusions as far as possible. Again, it is not an insensitivity to the value of metaphor and analogy in exposition that prompts the suspicion that existentialist language is frequently over-tolerant also of those. In sentences like 'we possess the present through encounter' (p. 116, *K.a.M.*) the adoption of the language of drama in the field of general philosophy has begotten a metaphorical mode of speech in which cogent argumentation or criticism is desperately hard. Distortion is inevitable when all relations come to be conceived on the model of inter-personal encounter.

Finally, an existentialist dramatic vocabulary tends on occasion illicitly to prescribe to the theologian what questions he should or should not pursue, where his inquiry should start and (worse still) where it should end. Bultmann writes: 'It is not for us to question [the] credentials' of the 'word of preaching', 'It is we who are questioned' (p. 41). Perhaps: but this alluring language of drama cannot justify the theologian's evasion of that abiding and ultimate question—'*on what grounds* ought I to assume an attitude of obedience before the New Testament and not before, say, the Koran?' On another page we read: 'I think I may take for granted that the right question to frame with regard to the Bible—at any rate within the Church—is the question of human existence' (pp. 191 f., *ibid.*), as if by the weightiness of existential utterance itself one could smother the thousand and one *other* questions—of historicity, integrity of text, interpretation

—which likewise clamour for their answer, and concern Churchmen as much as unbelievers. Here existentialism has become Bultmann's master, not his servant. So long as it provides the means of expressing what without its terms would be inexpressible, theologians can do nothing but respect it: but it is time to protest when it proceeds arbitrarily to impose limits upon critical examination, whether of doctrine or document.

The quest for a language that is adequate to describe our experience in all its multifariousness is the common task of philosophers and theologians. They must resist equally the artificial truncation of language on dogmatic positivist lines and any language ('inflationary' language, Isaiah Berlin would call it) which is given to the multiplication of metaphysical or theological entities beyond necessity, and from crying mystery where there is not always mystery but sometimes only muddle. In each case a defective linguistic instrument is an obstacle not only to clarity in exposition but also to the attainment of validity.

King's College
  Aberdeen
    SCOTLAND

XIII

MIRACLES[1]

PATRICK NOWELL-SMITH

I

Mr. Lunn throws down the gauntlet, several gauntlets, to the
'modernist'; but it is not on behalf of modernism that I
intend to take up his challenge. I shall confine myself solely
to the question of miracles, and to one aspect only of this
many-sided problem. First let me indicate the extent of my
agreement with Mr. Lunn:

(*a*) I am in full agreement with him about the value of
controversy and about the need, in controversy, for sticking
to accepted definitions. One can prove anything with
sufficient elasticity or watering down of terms.

(*b*) The problem must be attacked with an open mind,
that is to say, with a mind not disposed to reject evidence
because it conflicts with some preconceived theory. I have
known a very distinguished physicist to explain that Dr.
Rhine's experimental results in 'parapsychology' must be
false because such things just cannot happen. The parallel
which Mr. Lunn adduces between this attitude and that of
the Church towards Galileo is apt.

(*c*) I hold no brief for the Euhemerizing attitude of some
modernists. I do not altogether agree that it is illogical to
accept what seems credible in the gospel stories and to reject
the miracles, when the evidence is the same for both. It seems
to me that we are sometimes entitled to accept part of a
witness's story and reject another part. But I will not quarrel

[1] This was originally written as a reply to Mr. (now Sir) Arnold Lunn's article
'Miracles—The Scientific Approach', *Hibbert Journal*, April 1950, itself a
reply to an article by Professor H. Dubs in the same journal, January 1950.

with Mr. Lunn over this, since I reject Euhemerism myself for other reasons. Nevertheless, I must protest that to reject the thesis that Jesus was a man on to whom fabulous stories have been foisted is not to prove the Christian view that he was a Man-God. As Mr. Lunn knows, there is the alternative theory that he was always a God and that the growth of the gospel stories is not the progressive deification of a man but the progressive humanization of a God. However, Mr. Lunn was explicitly attacking the modernist view, and it is not fair to criticize him for not fighting his battle on two fronts at once. I mention this point solely as an illustration of Mr. Lunn's tendency to treat a convincing refutation of one view as a proof of another which is not the only possible alternative, a tendency of which I shall produce a more important example later.

So much for my agreement with Mr. Lunn. Whether modernists commit the fallacies of bad definition, the closed mind and Euhemerism I shall not presume to say. Let it suffice that they are fallacies; and now let us turn to miracles.

To put my cards on the table at once, I have no intention of trying to refute Mr. Lunn's explanation of miracles, since he has put it beyond the bounds of possible refutation. But I do not think that it *explains* and I am at a loss to understand it. In particular, I am at a loss to understand the distinction of the 'natural' and the 'supernatural' of which he makes so much in his explanation of miracles, but which he does not explain in its turn. But before coming to my main point I shall first summarize Mr. Lunn's argument and put out of the way two minor points. Mr. Lunn's main argument is as follows:

(*a*) A miracle is defined as 'an event above or contrary to or exceeding nature which is explicable only as a direct act of God'.

(*b*) Miracles certainly occur. (There is plenty of evidence for them, if only people will bother to investigate it instead of rejecting miracles out of hand.)

(*c*) Miracles are 'evidence provided by God to demonstrate the existence of a divine order'.

244

(*d*) Therefore we must believe that reality is not 'co-terminous with the natural order' and must answer in the negative the momentous question 'whether all phenomena recorded and witnessed by man are due to purely natural causes, such as the actions of the human will or physical causes'. Moreover, it is on the authority of the scientists themselves 'that we declare that a particular phenomenon is inexplicable as the effect of natural agents and must therefore be ascribed to supernatural agents'.

Before coming to my main point, I have two objections to make to this thesis: the first will certainly be familiar to Mr. Lunn and he has probably answered it elsewhere; the second is more important. In the first place, every religion has its own stock of miracles, some of which are as well-attested as the Christian miracles. Would Mr. Lunn deny that these miracles occurred? And, if he does, must it not be from some arbitrary standpoint such as he himself condemns? If he is willing to accept them, must there not be some flaw in the argument by which the devotees of other religions prove the existence of their Gods from such evidence? And might not this flaw appear also in the Christian case? Or are we to accept the God of Muhammad and the whole Greek and Hindu Pantheons?

My second, and more serious, point is that Mr. Lunn *defines* 'miracle' in such a way that, whatever scientists may say, it can well be doubted whether miracles have in fact occurred. If any scientist has said that a certain phenomenon 'is inexplicable as the effect of natural agents and must *therefore* be ascribed to supernatural agents', he is not speaking as a scientist, but as a philosopher; and whatever authority he may have in his own scientific field he is by no means a safe guide here. We may trust him, as a trained observer, accurately to describe the phenomenon; we may believe him when he says that no scientific method or hypothesis known to him will explain it. But to say that it is inexplicable as a result of natural agents is already beyond his competence as a scientist, and to say that it must be ascribed to supernatural agents is to say something that no one could possibly have the right to affirm on the evidence alone. Mr. Lunn defines a miracle, not merely as an event 'exceeding nature', but also as one *which is explicable only as a direct Act of God*. But to say that a phenomenon is a direct act of God is to offer an explanation, not to report its occurrence. Let us accept all the evidence for miracles; what this evidence shows is that extraordinary phenomena occur, and it is only in this sense that the evidence forces us to admit that miracles occur. If we define 'miracle' in the way that Mr. Lunn does, we could only be forced to admit the occurrence of miracles by means of some *argument*, such as Mr. Lunn himself offers. Mr. Lunn has, in short, smuggled his explanation of these phenomena into the evidence for them, and this he has no right to do. Evidence must be kept distinct from explanatory theory; otherwise, in accepting the evidence, we are already committed to accepting the theory. But, no matter how strange an event someone reports, the statement that it must have been due to a supernatural agent cannot be a part of that report.

II

As I have said, my main difficulty is to understand Mr. Lunn's distinction between the 'natural' and the 'supernatural'. There is, first, a certain inconsistency in his use of these terms. At one point he regards God's intervention as analogous to that of human beings. It 'does not violate the laws of nature but modifies some of the laws of nature by a process analogous to that by which the human will influences nature'. Here the human will is held to be, in some sense 'non-natural', if not supernatural. (Otherwise the analogy has no point). 'Natural' comes near to meaning 'physical' or even 'material'. But in the next paragraph the actions of the human will are treated, along with 'physical causes' as natural; so that the phrase 'natural order' cannot be regarded as co-terminous with the domain of physical science.

It is true that some scientists claim that, in the end, all explanation will turn out to be physical. I do not propose to examine this claim, as it is irrelevant. Mr. Lunn must be intending to attack a different thesis, namely, that all phenomena will ultimately admit of a natural explanation. It is vital, therefore, that he should let us clearly understand what he means by this phrase.

Mr. Lunn's belief that 'natural' explanations cannot be given seems to me to rest on an unstated, and therefore unexamined assumption as to the nature of natural science. He seems to believe that science is committed to certain definite *theories* and to the use of certain definite *concepts*—for instance, the concepts of matter and motion. But surely this is a mistake. Scientific theories are continually being overthrown; the scientific vocabulary is continually being revised and enriched. For example, 'Energy' does not mean for a scientist today what it meant for Newton; still less what it meant for Aristotle. In addition to explaining more and more with its existing battery of concepts and theories, science may advance by developing radically new concepts. The concept of gravity was unknown to Galileo and that of an electric charge unknown to Newton; and it is for this reason that if Newton himself said that such and such an event was inexplicable I should take leave to doubt him. Let us grant that Mr. Lunn has a right to say, on the authority of 'scientists', that no scientist can at present explain certain phenomena. It does not follow that the phenomena are inexplicable by scientific methods, still less that they must be attributed to supernatural agents.

It might be argued that I am cheating here by using the term 'science' in such a loose way that it can be used to cover any type of explanation. But this is not so. Science is committed, not to definite theories or concepts, but to a certain *method* of explanation. I do not say that this must be the only method; but I do not see what other there can be.

I may be doing Mr. Lunn an injustice in saying that he regards science as committed to definite theories and concepts rather than committed to a certain method. But so many of his points, both good and bad, seem to me to follow from this assumption that I cannot but attribute it to him. In the first place, his strictures on the absence of *Zetesis* in the attitude of some scientists seem to me to presuppose this view (as does the absence of *Zetesis* itself). It is true that some scientists refuse to admit any explanations that are not couched in terms of the orthodox scientific concepts of today; and it is also true that this is a mistake, a blindness fitly compared with that of Galileo's opponents. Mr. Lunn says: 'All evidence for such (i.e. supernatural) agencies must, on modernist assumptions, either be explained here and now as the result of natural causes or be referred to the science of the future to interpret in accordance with modernist pre-conceptions.' But there is an ambiguity here that must, I think, arise from the mistaken view of science that I have attributed to Mr. Lunn. If he means that, according to the modernists, science must either be able to explain everything here and now or be able, in the future, to explain everything *in terms now current*, he is right to object. But there is still the possibility that science may be able, in the future, to offer an explanation which, though couched in quite new terms, remains strictly scientific. And I shall try to show later that this is the only possible alternative to saying that *no* explanation is possible. Thus the breakdown of all explanations in terms of present-day science does not, as Mr. Lunn thinks, immediately force us outside the realm of the 'natural'; and we can only think that it does so if we make the mistake of equating 'science' with a certain set of theories. An explanation would still be 'natural' if it made use of quite different terms, provided that its method was scientific. If this be conceded, it is difficult to understand Mr. Lunn's distinction between the 'natural' and the 'supernatural'. For the problem is not whether science can explain everything in current terms, but whether the explanation of miracles requires a method quite different from that of science. Unless this latter thesis is proved, it is hard to see why miracles should be called 'supernatural'.

III

If the notion of the 'natural' is unclear, that of a 'miracle' is no less so; and that in spite of Mr. Lunn's explicit defini-

tion, At times he holds that a miracle is 'above, contrary to
or exceeding nature'; at others he holds that, in performing
miracles, God does not violate natural law. I find it hard to
reconcile these two views; at least the words 'contrary to'
must go; and with them the analogy between Acts of God
and human actions. Mr. Lunn sees that a fieldsman who
catches a cricket ball is not violating or suspending—he is
not even modifying—the law of gravity. And if God's interventions are analogous to those of human agents, they conform to natural laws. In this case they are in principle predictable (however great the difficulties may be in practice);
and the word 'supernatural' loses its force.

It might be argued that God's interventions are indeed
'lawful'; but that they proceed according to laws which are
not 'natural laws'; but at this point the difference between a
'natural' and a 'supernatural' law cries out for explanation.
There are many different kinds of scientific law—physical,
chemical, biological, psychological and so on. If supernatural law is another group alongside these, it is not
necessarily unscientific. But in calling it 'supernatural' Mr.
Lunn evidently means to imply that it is different, for
example, from physical law in a way in which a physical
law is not different from a biological law. Yet I cannot
imagine what this difference would be. If it is a law, it must
(*a*) be based on evidence; (*b*) be of a general type 'Under
such and such conditions, so and so will happen'; (*c*) be
capable of testing in experience. And if it conforms to this
specification, how does it differ from a natural law? The
supernatural seems to dissolve on the one hand into the
natural and on the other into the inexplicable.

And this is no *a priori* dogma; it follows from the nature of
explanation. It is, I think, a failure to investigate what is
involved in the notion of an explanation that leads Mr.
Lunn to leap at once into the supernatural. A scientific
explanation is an hypothesis from which predictions can be
made, which can afterwards be verified. It is of the essence
of such an hypothesis—a 'law' is but a well-confirmed
hypothesis—that it should be capable of such predictive

expansion. This is, incidentally, the burden of the old attack on *virtus dormitiva* and Bacon's *'tamquam virgo intacta, nihil parit'*. The type of explanation satirized by Molière and Bacon is futile because it merely repeats in learned jargon what has already been said in plain language in stating the phenomenon to be explained. A scientific explanation—any explanation—must do more than this. It must be capable of application to new phenomena. Now, Mr. Lunn's explanations are inevitably *ex post facto*; we can only recognize a miracle after it has occurred. Mr. Lunn may reply that it is 'illogical to exploit against an hypothesis consequences which are inevitable if that hypothesis is correct'. Certainly; but my argument is not intended to show that Mr. Lunn's hypothesis is false; it is intended to show that it is not an hypothesis at all. It is as if one were to say: 'Certain events in the past were caused by boojums; but I cannot tell you on what principles boojums operate or what they will do in the future; my hypothesis inevitably involves this consequence.' If anyone said this, we should have to treat his phrase 'caused by boojums' as simply a special way of describing the phenomena, moreover a misleading way, since it looks like an explanatory hypothesis. But in fact it is not. In the same way, to say that God's interventions in the natural order are 'lawful', but that we cannot use these laws for prediction is to retreat into an asylum of ignorance and to use the word 'law' in a most paradoxical sense.

To illustrate this let me turn to the example of Leverrier, which Mr. Lunn cites: 'If Leverrier had assumed that the planetary order is a closed system he would never have discovered Neptune.' True; and a valid argument against the exaggerated orthodoxy which Mr. Lunn and I both condemn and also against *a priori* proofs in the Hegelian manner of the number of planets that there must be. But the analogy with explanations in supernatural terms is invalid. For Leverrier discovered Neptune, not merely by saying: 'The planetary system is not closed; there is something outside.' He showed how the aberrations in the orbits of other planets could be accounted for; and his explanation involved a prediction that if astronomers examined a certain quarter of the sky they would find a new planet. And lo! it was so. It is here that the analogy breaks down; for Mr. Lunn's 'explanation' involves saying: 'Known laws and factors will not explain this phenomenon; there must be something outside; but I cannot tell you what this is or how it operates.' An explanation must explain *how* an event comes about; otherwise it is simply a learned (or a tendentious) name for the phenomenon to be explained.

Moreover, the new entity postulated by Leverrier was not of an altogether unknown type; it was another planet assumed to obey the known laws. I am prepared to allow Mr. Lunn much more than this (at least for the purpose of this discussion), and to admit that the present hypotheses of science can never be expanded to cover miraculous phenomena; that we may require new concepts and new laws. What I reject is the theory of science which makes it possible to claim that any phenomenon is essentially inexplicable, the leap to 'supernatural agencies', and the view that such agencies in fact explain the phenomena. If miracles are 'lawful' it should be possible to state the laws; if not, the alleged explanation amounts to a confession that they are inexplicable.

IV

Having said that miracles must be attributed to supernatural agencies, Mr. Lunn goes on to claim that they are 'evidence provided by God to demonstrate the existence of the divine order'. But what, in detail, can they prove? If we can detect any order in God's interventions it should be possible to extrapolate in the usual way and to predict when and how a miracle will occur. To expect accurate and detailed predictions would be to expect too much. But we must be able to make some predictions, however vague. Otherwise the hypothesis is not open either to confirmation or refutation. As far as I can see, we are limited to saying that God has in the past intervened in such and such a way. If Mr. Lunn would say more than this, I would ask how his method differs from that of a scientist. We would be faced, not with the supernatural, but with a new department of the natural, a department that might be as strange as electrical phenomena once were. But if he confesses that no predictions can be made, is not the phrase 'Act of God', which is introduced in order to explain miracles, in fact but a synonym for 'the miraculous'? We are back at the *virtus dormitiva* type of explanation. If 'Christ is risen' implies 'Christ is supernatural', we are entitled to ask what *other* attributes, besides rising from the dead, 'supernatural' connotes. We shall then be in a position to see whether a being that rises from the dead necessarily or probably has those attributes. Mr. Lunn passes from unusual or abnormal events (for which there is evidence) to the miraculous, from the miraculous to the supernatural and from the supernatural to God. He cannot mean each successive phrase to be a mere synonym for the previous one; each step in the argument is intended to explain the last and to add something more. But, to make use of an old-fashioned way of putting this, we have no right to postulate in the cause any power greater than what is necessary to produce the effect. The difficulty with the argument from miracles, as with other arguments for the existence of God, is that it is first claimed that certain evidence requires us to postulate an unknown X; we then call this X 'God'; and we then claim to have proved the existence of a being endowed with characteristics by no means warranted by the original evidence. Now science too does this. The gravitational theory says much more than is necessary to describe the fall of an apple. But we can test the truth of this 'more' by predicting how other bodies will behave. It is the absence of such a test for supernatural explanations that makes them at once unscientific and also non-explanatory.

It might be argued that I am in effect begging the question because my thesis amounts to saying that the phrase 'supernatural explanation' is a contradiction in terms. To assume this is tantamount to assuming that all explanation must be scientific. Now I certainly would not claim to be able to prove this dogma. To do so I should have to appeal to some premiss that would be equally unacceptable. All I can do is offer Mr. Lunn a challenge. Let him consider the meaning of the word 'explanation' and let him ask himself whether this notion does not involve that of a law or hypothesis capable of predictive expansion. And then let him ask himself whether such an explanation would not be natural, in whatever terms it was couched, and how the notion of 'the supernatural' could play any part in it. If he objects that I am in effect conceding his point by offering so very wide a definition of 'natural', my reply would be:

By all means; I do not wish to quarrel about words. I will concede your supernatural, if this is all that it means. For the supernatural will be nothing but a new field for scientific inquiry, a field as different from physics as physics is from psychology, but not differing in principle or requiring any non-scientific method.

The supernatural is either so different from the natural that we are unable to investigate it at all or it is not. If it is not, then it can hardly have the momentous significance that Mr. Lunn claims for it; and if it is it cannot be invoked as an explanation of the unusual.

Trinity College
OXFORD

XIV
VISIONS
ALASDAIR MacINTYRE

(1) The attempt to found religious belief upon the evidence of religious experience has traditionally taken two main forms. Among Protestants the appeal has usually been to the evidence of certain feeling-states. Among Catholic contemplatives and also among the more eccentric Protestant sects religious experience has been understood to include the seeing of visions and the hearing of voices. I want in this paper to defend three theses: *first*, that no experience less explicit than visions and voices could provide evidence for religious beliefs; *second*, that visions and voices could not in principle provide evidence of the existence of invisible and supernatural beings; and *third*, that, even if this were not so, over the claims made in connection with any particular vision or voice insuperable difficulties must arise. The logical issues that arise in the discussion can be treated for the most part in terms of visions and therefore I shall not often refer explicitly to voices.

(2) Contemplative theologians customarily distinguish three classes of vision, the external, the imaginary or the imaginal, and the intellectual. An external vision is one in which what appears appears as part of the environment and may be confused with the ordinary world of things and people. An imaginal vision is one in which what appears appears as an object of vision in some sense, but can be distinguished sharply from material objects. An intellectual vision is not a vision at all but a feeling of presence. For our purposes these can be reduced to two classes: first, those

visions which can properly be called such, that is, those where something is *seen*; and second, those where the experience is of a feeling-state or of a mental image, which are only called visions by an honorific extension of the term. It is worth making two observations initially. The first is that the classic contemplatives such as St. Theresa value intellectual visions the most highly and external visions the least so, whereas their ostensible evidential value is, it will be argued, if anything, the reverse, and from this it would seem to follow, as the argument will in fact entail, that whatever value visions may have, they possess it not because they are evidence. The second point to be made is that those experiences to which visions are customarily assimilated, namely hallucinations, are inappropriately chosen for the comparison. For we call an apparition of an elephant in a public house hallucinatory because we can compare its behaviour with the behaviour of the non-hallucinatory, normal elephants in the zoo, and it is the discrepancy with normal experience that justifies us in applying the term 'hallucination'. Whenever we apply the term there is an implicit comparison with the normal behaviour of what is ostensibly experienced and therefore, if we want to say, 'This *x* is hallucinatory', we must always be able to say what a normal case of *x* would be like. Now clearly we cannot do this with visions of, for example, the Blessed Virgin or the Archangel Gabriel. All experience of archangels is visionary and there is no normal non-visionary experience of them. Hence there can be no comparison with a normal case and lacking this we cannot call the vision hallucinatory. Indeed when we speak of 'a vision' we imply a visitant of an abnormal kind, rather than a normal being (an elephant or a rat) behaving abnormally.

(3) We can now return to our twofold classification of visions, and I want to argue that neither feeling-states nor mental images could provide evidence for religious belief even on the assumptions of the protagonists of religious experience. To uphold their case nothing less than visions (and voices) will do. The reason for this is that the point of

the experience is allegedly that it conveys information about something other than the experience, namely about the ways of God. Now an experience of a distinctively 'mental' kind, a feeling-state or an image cannot of itself yield us any information about anything other than the experience. We could never know from such experiences that they had the character of messages from the divine, unless we already possessed a prior knowledge of the divine and of the way in which messages from it were to be identified. The decisive evidence for the divine would then be anterior to the experience and not derived from it, whereas what we are concerned with here is how far the experience itself can provide such evidence.

We can approach this same difficulty from the question of the meaning of religious expressions. Either the believer who founds his faith upon religious experience learns the meaning of the religious expressions which he employs in his assertions from his experiences or he does not. If he defines their meaning ostensively by referring to his experiences, then we can inquire what there is in common between the word 'God' as he uses it and the word 'God' as it is used, for example, in the creeds. If he uses the word with the meaning that it possesses in traditional contexts such as the creeds, we are entitled to ask how he knows that it was the maker of heaven and earth who was manifested in his feeling-state. Surely nothing that occurs as a constituent of a feeling-state could provide us with satisfactory evidence on the basis of which either of these questions could be answered.

Behind these difficulties which arise from the claim that the divine is revealed in certain inner *Bewusstseinslage* lies one of the simplest and crudest difficulties of orthodox theism. If God is infinite, how can he be manifest in any particular finite object or experience? The definition of God as infinite is intended precisely to distinguish between God and everything finite, but to take the divine out of the finite is to remove it from the entire world of human experience. The inexorable demands of religiously adequate language seem to make of experience of God a notion that is a contradiction in terms.

The appeal to visions and voices is not, however, in quite the same difficulty here. For here there is no claim to an immediate experience of the infinite creator. There may be all sorts of difficulties about the relation between God and his messengers, but the primary claim that in a vision we confront a messenger and not God enables us to answer the question of how the information is conveyed by the experience. For here there is no esoteric interpretation of feelings, but information conveyed by a speaking figure in an ordinary language, Latin or Portuguese or whatever it is. The problem of the meaning of the religious expressions used by the apparition is not complicated by any attempt to define them ostensively in terms of the experience. Hence if we are to have an appeal to religious experience, it must be to visions rather than to feelings.

(4) There is, however, a further difficulty in the notion of religious experience which is peculiarly applicable to the claims made on the basis of visions. It may be thought that to treat a vision as a sign of the invisible is to accept in the realm of religious belief a procedure which we are accustomed to employ elsewhere. For certainly we do constantly infer the as yet unseen or the no longer seen from what we now see. If we infer fires from smoke, approaching trains from signals, why not gods from apparitions? The answer is that we can only infer the unseen from the seen when we have a rule of inference which entitles us to do so. The justification of any such rule can only be that we have grounds for believing in a correlation between the occurrence of the sign (the seen) and the thing signified (the unseen). So that in order to infer the divine from an apparition we should have to have experience of a connection between them in the way in which we do have experience of the connection between smoke and fires.[1] But what we experience and all that we experience is the vision, and if indeed we had the additional experience of the divine which we should need in order to assert that it was indeed the author of the vision, we

[1] Compare Hume's *Dialogues Concerning Natural Religion, passim.*, and *An Enquiry Concerning Human Understanding*, §§ X and XI.

should presumably not require the vision to tell us of the divine.

Could not the vision, however, be self-authenticating? If an angel appeared and announced himself as a messenger from God, would we not have grounds for believing him if we could find grounds for believing in his general reliability? And could we not find such grounds if the angel gave us verifiable information which invariably turned out to be correct? The fallacy in this argument is as follows. Suppose that the angel successfully predicted the winner of every classic race, appearing a week before the race in order to do so. This would justify us in inferring 'x will win the Derby' from 'The angel says that x will win the Derby', but the fact that the angel's predictions were invariably accurate would not justify us in any inference whatsoever as to the source of the angel's knowledge. We would not even be justified in saying that the angel *knew* the Derby winner, unless the angel told us the grounds for his prediction, and if those grounds were to be intelligible to us they would have to include no unverifiable assertions and hence no reference to invisible realities. Thus the angel's accuracy would be no warrant for accepting any distinctively religious utterance which he might make. Here we can restate Hume's point when he argues that from past traces of design in the Universe we can perhaps infer future traces of design but not an unseen designer.[2] From past phenomena we can infer future phenomena but not what belongs to a realm beyond phenomena. Visions are but one set of phenomena which may or may not be correlated with other phenomena, but they no more than any other occurrence lead us beyond the world of experience.

(5) The difficulties that we have so far encountered could be adduced against any vision whatever. Let us now pass on to consider some of the difficulties that inevitably arise over particular visions. Let us consider, for instance, visions of the Blessed Virgin Mary, such as that which William James[3]

[2] *loc. cit.*
[3] *The Varieties of Religious Experience*, Ch. X.

cites in the case of M. Alphonse Ratisbonne, a free-thinker who became a Roman Catholic in response to a vision. How did he know that it was the Virgin? Presumably only because she appeared in a Roman Catholic church and she looked like the religious paintings he had seen. But surely such an identification is inadequate? And yet what further identification could there be? These questions are not merely the doubts of the sceptic. They are raised also, for example, by the religious admission that such visions may well be wiles of the devil rather than messages from God. This rules out any assurance that M. Ratisbonne might have gained from the apparition announcing herself as the Virgin. What criteria does the believer invoke to distinguish true visions from false? The only criterion possible is presumably the congruence of the messages delivered in the vision with such theological doctrines as are already believed. If this be admitted it might be argued that visions could never be the original ground of a belief but yet might afford it confirmation. This will not do. Since we should only accept as genuine those experiences which did in fact afford confirmation to belief, the statement that genuine religious experience affords confirmation of belief would be an empty tautology.

Or consider the question as one of personal identity. Someone who appeared again after an absence of five years would have to be very much changed before we had real doubts as to his identity; but after two thousand years even Rip van Winkle would find it hard to gain credence of his identity. In the example of the Blessed Virgin, however, the case is worse. No one has authentic evidence as to what she looked like. So to identify her from religious paintings is to have no warrant that she who appeared to M. Ratisbonne is she who lived in Galilee as the mother of Jesus. The ordinary difficulties that arise in specifying the criteria of personal identity are intensified, for we normally judge of personal identity by standard tests. Is this the Tichborne heir? Does he resemble him sufficiently? Does he understand Latin? Does he remember his school days with the Jesuits? Only a correct answer to these three and other relevant questions would justify us in saying that this is indeed none other than the lost heir. Is this the Blessed Virgin? Does she look like her? We do not know what the Blessed Virgin looked like. Does she speak Aramaic? Appearances of the Blessed Virgin would be remarkably impressive if she did, but, to the best of my knowledge, in the classic apparitions of modern Mariolatry the messages delivered are always in the tongue of the recipient. Does the Blessed Virgin remember Galilee? What would be the appropriate criteria for testing her memory? We would have to have an independent source of information about matters on which she could be presumed to have special knowledge and we lack any such source. In so far as what the figure in the apparition said merely agreed with the Gospel narrative, we could have no guarantee that the source of the information was not the Gospel. It is clear that the difficulty is to find a ground for asserting that any given vision is indeed a vision of the Blessed Virgin.

There remains a final difficulty in the use of visions as evidence. If from premises reporting a vision we could infer ontological conclusions, the occurrence of rival visions would validate mutually exclusive ontologies. On visions of the Blessed Virgin some Roman Catholics have based beliefs about her present status and works. From visions of Krishna Hindus construct a theology which, if true, invalidates Roman Catholicism. We may note in passing that it is almost always Roman Catholics who have visions of the Virgin and almost always Hindus who have visions of Krishna and extraordinarily rarely, if ever, *vice versa*.

This completes the case against vindicating religious beliefs by referring to visions. If valid ground for religious belief is to be found, it must be found elsewhere. Equally, if there is to be a valid place in religion for visionary experience, it must be understood other than as evidence for belief.

University of Manchester
ENGLAND

XV

DEATH

A[1]

D. M. MacKINNON

To many contemporary philosophers it seems that claims to survive death must be described as nonsense statements, and that the philosopher's job is to lay bare their nonsensical character, and uncover the violations of syntactical propriety they contain. Of course, we do talk regularly of people surviving catastrophes and *escaping* death. We may even in certain unusual circumstances be justified in speaking of dead men as not really dead: in cases of catalepsy, and so on. But death itself is not something we can significantly speak of surviving. If we say we survive death, we do not know what we are saying. For we cannot stretch our lines of connection with ordinary usage far enough to establish the sense of it. The words are combined in a way that, if we attend to them closely, defies the possibility of our attaching sense to them.

When something is proposed to us for assent or dissent, we demand almost as a condition that we should have some idea of the sort of arguments relevant to establishing it. And, of course, such arguments must be internally sound— that is, they must not be self-contradictory, nor entail the denial of what we hope to establish by means of them. Now if it can be shown that arguments for the survival of bodily death, all of them, sooner or later take for granted the absence of the very condition of bodily death, then they can

1 The substance of this paper was originally given in the B.B.C. Third Programme.

have no power to establish survival. If it is the case that in order to think survival of bodily death, one has got to think bodily death away, then what one is thinking is not survival but simply the absence of the condition one is supposed to survive. To work this out in detail would involve the description of a whole series of arguments: to show how here in one way, there in another the reference to the body as something still there was allowed to creep back. There is no substitute for such pains. One would have to take some more or less traditional treatise on immortality and track out in the arguments the recurrence of references to some shadowy, ghostly counterpart of bodily existence: or the unacknowledged takings-for-granted of the continuance of the conditions of such existence.

One cannot, if one is honest, ignore the extent to which metaphysical arguments, like those concerning immortality, have gained plausibility from a refusal to attend to the logic of our language. How much indeed does our glib talk about survival owe to our refusal to reflect on the very significance of the pronoun 'I' itself. 'I survive'—but what is 'I'? Do I suppose that 'I' is the name of a kind of ultimate substrate of qualities, clad with its states much as a clothes-horse is draped with towels, shirts, etc.? Do I think that I am related to my biography in that kind of way? Yet much of our superficial talk about survival suggests that we do. Whether we think of the survival, or of the survivor, we are at once plunged into bewilderment. What exactly are we talking about?

One can certainly put a question-mark against almost every stage in the fabric of traditional argumentation on this issue. And yet one is somehow sure that that is not the end of the matter. I have already mentioned the importance of description, the description of arguments, the description of instances of proof, and so on. How odd it is that philosophers, who, where the exact sciences are concerned, are insisting more and more that we eschew the general formula and concentrate on the individual instance, should, where metaphysics is concerned, ignore their own rubric! Metaphysical arguments are so often treated as if they could be exhaustively set out in a formal scheme; whereas, of course, of all arguments they are surely the ones that require the most detailed and individual treatment. For in them, surely, so much more is set out, albeit indirectly, of the inwardness of the person whose arguments they are.

To put it very crudely, just what is it that is at stake for a person in this matter of immortality? What is it that is bothering him? Of course, you can show the queerness, the confusedness of the way in which the bother is expressing itself, when it does so by means of the traditional language of survival, and so on. You can discredit this means of expression by showing the logical confusions into which it plunges: but does that settle the perplexity, the issue in the mind of the bewildered person? Now I am not suggesting for one moment that when we think, there is a ghostlike something called our thought that tries now one form of expression, now another; rather like a stout man trying on suits off the peg, and discarding them one by one. The relation of thought to its expression isn't a bit like that. But isn't there something which we all of us know, a kind of confused knowing that we haven't said what we mean but that if we persevere, we might get the sense of what we are after through the criticism of what we've said?

Put it another way. Death is a clinical phenomenon. You can learn a great deal about it from text-books of pathology. medical jurisprudence and so on. But is it only that? Do we regard death as something about which we could learn everything we have to learn through a mere extension of the sort of information we can already pick up from the kind of text-books I have mentioned? Or have we anything to learn from poetry, from the language of religion and so on? Or are we to say that anything we find conveyed only by such language as religious persons use is somehow merely peripheral . . . the merest expression of private feeling and as such ultimately insignificant?

You see how the issue under discussion has been turned round, It is no longer a stretching or straining after inconceivable states of being. It has rather become a question of the way we regard the term of human life. Is it or is it not true that those who still mouth the logical vulgarities of traditional arguments concerning immortality do so because in the end they just cannot allow that the clinician has said or can say all that is to be significantly said about death?

Again, I know my description is not nearly detailed enough. How can it be when to make it so would involve me in a vast multiplication of individual instances? To understand the issue of immortality, you must look at the ways people talk of death: the ways they talk when they are defending a theory, the ways they talk when they are off guard and speak to themselves freely.

This issue, of course, does not stand alone. For all its intimacy to the individual, it cannot be isolated in the way the aim of an experiment can be. By translating the problem into terms of our human attitude to death, one does more than merely bring it down to earth in the sense of perhaps uncovering a little what is in people's minds when they bother about it. One relates the issue to all those manifold other issues that touch our relation to our neighbour. Such issues are only made explicit to us by means of language: so, too, the continually besetting problem of their place in the scheme of things.

Suppose we were as a kind of exercise simply to look at things people have said or written about death in relation to their lives as human beings. One could avert attention from all concern with speculation about what comes after, concern oneself with death as a factor in human life. One could call it a study of the logic of poetic and religious expression on the subject. It might be that such an exercise would open our minds a little to what drives people to speak so hazardously about survival and immortality. Such an enterprise would call for sympathetic imagination—for a readiness perhaps to widen our horizons. But I can see no other way to get at the inwardness of this problem than a readiness to take the strain of such a widening.

Of course, the question will remain how such expression

is related to that of the sciences and their commonsensical basis: the problem I referred to when I mentioned the place of human relations in the scheme of things, But at least one will have taken an important step towards curing oneself of the illusion that the stumbling speech of those who speak of immortality and survival (I except here the psychical researchers) is expressive of an attempt to gain knowledge of fact without the discipline of experiment and reflective analysis. One will have begun to track the language to its human source, to plot the experience of which it is the expression. The experience, indeed, *which takes shape through such expression.*

But what of proof? How does one prove, for instance, that the agony of a person suddenly, and as it seems to him irrationally, bereaved is not a bubble on the surface of things? How does one confer on grief itself the dignity of validity? The jargon is repulsive: but in the end perhaps just *this* is the real issue. I spoke of the bereavement as seeming irrational: I spoke of the protest. At such a moment a person may be simultaneously conscious of life as having form, direction, meaning. And yet as having no form, no direction, no meaning. The violence of the disturbance is due to the fact, not that meaning has never been found, but that suddenly it has been taken away—as if by a malignant practical joker. Some philosophers insist with good reason that such a phrase as 'the meaning of life' is empty of sense. But if they are altogether right, then the very anguish of spirit I have been describing is shown up as trivial and empty. And is this something we can allow? It is less a pinchbeck survival than the place of man in the world that is at issue. Almost we would beg the world that it does not treat our agonies as nothings.

Christian theology, which did so much to transform men's attitude to the after-life, speaks less of immortality than of resurrection, less of personal survival than of the life of the world to come. It speaks less of assurance that something will survive as of hope that 'all manner of thing will be well'. To develop this theme properly belongs not to philosophy but to theology, and above all to Christology, the pivot and centre of characteristically Christian theology. Indeed sometimes the man who is at all trained in this theology must be impatient of discussions of immortality, which studiously refrain from referring to the *event* of the death and resurrection of Christ. Clearly, however, that issue cannot be raised here.

But this at least can be said without prolonged invasion of the theological field. There is no escape at any point in life from the fear that our very seriousness about ourselves is sound and fury signifying nothing. The medieval schoolmen would have said: inevitably so, for man is poised between being and not being; he draws his existence wholly from the self-existent God. The movement of human thought must reflect man's situation in being. Because he is so poised between being and not being, he will never see his existence as something assured. Again and again, in taking stock of himself, he will not find easily the arguments which will assure him that his standing is secure. At their wisest the schoolmen would never allow that by a formula we could somehow escape the most fundamental conditions of our existence. In the end they would have said: the proof of the pudding is in the eating; a necessary implication of their insistence on the primacy of being over thought. And perhaps we must say the same. There is no other proof possible that a seriousness in life is justified than is found in living. One cannot by any magic escape the conditions of humanity, assume the absolute perspective of God. If it is better to arrive than to travel, we are still inescapably travelling *in statu viae*, to use the old phrase. And our perspectives are necessarily those of travellers, at least for most of the time. But there still remains a difference between the traveller who takes the measure of his road and the one who seeks to be oblivious of its windings.

King's College
  Aberdeen
    SCOTLAND

266

B²

ANTONY FLEW

'Whether we are to live in a future state, as it is the most important question which can possibly be asked, so it is the most intelligible one which can be expressed in language' (Butler, in the dissertation *Of Personal Identity*).

Surely Butler is right? Can we not understand the hopes of the warriors of Allah who expect if they die in Holy War to go straight to the arms of the black-eyed houris in Paradise? Can we not understand the fears of the slum mother kept from the clinic by her priest's warnings of penalties for those who die in mortal sin? Of course we can: they both expect —and what could be more intelligible than this?—that if they do certain things then they will in consequence enjoy or suffer certain rewards or punishments in the future. And if this future life is supposed to last for ever, then clearly the question whether or not it is fictitious (and if it is not, the consequent problem of ensuring that we shall pass it agreeably) is of quite overwhelming importance. For what are three-score years and ten compared with all eternity?

But surely, urges the sceptic, something crucial is being overlooked? For this future life is supposed to continue even *after* physical dissolution: even after the slow corruption in the cemetery, or the swift consumption in the crematorium. And to suggest that we might survive this dissolution seems like suggesting that a nation might outlast the annihilation of all its members. Of course we can understand the myth of Er or stories of Valhalla: but to expect that after my death

---

2 I have written at somewhat greater length on various themes touched on here in (*a*) 'Locke and the Problem of Personal Identity', in *Philosophy*, 1951; (*b*) *A New Approach to Psychical Research* (Watts, 1953), Ch. VII; (*c*) *Journal of the Society for Psychical Research*, Vol. XXXVII, pp. 79–80 and pp. 352–5; (*d*) 'Can a Man Witness his own Funeral?' in the *Hibbert Journal*, forthcoming. I hope some day to incorporate much of this, with a great deal of further material, in a book on *The Logic of Mortality*.

and dissolution such things might happen to me is to overlook that I shall not then exist.[3] To expect such things,
through overlooking this, is surely like accepting a fairy tale
as history, through ignoring the prefatory rubric 'Once upon
a time, in a world that never was . . .'?

Of course, this is slick, crude and unfair. But the excuse is
that it may serve to throw into relief two crucial points.
The *first* is that the essence of doctrines of personal survival
(or immortality)—and this alone is what gives them their
huge human interest—is that they should assert that we shall
exist after our deaths (for ever). It is thus and only thus that
they can provide the basis for harbouring 'the logically
unique expectation'[4] that we shall have (to put it as non-
committally as possible) 'experiences' after death. It is
important to underline this: both because some doctrines of
immortality have not been of this sort (Aristotle's, for
instance); and because some which actually started out as
doctrines of personal immortality have been so interpreted
by philosophers and theologians that they have surreptitiously
ceased to be anything of the kind.[5]

Now I am not at all sure that something of this sort is not
happening with Professor MacKinnon. In his sympathetic
anxiety 'to track the language to its human source, to plot
the experience of which it is the expression', he has been led
to deny 'that the stumbling speech of those who speak of
immortality and survival (I except here the psychical
researchers) is expressive of an attempt to gain knowledge of
fact without the discipline of experiment and reflective

---

[3] Cf. Lucretius:

> Debet enim, misere si forte aegreque futurumst
> Ipse quoque esse in eo tum tempore, cui male possit
> Accidere.
>
> <div align="right">(<i>de rerum Natura</i>, III, 861–3.)</div>

[4] John Wisdom in 'Gods': in *P.A.S.*, 1944–5; and in *Logic and Language*, First
Series (Blackwell, 1951).

Compare: (*a*) The protest of the Fundamentalist against 'that weasel method
of sucking the meaning out of words, and then presenting the empty shells in
an attempt to palm them off as giving the Christian Faith a new and another
interpretation' (quoted W. Lippmann *A Preface to Morals*, pp. 30–1). The
acids of modernism reinforce the 'acids of modernity'; (*b*) Ch. VI (i) above.

analysis'. Yet surely, though it is also expressive of so much else of agony and hope, essentially and fundamentally it makes a would-be factual claim that the logically unique expectation is justified. It is through this alone that it can console the grief of the bereaved: not by some general assurance that all will be well, for for him without the beloved nothing will be well again; but by its particular implication that one day they may both be reunited in a world to come.

The *second* point is that the great obstacle in the way of attaching sense to talk of a future life,[6] the reason why people suggest that it is self-contradictory to suppose we shall live after physical dissolution, consists in the often neglected fact that person words mean what they do mean. Words like 'you', 'I', 'person', 'somebody', 'Flew', 'woman'—though very different in their several particular functions—are all used to refer in one way or another to objects (the pejorative flavour of this word should here be discounted) which you can point at, touch, hear, see and talk to. Person words refer to people. And how can such objects as people survive physical dissolution? This is a massive difficulty: the desire to surmount or remove it has provided one driving force for many intellectual manœuvres; manœuvres for all of which, of course, there have been and are quite separate good reasons.

First, there have been attempts to show that person words have at most a contingent and not a necessary reference to ostensible objects; and hence that talk of people surviving dissolution is not self-contradictory. As Berkeley confessed, 'the grand mistake is that we know not what we mean by "we", "selves", "mind", etc.'[7] MacKinnon is right, I think, in saying that we can 'put a question mark against every stage of these arguments'.[8] Of course, they have

---

6 As so often nowadays the sceptic's first difficulty is with the meaning (and not yet with the truth) of the believer's faith. Cf. again Ch. VI (i) above.

7 *Philosophical Commentaries* (ed. A. Luce), p. 301.

8 For some of the oldest see Plato, *Alcibiades*, I, 128 ff.; an undeservedly neglected dialogue.

usually been obscured in the 'material mode of speech': they have appeared as arguments that people are—inexplicably—compound of two elements, body and soul (the latter sufficiently elusive and insubstantial to be a plausible candidate for survival after dissolution); and that the soul is the—real or essential—person.[9] This last equation is crucial: for unless I am my soul the immortality of my soul will not be my immortality; and the news of the immortality of my soul would be of no more concern to me than the news that my appendix would be preserved eternally in a bottle.

Second, it has been thought that the distinctively Christian doctrine of the 'resurrection of the body' (better perhaps reformulated as the 'reconstitution of the person') avoids this difficulty. But might not a sceptic argue that reconstituted Flew was only an imitation of the Flew that had been destroyed; and hence that I would not be justified in looking forward to the things that would happen to him as things that would happen to me? This sort of objection would be weakest against those who find reason to postulate 'spiritual' or 'astral' bodies which detach themselves from our 'physical' or 'earth-plane' bodies after death: since they could argue that death, even when followed by the dissolution of the ordinary body, is to be regarded as only an exceptionally drastic case of amputation.

Third, whether or not talk of people surviving dissolution is, according to present usage, self-contradictory; whether or not sense has been provided for such talk, it has been argued that we can attach sense to it. Indeed we can. But the difficulty is to attach a sense to it so that it will, if true, provide a basis for the logically unique expectation. In their present use person words have logical liaisons of the very greatest importance: personal identity is the necessary condition of both accountability and expectation; which is only to say that it is unjust to reward or punish someone for something unless (as a minimum condition) he is the same person who did the deed; and also that it is absurd to

9 Cf. Plato, *Phaedo*, 115C ff.: a revealing passage.

expect experiences for Flew in 1984 unless (as a minimum condition) there is going to be a person in existence in 1984 who will be the same person as I. The difficulty is to change the use of person words so radically that it becomes significant to talk of people surviving dissolution: without changing it to such an extent that these vital logical liaisons are lost. All I can say here is that it seems to me that this problem —which is often overlooked—is both immensely more difficult, and partly of a different character from what has often been thought.

The only substantial hope of finding a solution seems to lie in the surely necessary truth that people have 'private experience'. Since it is, surely, always significant (though often silly), to suggest—in the face of no matter how much 'behavioural'[10] evidence to the contrary—that a person really is in pain; it might be argued that 'private experiences' might occur disembodied (i.e. without anyone to have them). And if this were so it might be possible to suggest some manner of grouping such 'loose and separate' experiences so that each group might be called a disembodied person; in some (new) sense of '(disembodied) person' so designed that it would carry the requisite entailments. (It was this sort of thing which Berkeley and Hume were doing when they tried—and failed—to find 'the uniting principle which constitutes a person': though their own accounts of their admittedly unsuccessful efforts would have been very different indeed.) Furthermore, even if we succeeded in all this we should still have to find a way of identifying a disembodied person at time two with a person at time one, so that the latter might be justified in expecting the experiences of the former. A queer, quasi-legal problem this, to identify two people (in different senses of 'people') as the same person. And a disturbing one: for we assume too easily that all questions about personal identity must be straight

---

10 'Behaviour' is here used in the psychologist's often misleading sense: which includes not only all that we should normally call behaviour but also—what we so often and importantly contrast with behaviour—'linguistic behaviour' —what a person says.

questions of fact, even though some questions about the identity of things are decision issues.[11]

If the tricks cannot be done—and I do not myself believe that they can—then the apocalyptic words of Wittgenstein are to the point: 'Our life is endless as the visual field is without limit. Death is not an event in life. Death is not lived through.' Outside the visual field nothing is seen, not even darkness: for whatever is seen is seen within the visual field. When we are dead nothing is experienced, not even emptiness: for there is no one to experience. For each of us 'the world in death does not change, but ceases'.[12]

University College of North Staffordshire
ENGLAND

[11] A decision issue is one in which what is at stake is: not what the facts are; but what we are going to decide to call correct verbal usage is to be in the future, when the facts are thus and thus. Decisions made by courts are often of this kind. The point being made in the text is made in a less pemmican form in Flew, *loc. cit.* (*a*) and (*b*).

[12] *Tractatus Logico-Philosophicus*, 6.431 and 6.1411.

INDEX OF NAMES